Forms of the
Goddess Lajjā Gaurī
in Indian Art

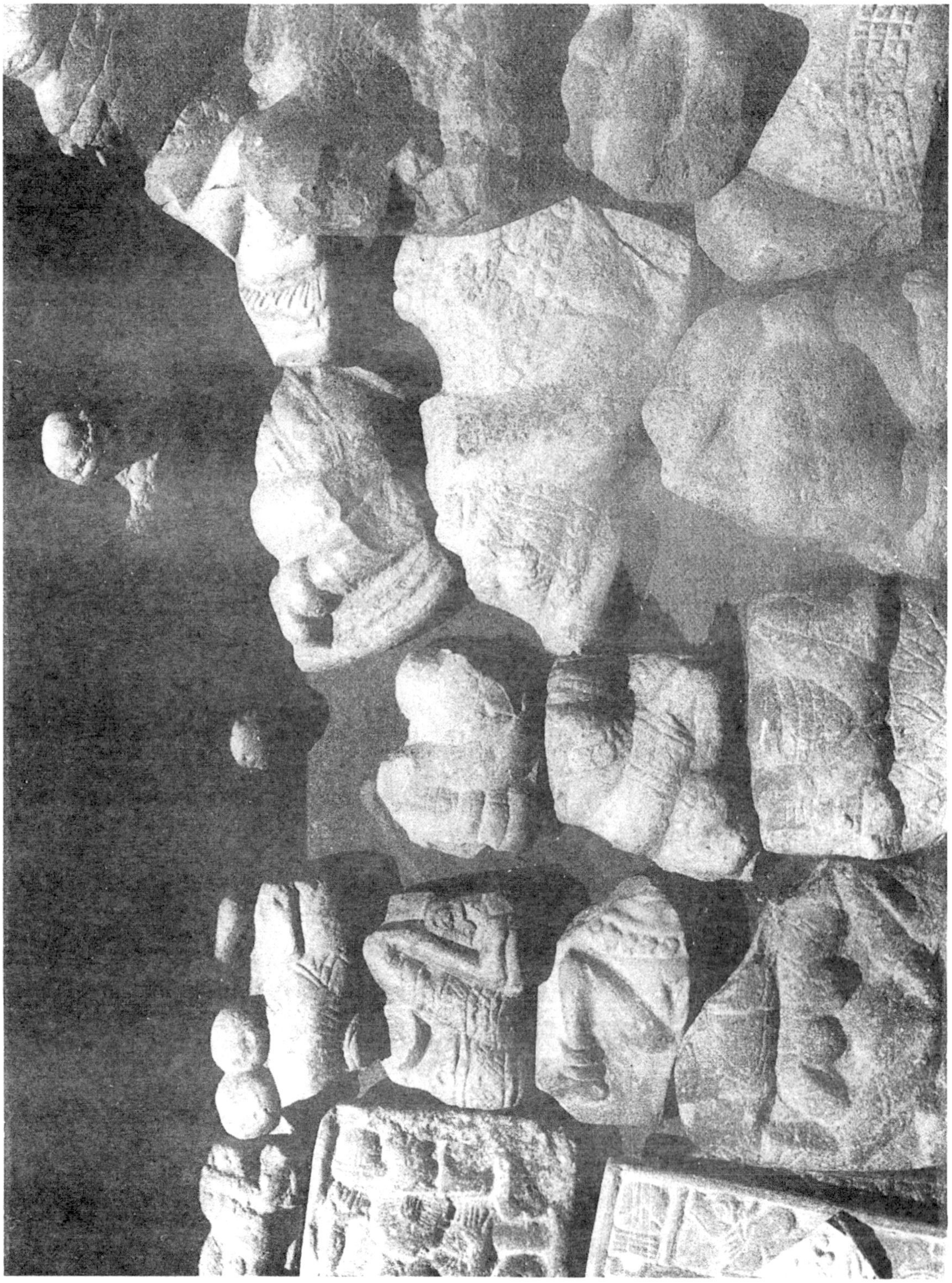

Forms of the Goddess Lajjā Gaurī in Indian Art

CAROL RADCLIFFE BOLON

MOTILAL BANARSIDASS
PUBLISHING HOUSE • DELHI
Email: naraina@mlbd.in • Website: www.mlbd.in
@mlbdofficial
+91 89 2999 9000

*Reprint: Delhi, **2024***

First Indian Edition: Delhi, 1997

ISBN: 978-93-5971-164-5 (Hardcover)
ISBN: 978-93-5971-670-1 (Paperback)

Printed & Published by
Rajendra P Jain *for*
Motilal Banarsidass Publishing House
A-44, Naraina Industrial Area, Phase I,
New Delhi–110 028 (INDIA)
Email: naraina@mlbd.in Website: www.mlbd.in
Tel.: (+91-11)4751 1592
Delhi Showroom:
4637/20, F-2, Hari Sadan, First Floor, Ansari Road, Daryaganj
Delhi–110 002 (Opp. Fire Station) ***Tel.***: (+91-11)4559 7999
Bengaluru Showroom:
1st Floor, 1/2 Rathnavilas Road, Basvanagudi, Next to Pai
Vista Convention Hall, South End Circle Bengaluru - 560004

Contents

List of Illustrations

Frontispiece: Ter Museum, Ter, Maharashtra

Map: Distribution of forms of Lajjā Gaurī in India (page xiv)

Illustration number, site, district, state, current location, size (inches, height precedes width), material, approximate date

FORM I

FORM II

FORM III

FORM III EARLY WESTERN CHALUKYA IMAGES

FORM IV

FORM I MULTIFIGURED REPRESENTATIONS

FORM IV MULTIFIGURED REPRESENTATIONS

FORM II MULTIFIGURED REPRESENTATIONS

FORM III MULTIFIGURED REPRESENTATIONS

OTHER MULTIFIGURED REPRESENTATIONS OF UNUSUAL TYPES

COMPARATIVE IMAGERY

Photo Credits

Carmel Berkson: 3. S. B. Deo: 4, 22. Sara Schastok: 12, 42. American Institute of Indian Studies: 15, 16, 19, 37, 48, 52, 77, 81, 82, 112, 115, 116, 117, 118, 119, 120, 121, 122, 123, 129. British Museum: 18, 28, 128. C. S. Gupta: 24, 25, 94. Devangana Desai: 33, 34, 71, 80, 86, 87. John C. Huntington and Susan L. Huntington: 38, 110, 111. State Museum, Lucknow: 39. Pat Shirreff-Thomas: 53. French Institute of Indology, Pondicherry: 54, 64. V. V. Krishna Sastry: 57, 104, 105. U. P. Shah: 65, 83, 84. U. P. Shah, Archeological Survey of India, Western Circle, Vadodara: 79. Department of Archaeology, Government of Maharashtra, Bombay: 73. Michael W. Meister: 85. Samuel Eilenberg: 98. Thomas Donaldson: 108. All other photographs by the author.

Dawn Tulach: Line drawings 10, 11, 31, 78, 92, 106, 107, 125.

Acknowledgments

I WOULD LIKE TO THANK the individuals and institutions who helped me with the research for this monograph. For financial support, I am grateful to the American Institute of Indian Studies, the Committee on Southern Asian Studies, and Department of Art of The University of Chicago.

For sharing many thoughts and images, I am grateful to: R. C. Agrawala, executive director, Museums of Rajasthan; Andrew Cohen, University of Central Arkansas; Marion Covey; Mitchell Crites, Vipasa Gallery, London; S. B. Deo, Deccan College; Devangana Desai, Bombay; R. C. Dhere, Poona; Margaret Egnor, Hobart College; Samuel Eilenberg; Sudha Gogate, Shreemati Nathibai Damodar, Thackersey Women's University; S. Gorakshekar, director, Prince of Wales Museum of Western India, Bombay; C. S. Gupta, Nagpur University; F. L'Hernault and Bruno Dagens, École Française d'Extrême-Orient, Pondichery; Marilyn Hirsh; John C. Huntington, Ohio State University; Susan L. Huntington, Ohio State University; Holly Hutchens; Stephen Huyler; A. P. Jamkhedkar, director of Archaeology and Museums for Maharashtra; S.C. Kala, Allahabad Museum; Vinod Krishna Kanoria; Stella Kramrisch, curator of Indian Art, Philadelphia Museum of Art; C. Margabandhu, Archaeological Survey of India; Ajit Mookerjee; C. Muley, director, Central Museum, Nagpur; M. S. Nagaraja Rao, director of Archaeology and Museums for Karnataka; N. Nagaswamy, director of Archaeology for Tamil Nadu; James Nye, University of Chicago; Maureen L. P. Patterson; A. K. Ramanujan, University of Chicago; I. K. Sarma, superintending archaeologist, Temple Survey Project, Madras; V. V. Krishna Sastry, director for Archaeology and Museums, Government of Andhra Pradesh; Sara Schastok, Northwestern University; U. P. Shah; B. V. Shetti, curator, Prince of Wales Museum of Western India, Bombay; V. H. Sonawane, M.S. University of Baroda; Doris Srinivasan, George Washington University; A. Sundara, Karnatak University; W. Zwalf, assistant keeper, Department of Oriental Antiquities, British Museum; the staff of the David and Alfred Smart Museum, University of Chicago; and the staff of the Epstein Archive, University of Chicago.

I would also like to thank Molly Kelly Ryan, who prepared the map on page xiv, and Ellen Walton for help with the final manuscript.

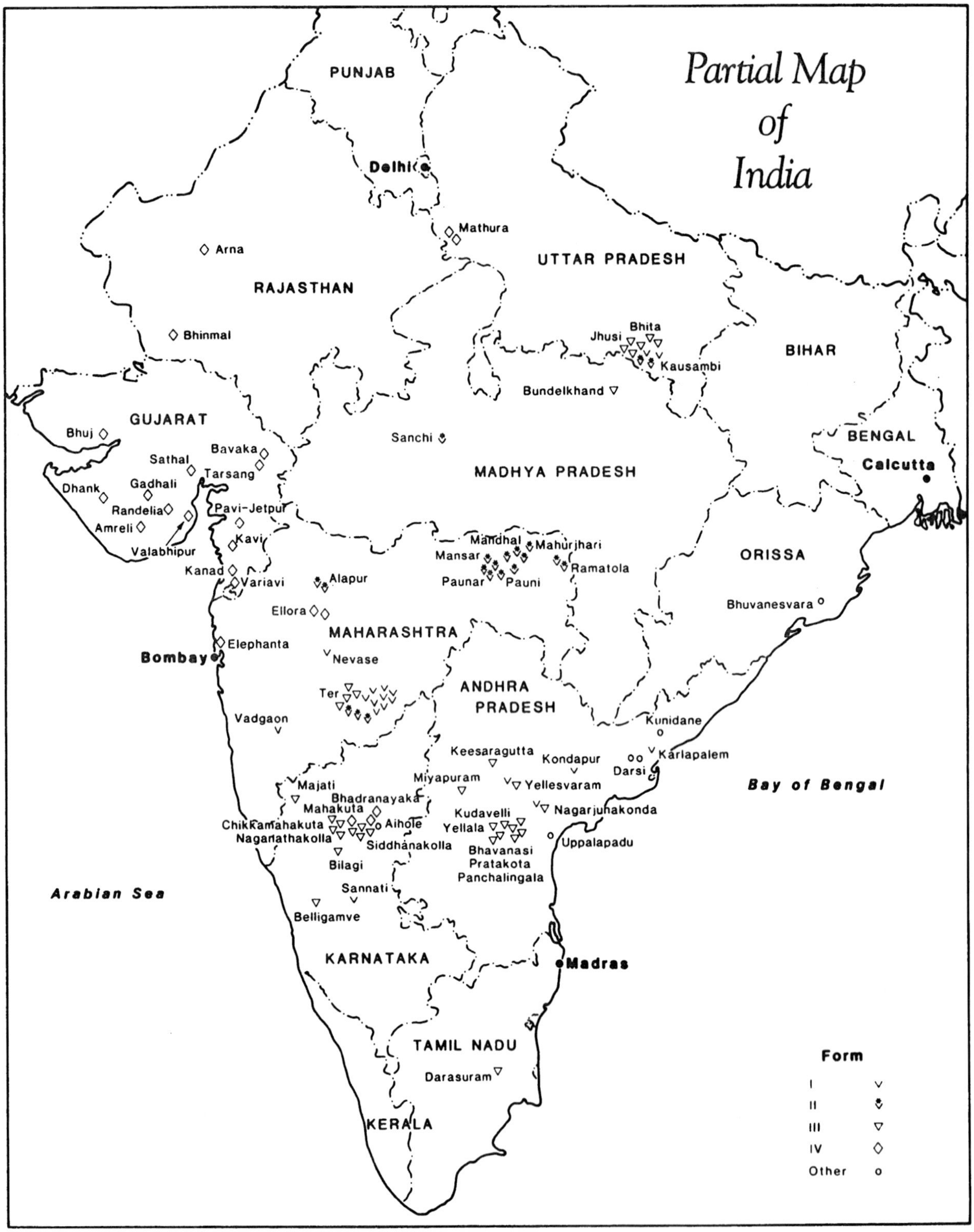

Partial map of India: Distribution of forms of Lajjā Gaurī

Introduction

STRIKING IMAGES OF A CERTAIN INDIAN GODDESS have been variously referred to as "the shameless woman," "the nude squatting goddess," "the mother goddess," or, because her historical name remains unknown, by more than twenty-five names, among them Aditi, Lajjā Gaurī, Reṇukā, and Nagna Kabamdha. The best-known images of this goddess have a female torso and a lotus flower in place of a head, while her legs are bent up at the knees and drawn up to each side in a pose that has been described as one of "giving birth" or "self-display," but there is actually considerable variety in the iconography of the image type.

Among the numerous names applied to this goddess, it is difficult to choose one, even for purposes of discussion, as she is not incontrovertibly identified by description and name in any ancient text or inscription.[1] Today her regional names vary; many are descriptive of a physical aspect of her images. The abundance of names may be due to regional replacements of a lost original name. For the sake of clarity and convenience, I will refer to her by the name most widely used in modern India, Lajjā Gaurī.

The icon of the goddess Lajjā Gaurī, a most sophisticated symbolic image drawing on epochs of artistic and cultural layering of meaning, illustrates a process of ongoing generational, cultural, and artistic imagination. The process is common to all images in Indian art but has not previously been a focus of investigation. Nor has a study of the forms, iconography, and iconology of Lajjā Gaurī images themselves been previously undertaken. Images have been published regionally in India, but there has been no cross-regional analysis. In this study I have proposed a schema of the iconographic forms of Lajjā Gaurī and investigated their symbolism, arriving at a conclusion about the meaning of the images. Because a much larger corpus of figures is documented here than has been gathered previously, such an art-historical study of the goddess is possible. I have carried it out with an interest in both the image-type itself and in the underlying issues that bear on the nature of Indian iconography, specifically as they affect this image. The larger question I addressed is the nature of iconographic formation of images of a deity—the factors, contexts, and contingencies that shape the metamorphosis in form and meaning of a symbolic image of a deity in Indian art. Until now, such issues have hardly been broached as a topic in Indian art history.

Primarily, however, this study is an investigation of the identity of the Lajjā Gaurī figure, the significance of her distinct iconographic forms, and her religious function. In the first two chapters the description of Lajjā Gaurī images set forth the necessary data for analysis. This formal and cross-regional documentation reveals that the figures conform to four broad iconographic configurations. The various types are particular to certain regions of India and certain periods of time, and the changes in the iconography of the image, though complex, can be traced through region and time.

THE STUDY OF INDIAN ICONOGRAPHY

India presents the unusual phenomenon of a traditional society that has produced religious art continuously from at least the third millennium B.C. to the present, within supposed canonical prescriptions, but actually with a great range and variation of forms. Besides the irrepressible creativity of the artists, this diversity is encouraged by the nature of a religious philosophy that sees myriad forms as fundamental expressions of the omnipresent nature of deity. Thereby, for example, one conception of deity, such as Śiva, may have 1,008 forms, and more. Furthermore, unlike many other religious iconographies, Hindu iconography seems exceptionally well documented by various ancient agamas, tantras, purāṇas, and epic and poetic literature as well. But these texts correspond only to the late stages of a long process of artistic creation and do not shed light on centuries of earlier versions of forms that served as prototypes for the developed imagery of the gods and goddesses. Many of the texts were probably transcribed as late as the seventh century, although their dates are not firmly set. They seem to be descriptive rather than prescriptive. No doubt after their creation they were consulted by priests and artists and served to fix and perpetuate a dominant version of each image of a god or goddess. Major reference books for Indian iconography have been compiled by drawing on such extant texts by T. A. Gopinatha Rao and J. N. Banerjea.[2] Unfortunately, no ancient text describing Lajjā Gaurī images is known.

Few scholars have attempted to grapple with the complexities of Indian iconography and to examine the many factors that bear on its changes. Ananda Coomaraswamy, father of Indian art history, in his study *Yakṣas,* contributed his understanding of the nexus of artistic formulation in Indian art, explaining that certain images and motifs are repeatedly drawn from a pretheological mythology and pool of imagery and are appropriated to a new but related use. In this way layers of interchangeable or associated meaning accrue to an image. Especially rich in this regard, for example, is the vast symbol language developed over epochs of time to express ideas related to the powers of water, symbolism pertinent to Lajjā Gaurī.

In an imaginative study, *The Golden Germ,* F. D. K. Bosch traced the process underlying the artistic formulation in Indian art that Coomaraswamy had examined. The evolution of a symbol in Indian art may be facilitated by a phenomenon Bosch calls "morphological resemblance," or "resemblance-elaboration." It accounts for the way in which visual elements of entirely different species or modes of being are translated into one another over time in a subtle process of seeing and elaborating relationships between certain prevalent forms endemic to the self-expression of the culture. The process works dialectically: images stimulate concepts and concepts stimulate the new conjunctions of images. Bosch focused part of his study of this process on the example of the formation of the *makara,* a composite Indian aquatic creature part gharial (an Indian crocodile) or elephant and part plant, whose use as a sculptural form spread throughout most of Asia. The formation of this symbolic and decorative motif, the *makara,* went through various stages, which may be traced step by step in ancient Indian art beginning with a plant form, the lotus node (parvan), which was elaborated into the open, birth-giving, jaw of the *makara.* Bosch concluded: "There are a great variety of mythological hybrids that are fixed features of the vocabulary of Indian art. Among them are found primordial and powerful symbols whose origins within the culture cannot now be traced, yet whose omnipresence within the art and culture indicate their usefulness within it."[3] Lajjā Gaurī, in artistic and conceptual ancestry, descends from a group of ancient popular symbols, among others, the lotus and the *pūrṇa kumbha,* or brimming pot. Conceptually Lajjā Gaurī has antecedents which may be, and in fact have been, traced back to the Indus Valley art of about 2500–1500 B.C. by scholars such as H. D. Sankalia.[4]

Recently scholars have begun to search deeper than ever before into the nature of Indian iconography and the forces that generated it, indicating a new interest in iconographic questions. For example, an important factor affecting the iconography of a particular deity is regional variation. In a recent publication Michael Meister examined the varieties of a certain image set known as the Saptamātṛkās and correlated their various modes to regional tradition.[5] Since different cultural regions of India interpret an image-type with variations that are endemic to it, the regional particularities of an image-type will be distinct. As an essential facet of the present examination of Lajjā Gaurī, I shall correlate the specific forms popular in certain periods and regions in order to establish the process of her iconographic changes.

A similar iconographic case study, based on Mahiṣāsuramardinī images of the Pallava and Chalukya areas of South India, was presented jointly by Gary Tartakov and Vidya Dehejia as a means of examining the questions of cross-regional, glibly assumed "influences." In fact, they proposed that such "influences" may be better understood as instances of cross-regional "sharing" of a vast traditional pool of forms for images rather than cases of direct dependence.[6] Language areas rather than dynastic areas, they propose (as have others), should be considered as the basis of delimitation of a cultural area within which sharing is facilitated: instead of seeking evidence of direct artistic influence as such, they conclude, in the Indian sphere we should consider a broader range of possible explanations.

The Tarr and Dehejia study and another by Joanna Williams both note the problem of informational gaps in Indian art history, of loss of actual objects that would complete the picture of development in iconography. This problem causes all proposals concerning the development of iconography, of course, to be theoretical and ultimately unprovable.

Williams studies the imagery still carved and painted on the colossal processional chariots used by the Jagganātha cult in Puri, Orissa. The carts' renovation demonstrates a process of iconographic change down to the present day. Williams's study of changes in "tradition" considers several factors bearing on iconographic formulation. One is the interdependence of the "receiver" of the imagery and the interpretation of its meaning: the identity of the gods carved on the chariots will differ according to the priest, the villager, the tribal, etc. Among multivalent interpretations, whose version was recorded by the ancient iconographers in their texts? Does an interpretation by one level of society invalidate the other meanings attached to the images? Williams argued that "we need not seek parsimony in iconological explanation in Indian art"; one source alone does not explain the origin of an image. Coexistence of definitions or inherent ambiguity must be accepted. The progressive changes in iconography through time and region reflect the meaning of an image to its particular audience.[7]

The four forms of Lajjā Gaurī I have identified show a broad progression through time and region from the minimal, and nearly aniconic to the fully human. The process of change is fascinating, especially given the comparable early aniconic configuration of the Buddha, before he was given human shape. The standard explanation for this aniconic phase of representation of the Buddha-presence was given by Snellgrove: the Buddha was first represented aniconically (by similar types of symbols of the popular culture as are used within Lajjā Gaurī images) due to the "philosophically radical doctrine concerning his true nirvāṇa essence, inconceivable, invisible form and human shape."[8] The early images of Lajjā Gaurī too may be read as expressions of the idea of something beyond the natural, beyond the human, which can most effectively be expressed by use of powerful macrocosmic and primordial symbols in combination with the familiar, universal, microcosmic reference point of the human body.

Like Hindu mythology, the image of Lajjā Gaurī communicates simultaneously on many levels. On the human level, the image of Lajjā Gaurī acts as a temporal reference point, that is, the female giving birth, an auspicious occurrence: she is the embodiment of human fertility. On the divine level Lajjā Gaurī is the embodiment of the idea of fertility, of generation, of life-force. On the cosmic level the image suggests universal laws and processes of generation of all life. Mythic narratives about Lajjā Gaurī exist as well. Most of these seek to explain her headless state, and these may only be modern, the inventions of villagers who have become alienated from the original intent and meaning of the image. Some others, however, may preserve a thread of her original meaning.

The artists creating images of Lajjā Gaurī drew on various ancient symbols of fortune, fertility, and life-force to communicate her power through their rich heritage of meanings. They used these symbols in new combinations couched within the female form in a birthlike position. As these historical-religious symbols and images were constantly reused and reincorporated, they formed a new and enriched religious context. In the process of recycling they became empowered cultural metaphors, visual morphemes in the language of Indian art.

Another underlying force bearing on artistic and iconographic formulation in Indian art is the frequent origin of a deity in a folk or village setting, and its subsequent elevation to an elite, pan-Indian, Brahmanical status. This process is one that can be traced in the reconstructed histories of a few icons, such as that of the goddess Hārītī who began her career as a horrible *yakṣī,* but the same process can be assumed, if it is no longer possible to reconstruct its steps clearly from remains of scattered images, for many others. Many major deities took their theological and artistic basis from the combinations of elements first found in minor village deities. The process of marriage of the "little tradition" (lower caste, village, or local) and the "big tradition" (Brahmanical, elite, pan-Indian) is well documented for literature, anthropology, history, linguistics, and history of religion in India, but not for art. Nonetheless, it was also of importance there.[9]

Though Lajjā Gaurī was obviously a popular goddess throughout India, her religious function remains unilluminated either by explanatory commentaries or any developed set of rites of worship. The practices that one can observe in village life where *grāmadevatās* continue to be worshiped as boundary deities, marking off and establishing the village locus and as guarantors of certain favors and boons (such as the birth of children or an increase in family fortune), are in many cases of ancient origin and are diligently continued, though in other cases their worship is of recent origin. Therefore, I have noted current rites of worship of Lajjā Gaurī and with caution accept that it is possible that current worship and beliefs reflect the original ancient modes.

THE STUDY OF LAJJĀ GAURĪ

Figures of the goddess Lajjā Gaurī range in size from two inches to over life-size and are made either of molded or hand-formed terra-cotta or of stone carved in relief. The larger images, made of stone, served as icons for worship in temple subshrines. Several are still worshiped today. The smaller stone or terra-cotta images may have been altarpieces in home shrines.[10] One was discovered buried under the altar of a fourth-century temple (Fig. 103).[11] The images, made between the second century and the eleventh century, range in quality from extreme crudity to great refinement, the finest being a seventh-century Early Chalukya example from a temple at Naganathakolla near Badami in Karnataka (Fig. 48). Images of Lajjā Gaurī have been found in most states of India, though they are especially common in Karnataka, Andhra Pradesh, Uttar Pradesh, Rajasthan, Gujarat, Madhya Pradesh, and Maharashtra, with concentrations in or around the towns of Nagpur, Ter, Kondapur, Kausambi, and Bhita. Lajjā Gaurī images are, in fact, not uncommon in Indian art. In this monograph about 125 images are studied. The relatively large quantity of figures, which is undoubtedly only a fraction of the number that exist, confirms the importance of the type, especially if compared, for example, to such well-studied images as Viśvarūpa, a form of Viṣṇu, of which only about fifteen stone-carved examples are known.

Lajjā Gaurī is almost always made to lie on her back, supine.[12] The toes of the recumbent figure are tensely splayed as if she is in the act of giving birth, yet there is no indication of pregnancy. Some scholars have concluded, however, that the goddess is simply indecent, shameless, and that the pose indicates sexual receptiveness. Nevertheless it should be noted that, although some do give birth miraculously, Indian goddesses are never pregnant in imagery or myth. The pose of Lajjā Gaurī is ambiguous, but probably intentionally so since the pose of sexual receptivity and the pose of giving birth are the same. The human form and the intercourse/birth pose are used as a metaphor for creation. In turn human parturition is used in this image as a metaphor for divine creation.

The divine (often haloed) figures of the goddess Lajjā Gaurī must be differentiated from mortal figures intended for erotic display. To miss this distinction is to miss the deeper meaning of Lajjā Gaurī images. They are erotic, but they are not merely or primarily erotic. A profound spiritual message is couched within a seemingly erotic display. This means of expression is familiar in Indian art, as for instance the copulating *maithuna* figures on the walls of the Khajuraho temples, which are meant to suggest the ecstasy of union with god.[13]

The image of Lajjā Gaurī has often been referred to as the "displayed female." However, while the legs are spread, actually nothing more than the vertical line of the pudendum is indicated. Nothing bawdy or ribald is intended, though certainly the image is sexually suggestive. But the intent is different from that of images in which the female opens her vulva with her hands. Such self-display by female figures on Hindu temples represents mortal behavior, sometimes in accordance with Tantric rituals.[14] These anonymous images are significantly different in expressive intent from images of the goddess Lajjā Gaurī. Lajjā Gaurī's pose is akin to, but distinct from that of such images in that Lajjā Gaurī never parts her sex organ with her hands as they do.[15] No doubt the artists who carved Lajjā Gaurī images were aware of the more simply erotic images, but they distinguished her image through incorporation of rich symbolism. Nevertheless, the assumption that Lajjā Gaurī is simply erotic has discouraged serious consideration of her iconography and meaning. Misconceptions about the image have become entrenched in literature. In fact the images are often not displayed by museums.

It is the spread-leg pose of the goddess that has provoked such confusion and many misconceptions. This specific *uttānapad* pose must be defined and explained since it is common to all the images of this goddess, which otherwise differ in possession of arms, a head, etc. While the figures may have a human head or a lotus head, while they may or may not have breasts or arms, their constant feature is the pose of the legs. In this pose the legs make an *M*-shape. They are drawn up to the sides of the waist as if to serve as a "stand" for the torso. The pose, as represented on most examples, is not anatomically natural or even possible as a yoga position, especially in the peculiar angle of the feet.

As applied by Kramrisch the word *uttānapad* exactly describes this image.[16] In *Ṛg Veda* (x.72.4) it is said that Earth sprang from the *Uttānapad,* the Creative Agency or Productive Power. *Uttānapad* in Sanskrit means "one whose legs are extended in parturition." It is the "name of a peculiar creative agency" (*Ṛg Veda* x.72.4); "vegetation, the whole creation of upward germinating plants" (Sāyaṇa).[17] The leg pose of all Lajjā Gaurī images may be described as *uttānapad.* The position of the body may be described as *uttāna,* which means "stretched out, lying on the back, sleeping supinely or with face upwards (*Ṛg Veda, Atharva Veda, Vāja Saneyi Saṃhita*); upright (*Śatapatha Brāhmana, Kātyayana Śrauta Sūtra*); turned so that the mouth or opening is uppermost (as a vessel), concave, (*Taittirīya Saṃhitā, Śatapatha Brāhmaṇa, Kātyāyana Śrāuta Sūtra*)."[18] Each of these definitions is given form in the image.

To avoid further confusion it is important to define what the *uttānapad* pose is not. It is not the pose of some of the *mātṛkās* who sometimes are represented seated with the legs spread wide and hanging down. That pose may be termed either *bhadrāsana* or *pralambapadāsana*. It is a sitting pose, as in the pose of the well-known image of the goddess Sarasvatī of the Kuṣāṇ period (c. first century) now in the State Museum, Lucknow. The *uttānapad* pose, in contrast, is used for figures meant to be lying on their backs, not seated and not squatting.[19]

"Nude squatting goddess," another descriptive epithet frequently applied to Lajjā Gaurī, is also inaccurate because nudity is not a constant feature of the type of image, and she never actually squats but lies supine. A few Lajjā Gaurī images made to be installed vertically in the walls of tanks or similar locations, therefore seem to squat. However, the vast majority of Lajjā Gaurī images are definitely supine, and this position is essential to their meaning. They are not intended to suggest a woman squatting to give birth. The normal birth pose in India is supine.

These Lajjā Gaurī figures are auspicious images giving blessing, rather than erotic or apotropaic images meant to ward off the evil eye.[20] The essential nature of this goddess is not as Universal Mother, Divine Woman, Personified Womb, or Mother Goddess, although she encompasses all these. More properly she is the elemental source of all life, animal and plant, and thereby she is the source of Fortune. She personifies the sap of life which in Indian philosophy is considered to be the vivifying element embodied in water, the support of all life. That she is creative power personified is apparent from the symbols employed in her form and their deep cultural and artistic significance.

In India women are traditionally revered for their special potential for reproduction. A large class of goddesses generically referred to as mother goddesses embody and idealize the "numinous power of the child-bearing principle."[21] The goddess considered in this study does broadly belong to the large grouping in Indian art of mother goddess figures, but among members of this group her meaning is most elemental.

Confrontation with the life-size nude figure of a voluptuous woman lying on her back with her legs drawn up provoked a predictable reaction from several nineteenth-century British surveyors for the Archaeological Survey of India. In 1881 John Faithful Fleet's reaction to such a figure at Mahakuta (Bijapur District, Karnataka) was published: "there is a somewhat notorious and very indecent headless stone figure of the goddess Pārvatī under the name Lajjā Gaurī."[22] E. W. West recorded that "Yellamma or Ellamma is a very favorite goddess in the Canarese country [Karnataka] and judging from the company she keeps, or rather from the classes that worship her, she is not a very reputable one."[23] West also mentioned that she is worshiped by circumambulation at an annual fair attended by 10,000 people at Ugaral (Belgaum District, Karnataka), and that she is the same as the Reṇukādevī of the Marathas.

Many images of Lajjā Gaurī have been published, often in the context of excavation reports wherein she is described as a "mother goddess," a "nude squatting goddess," or a "displayed female." Among the few serious considerations of the images an article by Stella Kramrisch, in 1956, related the physical form of one such image in the Alampur Museum (Fig. 52) to the descriptive epithets of Aditi Uttānapad found in the *Ṛg Veda*.[24] In 1960 H. D. Sankalia reported that C. Chapgar had seen a similar image at Siddan Kotte (Fig. 43) (now called Siddhanakolla) in Karnataka which he reported to be locally called Lajjā Gaurī, the name reported by Fleet in 1881, which Chapgar translated as "Shy Woman."[25] Sankalia reinterpreted the name Lajjā Gaurī as a euphemism for "shameless woman." "Shameless woman" is a mistranslation and a misnomer.[26] "Gaurī, goddess without reason for shame" or "Gaurī, goddess of modesty" or "innocent goddess" is a more correct translation of Lajjā Gaurī. Gaurī is a specific form of the goddess Pārvatī, Śiva's female counterpart, so Lajjā Gaurī may refer to a form of Pārvatī as goddess of innocence or modesty. Sankalia himself noted another Lajjā Gaurī image excavated at Nevase (Fig. 4), which he reported to be considered locally an *avatār* of Pārvatī.

In response to Kramrisch's article Sankalia stated that this type of image could not be accepted as the Vedic goddess Aditi since the earliest such image is considerably post-Vedic. He suggested that, rather than having an Indian origin, the source for the image had come from Egypt. In his discussion of the "shameless woman," Sankalia did not differentiate between the form or function of the goddess in India and that of various erotic figures in Indonesia, Egypt, and elsewhere. In fact, he grouped them as one in meaning. He also related European images of females opening their vaginas with their hands, published earlier by M. A. Murray, to Lajjā Gaurī.[27] Murray and Codrington had discussed Lajjā Gaurī figures in relation to the Roman Baubo and other fertility figures which Sankalia also believes similar to Lajjā Gaurī.[28] Erotic images of females sexually displaying themselves occur in many cultures although their specific functions vary. The fact that Lajjā Gaurī is a goddess with a pose and features distinct from such erotic figures separates her from the images of mortals with whom she is sometimes grouped.

Jagdish Narain Tiwari included a chapter, "The Nude Squatting Goddess of India," in his dissertation "Studies in the Goddess Cult in Northern India with Special Reference to the 1st to 7th centuries A.D."[29] Tiwari exhaustively discussed earlier opinions and reviewed the debate of foreign or indigenous origin generated by Sankalia in response to Kramrisch's article. This kind of debate is classic in Indian art history, calling to mind the debate over the origin of the image of the Buddha between, originally, Ananda Coomaraswamy and Alfred Foucher.[30] Tiwari evaluates the difficulty of resolving this argument about the origin of Lajjā Gaurī and states that the two theories are not exclusive. Nonetheless, he asserts that the name Aditi cannot firmly be applied to the goddess, and postulates that the origin of the goddess may have been the inspiration of a local priest since she is not described in any known ancient text.

In 1978 R. C. Dhere published in Marathi a serious consideration of the goddess Lajjā Gaurī including a collection of sixteen images.[31] His study records the many regional names of the goddess and studies their onomastics and meaning. Dhere also provides much information on the cult centers of Lajjā Gaurī, the modern regional myths about her, and sociological information about the castes that worship her now and the ways in which they worship her. Dhere accepts Kramrisch's association of the figure with Aditi of the *Ṛg Veda* as one among many conceptual sources for the figure, His study is religious, linguistic, and sociological rather than art-historical and does not include consideration of questions of iconographic formation and change, or of the process of Brahminization as studied here.

Without texts to explain the images, the images themselves must be relied upon to communicate their meaning. Symbolic parts (lotus, pot, *uttānapad* pose) which are combined to form Lajjā Gaurī images are understood from the other contexts in which they occur. They are part of a known language of Indian art. The provenances and stylistic dating of Lajjā Gaurī images document regional and chronological patterns of her importance. In the absence of texts, the dates and origins of the images must be used to trace the changes in and spread of her cult and related changes in the iconographic features of her images. Or, as Michael Meister has written: "Visual images follow a visual language. Literary sources often can only provide a background for what visual sources are trying to say. We must look for the mechanisms which operate in the visual sphere and the means by which visual forms are then adapted and used for political, cultural, and cult purposes."[32] The context of the in situ images of Lajjā Gaurī also aids our interpretation of the meaning of the goddess.

Notes

1. Gopinatha Rao, 1968; Banerjea, 1974.

2. Nor is she identified in any secondary iconographic study. Banerjea, 1974, 489–90, briefly refers to a Gupta seal depicting a goddess with a lotus emerging from her neck, but no references are provided.

3. Bosch, 1960, 27, 99–106.

4. Sankalia, 1978.

5. Meister, 1986.

6. Tartakov and Dehejia, 1984.

7. Williams, 1984, 301.

8. Snellgrove, 1978, 24; however, this explanation is questioned by Huntington, 1985, 70, 72–73, 87, 98–99, 113, 123, 173.

9. See Eschmann, 1978, 82 note 9 for a full bibliography on this point.

10. Sircar, 1980, 14, suggests that the terra-cottas were purchased for worship on particular occasions and were kept thereafter in the home. Another possible use would be as a votive offering, that is, a gift made in fulfillment of a vow made in prayer after the prayer is answered.

11. Sarma, 1987, 238. Discussed here on page 45.

12. An exception is seemingly found in Gujarati Lajjā Gaurīs and their relatives in Maharashtra and Rajasthan, wherein the Form IV human-headed goddess is represented vertically in situ in walls of bathing tanks, for example, that from Dhank (Fig. 82). It may be that the location of the images requires this adjustment, which makes the goddess appear to squat, when it should still be understood that she is supine. Other examples from Andhra (Figs. 104–7) enthrone the goddess when she is represented in a group of deities. In these she is not represented as supine at all.

13. Desai, 1975.

14. Donaldson, 1985, 40, explains the figure type's purpose as auspicious and apotropaic.

15. Sircar, 1980, 14–15, notes the important difference of function of Lajjā Gaurī and a squatting human female figure carved on a pillar of the Venkateśvara temple.

16. Kramrisch, 1956, applied the term to the image.

17. Monier-Williams, 1976, 177.

18. Ibid.

19. Sivaramamurti, 1982, 24, wrote that the Alampur Museum Lajjā Gaurī (Fig. 52) is seated in the pose known as *utkuṭikāsana*. This, he claims, is the continuation of the same pose of seated goddesses and even of the Sun god, Sūrya, in the earliest Kuṣāṇa sculpture from Mathura. The equation of that pose with the pose of Lajjā Gaurī is inaccurate, as the Lajjā Gaurī figure is supine and not seated.

20. Donaldson, 1975, 89.

21. Neumann, 1955, 138.

22. Fleet, 1881, 103.

23. West, 1881, 245; regarding her worship, Nagaswamy, 1978, 134, notes that her image in Darasuram is worshiped today

by all castes. Narasimhaswami, 1952, notes that the Ikṣvāku Queen Mahādevī Chāṁtamūla worshiped her in the late third century.

24. Kramrisch, 1956.

25. Sankalia, 1960, 111.

26. Sankalia's article has led to gross misunderstanding. For instance, the *Times of India,* 14 September 1983, printed a bombastic summary of his article with Sankalia's byline, discussing the evidence for the ancient practice of squatting to give birth and including two miscaptioned photographs.

27. Murray, 1934.

28. Codrington, 1935.

29. Tiwari, 1971, chap. 4. Recently published as *Goddess Cults in Ancient India with Special Reference to the First Seven Centuries A.D.*, Delhi, 1985.

30. Coomaraswamy, 1972, reprint of article first published in *Art Bulletin,* 9, no. 4, 1927; and Foucher, 1905–51.

31. Dhere, 1978.

32. Meister, 1986, 246.

I

Forms

FOR PURPOSES OF DISCUSSION, description, and documentation it is useful to define the four apparent iconographic categories of figures of Lajjā Gaurī. These categories may be conceptualized as progressing from a minimally anthropomorphic form toward a completely anthropomorphic goddess. These humanizing changes in iconography have some correspondence, but not a simple correspondence, to chronological progression, as will be discussed. Only two figures studied actually fall between the four broad categories as defined (between Forms II and III; Figs. 20 and 96), but it must be noted that virtually every figure is unique in its treatment of detail or style. The four categories are:

Form I	*Uttānapad* pot
Form II	Lotus-headed without arms
Form III	Lotus-headed with arms
Form IV	Anthropomorphic

Each form will be generally characterized before proceeding to descriptions of individual images in each group. The elemental figures referred to as "*uttānapad* pot," and designated Form I are characterized by human legs in *uttānapad* pose with a shape above the legs that resembles both a pot and a female's lower torso with pudendum, abdomen, and lower rib cage topped with a lotus flower (Fig. 1). The figure has no upper torso so it lacks other human female features; there are no breasts, arms, or head. The pot torso is set with its mouth upward and holding a lotus flower, like the brimming vase, or *pūrṇa kumbha*, familiar in Indian art. The emphasis is placed on the metaphor of the body as vessel. In every example of this type the pot's top holds a lotus flower, although in some examples the flower is only visible by viewing the piece from the edge above the figure.[1] This image-type fits the definition of both *uttānapad*, one whose legs are extended in parturition, and of *uttāna*, turned so the opening is uppermost, like a vessel. Perhaps the linguistic double meaning of pot/womb was the inspiration for the visual double entendre embodied in Form I Lajjā Gaurīs.

Form II figures are like those of *uttānapad* pot Form I except that the torso extends up to the shoulders and includes breasts (Fig. 18). There are no arms or head in images in this group, but the lotus is elevated to sit atop the shoulders.

In Form III the figures are all lotus-headed with otherwise anthropomorphic female bodies with breasts and two upraised arms on the full torso with each hand holding a lotus bud, and legs in the *uttānapad* pose (Fig. 48).

In Form IV the figures of Lajjā Gaurī are totally anthropomorphic, with a human head and a full natural female torso, with raised arms, each hand holding a lotus bud as in Form III, and with legs in the *uttānapad* pose (Fig. 67).

In addition to representations of individual figures, images of each Form also occur in assemblages of figures carved on plaques (e.g., Fig. 98). These are discussed in chapter 2. These more complex representations deserve special examination; their provocative combinations of figures throw light on the meanings of the images of Lajjā Gaurī by giving her a context.

Before proceeding it must be noted that dates provided for images in this study are most often approximate to a century. Their dating is rendered problematic by several facts: first, the absence of a face and treatment of facial details that would otherwise be partially relied upon to suggest a proper period/style dating; second, the absence of an established iconographic-regional-temporal schema, which evidence would otherwise be relied upon as a part of one's judgment for establishing the date of a piece of Indian sculpture (and for which this study is the first attempt for this image-type); third, the apparent range from popular production to images of royal patronage that invalidates the consideration of the quality of the carving as dating criterion. Most Lajjā Gaurī figures are manifestations of the major regional/period styles familiar to Indian art historians. The cruder examples, however, reflect local, timeless styles and are more difficult to date. A few images have been roughly dated by excavation stratigraphy, as will be noted when such images are discussed. One image from Nagarjunakonda (Form III?) has been dated to the third century by paleography and content of its inscription, which accords with its style and its site's active period (Fig. 42). In fact, many images are dated by the correspondence of their style to their site's known active period. An image at Alandgunjoti, Gulbarga District of Karnataka, has been reported by Dhere to be Later Western Chālukya. He dated it to 1082 by association with an inscription, which he unfortunately did not identify as to its location, nor did he translate the inscription or explain its relevance.[2] Opinions of regional experts who have published particular images of Lajjā Gaurī are discussed.

To outline the regional and chronological associations discovered for the four Forms described: the *uttānapad* pot Form I goddess is the major early form popular in the south. It was made in the third century and the fourth century but not thereafter. Form II, the full-torsoed, armless, lotus-headed image, was made primarily from the fourth to the ninth century except that there are two examples that may possibly be second century. The predominant Maharashtrian-type figure, especially in the central area around Nagpur, is Form II, carved either individually or in groups. The human-bodied, lotus-headed Form III goddess was made from the fourth to the tenth century. Form III figures were made in Madhya Pradesh and Gujarat as early as the fourth century and were made with great refinement of details during the Early Chalukya period in the late seventh century in Andhra and Karnataka; they continued to be made in the south until at least the ninth century. Twice as many images of Lajjā Gaurī exist from the later period, sixth to tenth century, than from the earlier period, second to fifth century, indicating an apparent rise in her popularity and importance or in image use in general. One very distinct image of the human-headed Form IV figure was made in Mathura in the second century (Figs. 66–68), but the major period of their production in Gujarat was sixth to seventh century, with the addition of attending maids or accompanying gods. In the south the lotus-headed Form III Lajjā Gaurī is seen in multifigured plaques from the fourth to the seventh century in Andhra, Karnataka, and southern Maharashtra. Form IV, Lajjā Gaurī with a human head, is a northern type only, never made in the south. To generalize from this complex history of regional types of the icon: Form I is only early and only southern, Form IV is only late and only northern, Forms II and III are not exclusively northern or southern, and were made between the fourth and tenth centuries.

Of 124 examples surveyed, including some fragments, by coincidence 62 are from northern sites and 62 are from southern sites. Of the 62 northern examples 48 are stone and 14 are terra-cotta. Of the 62 southern examples 51 are stone and 11 are terra-cotta. This evidence refutes assumptions often reiterated in the literature that Lajjā Gaurī figures were made mostly in the south and that they were made mostly of terra-cotta. The assumption that they were mostly terra-cotta is partially based on the further misassumption that they were only produced as popular village art as opposed to more expensive and even royally patronized stone images worked in the dynastic (or tempo-regional) style.

The rest of this chapter is devoted to the physical description of specific images of each form that have been studied. The significance of the regional and chronological occurrence of images will be discussed in the conclusion of the book.

FORM I: *UTTĀNAPAD* POT

The most elemental and symbolically potent Lajjā Gaurī representation is the *uttānapad* pot goddess, Form I (Figs. 1–17, 73). This is the personified *pūrṇa kumbha,* or brimming vase of fortune, depicted in an unusual manner, like a visual pun or optical illusion: the *uttānapad* legs are joined to a truncated torso that may be perceived either as the pudendum, belly, and lower rib cage of a female figure or as a traditional *pūrṇa kumbha.* Each potlike lower torso is topped by a lotus flower. The vase brimming with lotus flowers is a traditional symbol of fortune, life, and procreative power in Indian art. In this culture, as in others, "Pots, like human beings to which they are compared metaphorically [as having a hip, foot, neck, etc.], are [considered to be] containers of power and life force."[3] The legs of Form I figures, which serve as a cradle for the pot, make the potlike lower torso partially anthropomorphic. None of the Form I images has breasts, arms, or head. The belly portion is provided with the detail of a *mekhalā,* or jeweled girdle, such as that typically worn by a woman or a goddess or as would serve as the decoration of a *pūrṇa kumbha* motif around its hip (e.g., Fig. 113).

Form I images are small and are made of terra-cotta or stone. Most of the examples of the *uttānapad* pot Form I that have been examined are carved in stone; in fact, the majority of all types of Lajjā Gaurī images are stone. Tiwari's idea, which is one that has been generally assumed true, that most of the images of this goddess are terra-cotta, thereby indicating the low status of the goddess and worship by low castes, is doubly erroneous in that first, most images are stone, and second, terra-cottas are known to have sometimes been royally patronized.[4] In size, Form I images range from two inches square, to widths or heights of five to six inches on a side. Several images of this group have been dated by stratigraphy to the third century. The largest number of examples of this type are from Ter (Osmanabad District, Maharashtra). Other sites from which multiple Form I figures originate are Sannati (Medak District, Karnataka) and Kondapur in Andhra. All of the twenty intact examples (and many fragments) studied were found at southern sites, except one from Kausambi in Uttar Pradesh, which could have had a southern origin as will be discussed later. Other find sites include Vadgaon and Nevase in southern Maharashtra and Yellesvaram in Andhra.

Many *uttānapad* pot–type figures are carved in relief against a rectangular or square plaque background. Examples with such a plaque format from Ter (Figs. 1–3,)[5] Nevase (Fig. 4),[6] and Yellesvaram (Fig. 5),[7] constitute a distinct subgroup within Form I because in each plaque the area beneath the legs of the pot figure is incised with lotus petals. The sex parts of the female figure are centered where the seed pod of the incised lotus flower would arise, clearly suggesting an analogy of their generative aspects. The border around the plaque is ridged and patterned. The lotus flower that issues from the pot belly is at the top of the plaque. In these examples, as in virtually all examples of all Forms, the legs are ornamented with anklets, the navel is indicated, and a patterned cloth is "woven" through the legs so that it passes over both thighs and, it is understood, behind the back.[8] The soles of the feet are turned up toward the viewer at a sharp, unnatural angle. The consistent repetition of all these details indicates that they bear essential meaning. Other plaques within Form I do not have the lotus petal detailing of the lower portion just described (Fig. 6) (Ter Museum RC 9.119), but are left plain, possibly unfinished. Otherwise all details are repeated. The Nevase image, now kept in the Deccan College Museum, is dated by excavation strata to A.D. 100–300. Within this range I would date it to late third to fourth century rather than second century, by its style of carving, which seems well defined as is typical of a slightly later handling. I would date the other Form I figures of this subgroup to the third to fourth centuries also.

Three terra-cotta images discovered at Sannati in Karnataka seem to have been made from one mold (Fig. 7), while others from the site show variation within Form I. Sannati is well known for recently unearthed Buddhist sculptures in the Kṛṣṇa Valley style datable between the first and third centuries, and these probably should be dated within this period too.[9] Few duplicate figures of Lajjā Gaurī have been documented.[10] A terra-cotta fragment from Kondapur (Fig. 8) and another fragment from Ter (Fig. 9) (Ter Museum RC 1.258)[11] also seem to be identical images (though each is now a fragment) and could be from the same or duplicate molds.[12] Both are $3\frac{1}{2}$ inches in height. Each has lotus pads beneath the feet and a pot brimming with lotus flowers in each upper corner; each is draped with a cloth across its "hip," or widest part, in analogy to the *mekhalā* worn by the goddess. Since the opposite has been assumed, the point should be stressed that the iconographic variety among examples seen in details within a Form, is more common than the repetition seen in the few duplicate images that exist. The images are, in fact, virtually all unique in their detail. For example, another Form I terra-cotta relief from Ter (Fig. 10) (Ter Museum 785.C2) has lotus rosettes placed to either side of the figure, not only in the upper corners but also below; thus it is similar to the examples just mentioned but not identical.[13] Another terra-cotta example from Nagarjunakonda (the second from this site) (Fig. 11), which has been misdescribed as "*stūpa*-headed," probably because the observer did not see the lotus details of the upper portion and assumed its Buddhist use because of the site's preponderent Buddhist dedication, is similar to the figure just described with four lotus rosettes.[14] A stone (whitewashed) Lajjā Gaurī from Karlapalem, Guntur District, A.P. now in the Victoria Jubilee Museum at Vijayawada, Andhra Pradesh, is more potlike than any other example (Fig. 12). The unusual feature of this relief is that the legs are joined at the upper shoulder of the pot rather than below as in all other examples. This image most clearly enunciates, therefore, the *pūrṇa kumbha* ancestry of the Lajjā Gaurī figures. The variety of iconographic detail of the Lajjā Gaurī figures suggests that the artists followed no text and that the images were quickly adapted to regional or other requirements.

The only large figure that may be a Form I example is the stone Nagarjunakonda piece (Fig. 42). When it was first published the lower torso looked very much like a legged amphora with a belt and was so described.[15] When another piece of the image was later found it was joined to it above the amphoralike abdomen. The image's appearance and, in my schema, its form-type were thereby changed. It is clear since the pieces were joined that the image originally continued above the waist, although how far is not known since it is still incomplete. The *channavīra* (body jewelry that hangs from the neck, crosses between the breasts, passes around the waist and up the back) on the restored fragment suggests that this goddess may have originally been more like the Chalukya figures (Form III) (see Fig. 48), which regularly have such ornamentation. This type of body jewelry would imply (necessitate) a full upper torso and culmination in a lotus or human head. The Nagarjunakonda example should probably not be classed as *uttānapad* pot Form I despite its early date of late third or early fourth century, which is firmly established by several factors including its site's known active period, the fact that the carving style coheres to the later part of that period, and its inscription's content and paleography. I shall consider it in greater detail in the Form III section dealing with lotus-headed figures with arms since I believe that was its original appearance.

If one inverts almost any of these Form I examples, one notices that the potform belly area also looks very much like either a closed lotus bud or a phallus. The slit seems to serve as the opening of the vagina and of the penis or lotus bud. This composite image formed of the large bud and pot, or phallus and womb, is surprising but not atypical of Indian art in general where clever visual double entendre is common, as for example in an image in Ajanta rock-cut *vihāra* I of bodies of four deer sharing one head, or in the bodies of four wrestling *gaṇas* sharing two heads at Badami rock-cut temple I and elsewhere, or in the frequently encountered elephant-bull where the two affronted bodies ingeniously are carved sharing one head which can be seen as either a bull's or an elephant's. These examples are, admittedly, a different class of optical illusion than Lajjā Gaurī images because they are merely physical conjunction (though some philosophical interpretation is possible even for these), whereas the Lajjā Gaurī figures play not only physically but also play on symbolic and sexual meanings. Viewed from the "head" end it seems that within the female body of Lajjā Gaurī a phallus is enclosed in the womb area, or a lotus bud is within the *kumbha,* or pot.[16] Indian literature, poetry, speech, and language itself also abound in punning, paradox, and multiple meanings, a simple relevant example being the word *kumbha* which means both pot and womb.[17]

In her discussion of cultural metaphors in the tenth-century Tamil text, *Tirumantiram,* Margaret Egnor notes that modern informants familiar with ancient texts said that a metaphor for the vagina is either an open flower or a ripe fruit, that the womb is described as a lotus flower which opens and closes rhythmically (in response to the presence and absence of the sun), and that the womb is called the *yoni,* or the vessel which receives. The penis is called a closed bud, or a green fruit. All of these associations are given form in Lajjā Gaurī images. Egnor further says that the *Tirumantiram* rather simply describes conception thus: "After the bud joins the flower, it blossoms."[18] Lajjā Gaurī images of all Forms (Figs. 3, 21, 93, for example) seem to suggest the union of the bud and the flower, the phallus and the womb. The phallus is clearly represented within Form III images from Naganathakolla (Fig. 48), Kudavelli (Fig. 52), and Darasuram (Fig. 54), but can be identified in almost all of the images. The inclusion of the bud/phallus should probably be credited to the creative imagination of the artist drawing on such well-known cultural metaphors.

In the sanctum of a Śiva temple, union is symbolically visualized with the phallus (*liṅga*) rising away from the womb (*yoni*) that forms the surface of the altar.[19] The body of Lajjā Gaurī itself served as an altar and in these images within her body, union seems to be cleverly represented as a visual union of body parts and/or symbolic elements. Although the visual representation is quite distinct from that of the *liṅga* and *yoni,* a general conceptual basis may be shared.

Three other figures of the *uttānapad* pot Form I goddess from Ter and Bhita (Figs. 11–14) give more emphasis to the figures' upper portion, elongating the waist in a way that seems intended to suggest a rising phallus.[20]

A few unusual examples of Form I Lajjā Gaurī merit special description because of their distinct and revealing details. The first of these is a plaque from Jayaramswami Vadgaon (Satara District, Maharashtra) (Fig. 73), which bears a "multifigured representation" including Lajjā Gaurī in Form I in the upper area of the rectangular stone. Lotus petals are not incised below her, though the intention may have been to finish the plaque with this detail in the manner of a group of Lajjā Gaurī plaques already described (Figs. 1–4). Added to her right side is a couchant bull carved upright and in high relief; that is, the bull crouches on the same ground upon which the goddess is supine.[21] This relative positioning of Lajjā Gaurī and the bull, which is repeated in many examples, clearly indicates that the goddess is meant to be worshiped in a supine position. A bull, along with other figures, is often added to multifigured plaques, as is discussed in chapter 2, but this particular pairing of only the bull and a Form I goddess is unique. The plaque is difficult to date, but may be c. late third to fourth century, judging by its sculpture quality which is comparable to that of the figure from Nevase which is stratigraphically dated (see Fig. 4).

In regard to the Vadgaon plaque, Dhere suggests that the association of the goddess with the bull is as goddess of fertility with god of virility: the bull, archtypical symbol of virility, who plows the earth and the female figure, Pṛthvī, the earth personified as a goddess.[22] The same association of bull with Lajjā Gaurī is found, with quite a different arrangement and scale, before the Ellora rock-cut Śiva temple 21 (Rameśvara) (Figs. 74–75). There a life-size Nandi bull is carved on top of a monolithic stone platform, the most prominent side of which, on approaching the temple, is carved with the image of Lajjā Gaurī in the anthropomorphic Form IV (see pages 39–40). On many other multifigured plaques (see chapter 2) a bull is also included. The association of the bull to Lajjā Gaurī is apparently important since he is her frequent companion. Although Dhere's interpretation is likely within the cultural context of Indian symbols, it is not specifically defensible. The interpretation he gives is fundamental even in examples in which the bull is obviously Nandi. In many other representations the bull is clearly Śiva's vehicle (*vāhana*) Nandi because it is oriented toward a Śiva *liṅga,* as for example in Figures 99 or 103 and especially as at Ellora 21 (Fig. 75). In the Vadgaon example his exact identity and meaning remains uncertain.

A second example is unusual for its design and provenance. The *uttānapad* pot goddess from Kausambi in Uttar Pradesh is the only northern example of Form I, so one would suspect that it was originally made in the south and traveled to the north (Fig. 16) as mentioned earlier. Against its southern origin, however, is the fact that its design is distinct from southern types especially in the detail: above the abdomen is carved a design that may represent a lotus in full bloom, and above this a triple arch with striated patterns, such as are not found on southern examples. Perhaps the arches served as the frame for the images as they do in an example from Kausambi, now in the Indian Museum, Calcutta (Fig. 21). The arch reminds one of those seen over the heads of several early northern Kuṣāṇ period mother goddesses from Mathura (for which there is not an accepted explanation), which visual similarity further supports the probability of a northern origin of this figure. The abdomen area is damaged, but the *uttānapad* legs are clear with a cloth around each thigh. This terra-cotta measures about $2\frac{1}{2}$ inches.

The third unusual example is also the smallest of all Lajjā Gaurī images (Fig. 17), seven-eighths of an inch square. It is the only example yet found made of green faience, and the only one that has a pinhole at the top, suggesting that it was worn as a pendant or an amulet. The figure has an emphasized slit of the pudendum, and the *uttānapad* pose supports an amphoralike pot. It is difficult to tell, due to its condition, whether the round shapes to the side of the amphora's "waist" are breasts, foliage, or pot handles. This piece is in the museum at Ter.[23]

The minimally anthropomorphized Form I goddess as *uttānapad* pot is clearly visually related to the pan-Indian symbol of the *pūrṇa kumbha*, the brimming pot. The brimming pot issuing a riot of lotus life is one of the most familiar of all auspicious symbols of Indian art seen in Buddhist, Hindu, and Jain art. The symbolic ancestry of the *pūrṇa kumbha* and its relevance to the meaning of Lajjā Gaurī will be discussed in chapter 3.

The *uttānapad* pot Form I of Lajjā Gaurī focuses on the personified womb (pot) to suggest the elemental female power of reproduction. In other forms not only the womb but also the entire female body with nurturing breasts and arms is represented suggesting the emanation of female power from these parts as well. In Form II, which is armless, the breasts seem more important than the arms in suggesting motherly nourishment. Compared to the other Forms, *uttānapad* pot Form I is more purely an icon of reproductive power. The other forms more broadly encompass the idea of motherhood—reproduction and nurturing—by inclusion of breasts and a more nearly human body with arms.

Form I was the major early type of Lajjā Gaurī popular in the south in the third and fourth centuries and was not made thereafter nor was it made elsewhere. Forms II and III seem to have succeeded it, but the lotus flower "head" they include, must be understood partially in reference to the pot bearing a lotus flower of Form I which symbolizes abundance of life. Although the torso of Forms II and III is no longer a pot but a human torso, the lotus culmination is retained with the same meaning as in Form I.

FORM II: LOTUS-HEADED WITHOUT ARMS

Form II Lajjā Gaurī images (Figs. 18–31) have the *uttanapad* pose of the legs on a torso that is not potlike but more human in form in that the torso includes the abdominal area, which is ornamented with a girdle and has a carefully indicated navel, breasts, often a necklace, and, consistently, a lotus in the place of a head. The legs of Form II do not cradle the abdominal area as they do in Form I images. In Form II the figure has no arms.

Like the *uttānapad* pot Form I images, Form II images are all small, measuring either about two inches or about five inches on a side. Almost all are stone, in fact only two examples, one from Ter (Fig. 18) and another from Kausambi (Fig. 19), are hand-modeled terra-cotta. The stone figures are from the following sites in Maharashtra: Ter, Mahurjhari, Paunar, Mandhal, Mandapuri, Hamlapuri, Ramatola, Pauni, Mansar, and Alapur, and from Sanchi in Madhya Pradesh and Kausambi in

Uttar Pradesh. Fourteen other Maharashtrian examples that I have not seen have been reported from Nandapur, Mandapuri, Valad, Nagara, Supala, Buldahana, Chandrapur, and Bhambragarh in the districts of Nagpur, Wardha, Bhandara, Amaravti, and Chandrapur. Four additional images from Madhya Pradesh are in the Archaeological Survey of India Collection at Malhar (Bilaspur District), Madhya Pradesh,[24] and one image from an unknown site is in the Kanoria Collection in Patna, Bihar (Fig. 20).

Of thirty-four images, only the two buff terra-cottas with a red slip from Ter (Fig. 18) and Kausambi (Fig. 19) have been given an early date, first to third century, by H. D. Sankalia, but these have been dated as second to third century by S. C. Kala[25] and by Douglas Barrett in comparison with a large number of southern terra-cotta figures.[26] These may in fact be the two earliest Form II figures, but I would date them second to third century in agreement with Kala and Barrett. Following Sankalia, as many scholars have, Mukhopadhyay dated a stone figure from Kausambi (Fig. 21), now in the Indian Museum, Calcutta, to first to third century.[27] A more appropriate date for this visually distinguished figure, judging stylistically, may be fourth to fifth century. The rest of the Form II lotus-headed Lajjā Gaurī figures are from northern locations in Maharashtra and nearby Kausambi in U.P., and are dated fourth to sixth century. Two were found at Alapur near Bhokardan in Maharashtra and one of these was found in excavation. According to stratigraphy it is dated by one scholar to the fourth to fifth century and by another to fifth to sixth century (Fig. 23).[28] The other Alapur image (Fig. 22), which is similar to the excavated example, was a surface find.

All four Forms of Lajjā Gaurī are found in Maharashtra, but the lotus-headed Form II, in which the goddess is armless, was evidently very popular in this region, especially around Nagpur (which is in the center of India within Maharashtra), in the fourth to sixth centuries, judging from the large number of these images found there. No Form II figures have yet been found in Gujarat, or Karnataka, and just three are known from Kausambi in Allahabad District of Uttar Pradesh. From Andhra there are two examples of a Form II Lajjā Gaurī included in a multifigured plaque (Figs. 104 and 105). (These will be described in chapter 2). Form II is the predominant Maharashtrian form.

Within the grouping of lotus-headed, armless Form II images there is a great diversity of details. In the simplest version the armless torso rests on the spread *uttānapad* legs; a lotus, sometimes looking like a ruff, rests just above the breasts. Such examples are one from Ter (Fig. 18),[29] two from Kausambi (Figs. 119, 21),[30] and two from Paunar (Figs. 24 and 25).[31] In these the goddess wears anklets, but there is no cloth woven through the thighs. The Kausambi example in the Indian Museum (Fig. 21), mentioned above as datable to the fourth to fifth century, is especially dignified in the upright posture of the female torso and the crownlike treatment of her lotus. It is stone, carved against a round background which has a patterned edge.

In another type of Form II image a lotus flower or bud is added to either side of the lotus head; even without the arms the lotus flowers by the "head" are in the same location as they are in Form III in which the hands hold the buds. The Form II figures from Sanchi (Fig. 26),[32] Ter (Fig. 27),[33] two from Alapur (Figs. 22 and 23),[34] and Pauni[35] (Fig. 28) are otherwise like the first simple group just described (Figs. 18 and 19, 21, 24 and 25), which only lacks the lotus rosettes by the lotus head. One of the two Alapur examples (Fig. 23) includes the cloth around the legs.

A small oval relief (height $3\frac{4}{5}$ inches) of Lajjā Gaurī in the Kanoria collection, Patna, is a unique depiction, basically Form II, lotus-headed, without arms (Fig. 20). The image varies from the normal

Form II figures in that lotus rosettes, which in other examples are placed to the sides of the lotus head, here are placed to the sides of the shoulders joined to the figure. This particular example is similar in its outline to the anthropomorphized *śrīvatsa* from Enadi (Fig. 125) with similarly abstract arms.

Two interesting examples from Ramatola (Bhandara District, Maharashtra) are now kept in the Central Museum, Nagpur (Figs. 29 and 30). Like the figures mentioned above from Kausambi and Ter, in these two examples the armless goddess has a lotus flower to either side of her lotus head. These two, however, are quite different in that in either Ramatola example the figure is placed to the right side of a wide rectangular stone plaque which includes two miniature tanks, or *kuṇḍa,* on the left side of each. One tank is rectangular, the other is square, and in the larger of the two plaques there is a third tank below the goddess. Each tank has a hole cut through its side wall nearest the figure. Muley has suggested that these are like a tank near the goddess, as would be standard in a temple setting, for bathing.[36] Water poured into the tank runs out the hole onto the goddess. The inclusion of the tank on the plaques emphasizes the importance of worship of the figure and also of worship of the goddess near a source of water for ritual bathing. The importance of a water source near the goddess is also evident from observation of the physical circumstances of the large Lajjā Gaurī images that are still in worship: all are near a tank, river, pond, or in a step well.

Four other examples of lotus-headed Form II images are multifigured relief plaques that each bear lotus rosettes to either side of the goddess's lotus head like others described (Figs. 22 and 23, 26–30), but with the addition of a bull to the right of the goddess and originally in each case a devotee to her left (Figs. 93–95). The bull's back is seen from above for he is couchant next to the supine goddess. This inclusion of the bull and his position recalls the Vadgaon example of Form I (Fig. 71), but here the bull is smaller than the goddess rather than of equal size. These four examples are from Maharashtra: one is from Hamlapuri (Nagpur District),[37] two are from Paunar (Wardha District) (Figs. 92 and 93),[38] and one is from Mansar (Nagpur District) (Fig. 93).[39] These are similar in style to those previously described of the fourth to sixth centuries and must be contemporary with them. Other examples of lotus-headed Form II figures of later dates are found in multifigured plaques that have variations in iconography. These figures (Figs. 91 and 92, 98) will be discussed in chapter 2.

Most of the Form II images described above are datable between the fourth and sixth centuries, but a few other individual representations of Lajjā Gaurī are clearly later in date. For instance, a large stone Form II Lajjā Gaurī of good quality is now in worship at Sharadaāśrama at Yeotmal in Maharashtra, although it is originally from Mahurjhari near Nagpur in Maharashtra (Fig. 31).[40] Its style compares well to that of several Early Chalukya period images, and thereby it should be dated to c. seventh century. The similarity to Chalukya examples is stylistic only. It is iconographically distinct; the only form of Lajjā Gaurī made by the Early Chalukyas was Form III (with arms). The area of this image's provenance, furthermore, was never within the Chalukya realm, so it cannot be credited to their direct influence. The only Form II figures to date later than the seventh century, in my opinion, are the four examples from Malhar in Madhya Pradesh, which stylistically may be dated ninth to tenth centuries, as suggested by O. P. Misra.[41] The Malhar figures have a treatment of volume and mass that is distinct from that of the earlier examples; it is at once heavier but more contained and crisply delineated in the early medieval manner typical of Central Indian sculpture in general.

FORM III: LOTUS-HEADED WITH ARMS

Form III figures of Lajjā Gaurī (Figs. 32–64, 99–103, 106–7) are all lotus-headed with otherwise human female bodies. The legs are in the *uttānapad* pose, the arms are held up by the sides of the lotus head with a bud in each hand, and the torso includes breasts. The difference between Forms II and III is the inclusion of arms in Form III. It may be noted that Lajjā Gaurī never has more than two arms as many Hindu goddesses do. In fact, the image of a goddess without arms in Indian art (Forms I and II) may be unique. Whereas multiarmed Hindu goddesses and gods hold an attribute in each hand to express a particular power, and a superhuman cumulative power, it may be the intention of their omission in Forms I and II of Lajjā Gaurī to suggest that her elemental power of fertility and creation cannot be symbolized by hand-held attributes, but is expressed through her body, locus of her particular power. When the goddess has two arms in Forms III and IV she holds lotus buds or flowers, an appropriate attribute expressing pure generation. The buds held to the side of the mature blossom-head suggest the potential of new life. A similar suggestion of the life cycle is also seen in the depiction of the *pūrṇa kumbha* motif at such sites as Nagarjunakonda and Sanchi, where consistently the pot holds a lotus bud, a fully bloomed lotus, and a wilting flower symbolizing infancy, maturity, and old age or death.

Whereas the lotus-headed Form II image was popular in Maharashtra, Form III predominates further south with only a few examples found in the north. All of the Early Chalukya period (late seventh century) examples found in Karnataka and Andhra states are of this Form, but there are also earlier and later examples from other regions.

A unique figure from Paunar in Maharashtra (Fig. 96) iconographically falls between Forms II and III, not conforming to either type. In this small multifigured stone plaque, $5\frac{1}{4}$ inches by 7 inches, the goddess in *uttānapad* pose has breasts and a lotus head.[42] Her unique feature is that out of the fully blossomed lotus head there grows to either side a lotus stalk with a bud. The stalk touches the top of each raised knee in exactly the manner of the arms holding a bud in Forms III and IV. From this representation it is a small step to substitute arms for stalks and to place a lotus bud in each hand, which is standard for Form III figures. It is unlikely, however, that this figure represents an actual iconographic intermediate step leading toward substitution of arms for the stalk since the example is one of a kind. Certainly, however, in images where arms are added, they often do have a sinuous lotus-plant quality. Note, for example, that in the Naganatha figure (Fig. 48) the stalk of the lotus bud held in each hand wraps around the wrists as bangles, and the fingers of the hands bend like lotus tendrils. In Indian poetry a young girl is often described as being like a tender vine and in this image the metaphor seems to be visualized. In this relief from Paunar the goddess wears a leaf-patterned necklace further emphasizing the visual conflation of the female and nature. The plant parts of Lajjā Gaurī images seem to relate her to the irrepressible reproductive force of nature related to human and divine creation by visual metaphor. The use of the lotus, symbol par excellence of endless, pure generation of life, makes this meaning clear. Final details of the multifigured plaque from Paunar are the bull on her right, as in examples previously described, and to her left a kneeling figure of indeterminate sex, which may be a devotee. The devotee is standard on many plaques by the side of the goddess, while the bull is found on the other side of the goddess.

Form III figures are either small, about $2\frac{1}{2}$ or $5\frac{1}{2}$ inches, or they are much larger, about 37–41 inches square, that is, life-size. The large images are stone and were used as the icon in a temple subshrine as is evident from several in situ images, found at Siddhanakolla (Fig. 43) (Karnataka), Belligamve (Fig. 61) (Karnataka), and Alampur (Fig. 46) (Andhra). Other images still in worship though not in their original location are at Darasuram (Fig. 54) (Tamil Nadu), and Yeotmal (Fig. 31) (Maharashtra). Undoubtedly, there are others of which I am unaware. An image from Kudavelli (Fig. 52) now kept in the Alampur site museum is carved of a piece with its altar. The Form III Lajjā Gaurī is mainly found in Karnataka and Andhra Pradesh but also in Maharashtra, Uttar Pradesh, and Gujarat. One figure in worship now in Darasuram in Tamil Nadu, is the only example found in that state and is thought to have been made in Andhra.

The small terra-cottas of Form III and a few small stone images are from the northern sites whereas all of the large stone figures of Form III and a few small stone figures are from the south. Only one small terra-cotta in this iconographic grouping is from the south: Yellesvaram in Andhra Pradesh (Fig. 32).[43]

Form III is the largest group of surviving examples. I know of thirty-five individual images (and more Form III images are found in multifigured plaques surveyed as well), whereas I know of only eighteen Form I examples, thirty-two Form II, and twenty-three Form IV images. Of all Lajjā Gaurī images scholars have assigned the earliest dates to northern Form III terra-cottas. One example of such a supposedly early terra-cotta is an especially crude round plaque, $4\frac{5}{8}$ inches in diameter, in the Indian Museum, Calcutta, from Bhita (Fig. 33) that has been dated to the first to second century (Kuṣāṇ period) by Sankalia and by subsequent scholars who followed his opinion. It is, however, important to note that upon its excavation Marshall dated it Kuṣāṇ to Gupta period or first to fifth centuries.[44] In this case Marshall's broader dating is more appropriate because of the crudity of the piece and resultant difficulty in dating it. Sankalia's date was based on circumstantial evidence of the excavation that seems undermined by Marshall's opinion. I would prefer a later dating for this example from Bhita given the fact that all others of this form are later.

The goddess in this Bhita example has her empty hands held up (the right forearm is broken off), an emphasized pudendum, large anklets with an incised criss-cross design, a deep navel, appliqué girdle, and the plaque has borders decorated with incised and punched designs. It was hand-modeled and given a red slip. Other images in Form III that have been dated early are six images from Kausambi kept in the Allahabad Museum, all dated to the second century by Kala, though he provides no reasons in his catalogue.[45] I believe the Form I type was the original conception because of its dependence on earlier symbols, its simplicity, and the style of individual figures. This point will be discussed in the conclusion to this study.

I know of eleven images of Lajjā Gaurī from Kausambi made of terra-cotta or stone including four fragments (Figs. 16, 19, 21, 34, 37, 39, 40). Kausambi was a great Buddhist center, located thirty-two miles southwest of Allahabad on a bank of the Jamuna river, now part of Uttar Pradesh. It was inhabited from 600 B.C. until about A.D. 400. It is therefore not surprising to find a range in quality of the pieces and of dates for these figures of third to fourth centuries, and to find that three forms of Lajjā Gaurī were made there (I, II, and III). Of the eleven images, four are Form III. Unfortunately, of 323 human figures in terra-cotta included in the site's excavation report, no images of Lajjā Gaurī were reported so that their datable strata are unknown.

The Patna Museum possesses a rectangular plaque (no. Arch 7716) from Kausambi with Lajjā Gaurī (Fig. 34).[46] It is identified as Kuṣāṇ period by Gupta and Shere, although no reasons are provided in their catalogues. It is again a very crude and damaged terra-cotta covered with a red slip in which the empty hands are held up by the sides of the head. The Kuṣāṇ date is possible, but the figure could date later, perhaps the third or fourth century. The border is ridged all around. The example is badly worn and its head now looks like a plain disk, but there are some remnants of lotus petals on it. Examples that have been described as disk- or mirror-headed, such as the one from Kausambi in the Patna Museum, actually all have surviving traces of lotus petals on the disk (Fig. 34). Only one example of Form III in worship at Bilagi in Karnataka —which seems to be modern—does have a plain disk head. It is extremely crude and perhaps should be considered iconographically corrupt (Fig. 35). Similarly, an image from Amreli in Gujarat seems disk-headed, but this is probably due to damage to the stone.[47]

Similar to the Kausambi image in the Patna Museum (Fig. 34) in the angular pose of the arms and legs is a stone image from Bundelkhand (Fig. 36) which has been dated to the second to third century in the catalog of the State Museum, Dhubela, presumably by its style. The Bundelkhand image has the lotus details of the head intact, that is, turned toward the viewer like a wheel. This plaque is about 5 inches square.[48] A large fragment of a Lajjā Gaurī from Kausambi and now in the Allahabad Municipal Museum (no. 5034) (Fig. 37) also has the angular pose of the arms and legs and the same general roughness. These four figures (Figs. 33, 34, 36, 37) form a type group related by the angular arms and legs and the full view of the round lotus head (where intact). They are from three sites: Bhita and Kausambi in Allahabad District of U.P. and nearby Bundelkhand in Rewa District of Madhya Pradesh. I would date them within the range of third to fourth centuries, the Bhita example possibly being somewhat later, fourth to sixth centuries.

An example from Jhusi, U.P., now in the Allahabad Municipal Museum (no. 4617), is a hand-modeled, red-painted terra-cotta, 5 by $5\frac{1}{2}$ inches (Fig. 38). It has been dated to the second century by two scholars, and to the first century B.C. by another scholar.[49] I would date this image c. fourth century by comparison to an image from Kausambi (Fig. 39) in the State Museum, Lucknow, discussed hereafter. In both the lotus head is given a special crownlike treatment. The back of the Jhusi figure is flat. The upper arms and the lower part of the legs are broken off. The navel is an incised cross, the nipples are stippled, as are the necklace and girdle. The pudendum is heavily emphasized. This piece has been published extensively.[50] The lower torsos of these Form III figures are not potlike at all, but are narrow-waisted.

The mentioned terra-cotta, a fragment, from the site of Kausambi, now in the State Museum, Lucknow (79.15.6) (Fig. 39), is dated by the museum to about fourth century, the late Kuṣāṇ period, which date I agree with judging by its lively style and quality and by the similarity of these to the excellent large terra-cotta Gaja Lakṣmī republished by Harle, from the same site.[51] These images share a great stateliness and similar bold style. This terra-cotta is painted with a shiny red slip. The fragment is about 8 inches in height. The lotus head is again a half-open flower worn like a crown with its seed pod carefully indicated. The lotus head leans forward slightly and is based in a lotus filament necklace. The breast is quite carefully formed. The surviving upraised hand in this case is empty rather than holding a lotus and the arm is adorned by many bangles. The curved frame has a ridged edge.

One last Lajjā Gaurī of Form III from Kausambi is kept in the Patna Museum (no. 7606). The red sandstone figure is 5 by $5\frac{1}{2}$ inches with a very eroded surface (Fig. 40). The feet are not visible in the museum mount. The head is a lotus, though details are unclear.[52]

The site of Ter, which, like Kausambi, was also a major early Buddhist site at which Buddhism coexisted with Hinduism, has yielded examples of Forms I, II, and III, and it is the only site to have produced such a range of forms. Only the human-headed figures of Form IV that are common to Gujarat do not occur at Ter or, for that matter, anywhere in the south. Ter Museum figure no. 9.147 is stone, $2\frac{3}{4}$ inches square, of Form III with a lotus head, arms, and breasts, wearing a jeweled girdle, a cloth woven through the legs, and with a deeply incised navel (Fig. 41). It may be dated c. fourth century by its style.

Some of the stone figures of Form III are datable by style, by their known place of origin where artistic activity was alive within a certain time period, or by a combination of such evidence, as cited for examples discussed. For example, twelve Form III figures, yet to be discussed, are datable to the late seventh century because they are from Early Chalukya temple sites and are carved in the Early Chalukya style (Figs. 43–52, 54–59, 61, 64).

Although there is a great range in quality of carving of the Form III figures from crudest (Fig. 34) to most refined (Fig. 48), in iconographic terms they are consistent. They are in *uttānapad* pose with the soles of their feet turned up sideward. They wear a jeweled girdle, anklets, armlets, bracelets, and a necklace. Each upbent arm rests behind the knee, and each hand holds a lotus bud at the side of the lotus head. A cloth is often "woven" around the thighs and behind the back. The "head" is a fully blossomed lotus flower. It may be represented as if seen from the side edge or turned "full face," wheel-like, toward the viewer, or half open and crownlike as in the Jhusi and Kausambi examples.

Most of these Form III lotus-headed figures were made between the seventh and the ninth centuries, and all of the large stone altar figures were made within this period except that from Nagarjunakonda of the early fourth century.

Form III?: Nagarjunakonda Lajjā Gaurī

An inscribed marble image of Lajjā Gaurī was discovered in 1940 on the north slope of Nagarjunakonda hill at the extremity of the remains of the pillared hall of a Hindu temple (Fig. 42). It was reported by H. K. Narasimhaswami.[53] The one line Prākṛt inscription on the lower rim of the stone is written in Brāhmī and reads: "Success! [This image is] caused to be made by Queen Mahādevī Khaṁḍuvulā, whose husband and children are alive and who is the wife of Mahārāja Siri Ehuvala Chaṁtamula."

Unfortunately, the inscription does not give the name of the goddess, but it suggests that this woman's fortune in having her husband and children living is due to her worship of this goddess and, by extension and because the figure was probably placed within a temple shrine, that by worshiping this image other women may achieve the same auspicious state.[54] This, we know, is the motivation for worship of such images in India today.

The script is identified paleographically as third century or early fourth century. The reign of the mentioned Ikṣvāku King Ehuvala Chaṁtamula is variously set as c. A.D. 261–58, 320–44, 333–57, or 326–50.[55] This figure was found near the Nodagiśvaraśvamin temple (site 127). An inscription on a *dhvajastambha* (temple pillar) found at the same site says that the temple came into existence during the rule of Ehuvala Chaṁtamula, which further confirms the date of the image found here.[56] Like other Lajjā Gaurī images this Lajjā Gaurī figure was found at a predominantly Buddhist site in the small Hindu temple area.

This large marble image is damaged and is still missing its upper portion.[57] The legs and abdomen are preserved. The abdomen sits like an amphora on the stand of the thighs. Narasimhaswami noted that "the belly resembles the decorated *pūrṇa ghaṭa* (brimming vase), the representation of which is a common feature in the Buddhist sculpture of this period at Nagarjunakonda" (Fig. 113).[58] The vulva is indicated by a line. The ankles are heavily ornamented with bangles, and the belly is adorned by a detailed, jeweled girdle. The feet have the soles slightly turned up with the toes tensely splayed. A *channavīra* adorns the remaining fragment of the upper torso. The image is carved in relief from a flat-backed slab.

Since the image is broken we cannot tell whether it culminated with a lotus on top of a pot-abdomen of Form I, or a lotus on top of a full torso with (Form III) or without (Form II) arms, breasts, or even a human head (Form IV). The image may have been Form I, as we would expect from its early date and southern origin, but due to its fragmentary state we cannot be certain it was not Form II or III, or IV. Of the early Lajjā Gaurī images it is the only life-size one. Life-size Lajjā Gaurīs are, however, standard for the Early Western Chalukya period (seventh century) and there are a few life-size examples which date later. A significant detail is the *channavīra* worn by the figure for other than this example only the Chalukya Form III images are ornamented with a *channavīra* (see Figs. 43 and 48 for example); none of the Form I, II, or IV images wears a *channavīra*. This suggests that the Chalukyas were looking to the Nagarjunakonda piece, or similar ones, as their model. The cultural admiration of the Ikṣvākus by the Early Chalukyas has been discussed by S. Settar.[59]

The body of this image would have filled an altar, as does that of the Kudavelli image in the Alampur Museum (Fig. 52), the Siddhanakolla figure (Fig. 43), and another still in worship at Alampur (Fig. 46). These were probably worshiped by circumambulation and application of ghee as the Siddhanakolla and Alampur (Bala Brahmā temple) images still are today.

The powerful image of a large woman on her back in a birth-giving pose in the sanctum of a temple subshrine relates conceptually to the physical suggestion of the initiate's pure rebirth into the spiritual world as described by Eliade: "The initiate is the newborn infant."[60] Such visual metaphor in Indian art is constantly used to relate the experience of the microcosmic and the macrocosmic spheres, so deftly integrated to "personalize" the religious experience of the believer.

Form III: Early Chalukya Lajjā Gaurī Images

The goddess Lajjā Gaurī was especially important to the people ruled by the Early Chalukya kings during the last two decades of the seventh century as is apparent from the number, size, and quality of her images made at this time. The Early Chalukya kings ruled over areas of the Deccan plateau, which today comprise parts of the states of Karnataka, Andhra, and Maharashtra. From this period and area of India there survive twelve large stone images of Lajjā Gaurī, all of which share a common iconography: they are Form III lotus-headed figures with arms and breasts included on the anthropomorphic torso, and with legs in the *uttānapad* pose. Although the Chalukya-period images are only of Form III, the Form was also made outside the Chalukya region in earlier and later centuries as described. All of the Chalukya-period examples are large, three to four feet, and are carved in relief in stone. No small Lajjā Gaurī images or terra-cottas from the Chalukya period and region are known. The large size, the choice of stone for Lajjā Gaurī images, and the care taken in carving them indicate their considerable importance at this time. Furthermore, a subshrine was specially built to enshrine Lajjā Gaurī in front of some seventh-century temples dedicated to Śiva. The Lajjā Gaurī subshrine was symmetrically paired to a subshrine housing the Saptamātṛkās (Seven Mothers).

Several of the Chalukya images are still worshiped at sites where temples of the period stand. These temples provide an important context in which to study the role of Lajjā Gaurī. Two Chalukya-period temples, the Lakulīśa temple at Siddhanakolla and the Bala Brahmā temple at Alampur, still in worship, retain images of the goddess. They are visited by childless women or couples seeking the blessing of fertility. (The tradition of such temples continues in India today). One of the images, that at Siddhanakolla, is in its original location. Every Chalukya site, except Badami and Pattadakal, has at least one major image of the goddess. Records exist of the original location of three subsequently displaced Chalukya images of Lajjā Gaurī. From these in situ and recorded locations a pattern emerges: Where Lajjā Gaurī was or is still in worship at a Chalukya temple site, she is housed in a subshrine of the main Śiva temple, and she is accompanied by images of the *Saptamātṛkās* in a subshrine opposed to hers.[61] The Seven Mothers' shrine is (or was) guarded, in two cases, by goat-headed male figures. Several of these temple sites are known to have been Pāśupata in dedication, including Siddhanakolla and Mahakuta. Ellora cave temple 21, where Lajja Gaurī is carved in situ, is also known to be a Pāśupata dedication, and Elephanta, where an image of Lajjā Gaurī was found, was also probably Pāśupata.

Siddhanakolla

The image of Lajjā Gaurī that is, without question, in its original location is at Siddhanakolla, a site in the hills outside the major Chalukya temple town of Aihole in Karnataka. There stands a late seventh-century Chalukya temple dedicated to Lakulīśa, founder of the Pāśupata sect, as determined by the image of Lakulīśa in the projecting arch (*śukhanāsa*) on the front of the temple's curvilinear spire (*Nāgara śikhara*). To the southeast of the temple is a natural grotto. The goddess, locally called Lajjā Gaurī, is carved in relief from the rock floor of this grotto (Fig. 43).[62] A spring originates above, falls alongside the goddess, and runs down the mountain.

The image here has a broad lotus head.[63] Her two hands are raised to either side of her head, but they are empty rather than holding a lotus bud. A cloth is threaded through her legs and behind her back, which is a detail of her iconography consistently included by the Early Chalukya artists and also frequently (though not consistently) found in images from other regions and of other Forms. She wears anklets, bracelets, *channavīra,* and has her feet flexed up, showing their soles. Her leg pose makes the *uttānapad M*-shape. The life-size image measures 32 inches in height and 39 inches in width. A Śiva *liṅga* now stands on a *pīṭha* nearby the monolithic Lajjā Gaurī. The age of this *liṅga* may be seventh century or later.

A crude headless image of Lajjā Gaurī is carved into a rock on the side of a stairway that leads up the mountain toward the temple (Fig. 44). This styleless image seems to be post-Chalukya and must be merely a path marker and not an icon itself as it is carved in an abbreviated fashion omitting any sort of head. It measures 18 inches in height and $17\frac{1}{2}$ inches in width. Worship of the main Lajjā Gaurī image at Siddhanakolla, I am told, is performed by ablutions of ghee applied to the pudendum.[64] Also, miniature dolmenlike "houses" to be filled with children are built by women or couples making pilgrimage to the site along the same path that leads from the stairway across the mountain top for a mile before the temple is reached.

Just northeast of the temple stands a simple structural subshrine housing a set of Saptamātṛkās, Chalukya in style, carved on one long stone slab. The subshrine's entrance is guarded by two goat-headed sentries carved in relief (Fig. 45) that may be identified either as Dakṣa (son or father of the goddess Aditi and father of Gaurī) or Naigameṣa (son, brother, or playfellow of Skanda).

Based on comparisons with Chalukya remains elsewhere, the Lajjā Gaurī in the grotto and the structural subshrine date, along with the Lakulīśa temple at Siddhanakolla, to the late seventh century. The subshrines, one natural and the second structural, were probably both a part of the original temple plan.[65] The location of the temple, outside a major temple center, Aihole, is significant. Other temples where this goddess was worshiped are also isolated, often in a glen outside a major center. "The shrine of any mother goddess without an *identificatio brahmanica* is outside the village."[66] However, in this case Lajjā Gaurī seems to have been given Brahmanic status by association to the temple. Lajjā Gaurī images at Mahakuta, Naganathakolla, and Chikka Mahakuta are also at remote sites where springs are found. The springs may be associated to Lajjā Gaurī's function as source of waters, and thereby fertility.[67]

Alampur

Another Chalukya-period lotus-headed Form III Lajjā Gaurī is in worship at Alampur in Kurnool District of Andhra, inside a modern subshrine that has been added to the main Śiva temple at the site, the Bala Brahmā temple built during the seventh century under the Early Chalukya rule (Fig. 46). She has a lotus head. She holds lotus buds up on either side of her head, the stalks of which wrap like tendrils around her wrists and upper arms, making bracelets and armlets. The image measures about $3\frac{1}{2}$ feet square and is clearly carved in the Early Chalukya sculpture style.

The Bala Brahmā temple is, like the Lakulīśa temple at Siddhanakolla, a Chalukya-period, Śiva temple dating about A.D. 660–90.[68] An extraordinarily fine set of Saptamātṛkās, each carved individually, is kept in an area that once was outside the temple, but is now enclosed by modern additions and joined to it.[69] The style of carving of this set and minor decorative details on the figures are the same as that of the Lajjā Gaurī image.

As it was originally built, the temple included two subshrines within its encompassing wall. These still stand but are complicated by the addition of modern structures. The subshrine at the southeast corner is a long rectangular shrine with one curved end (*gajapṛṣṭha*) with its entrance on the north, its long inner side to the left of the entrance axis of the temple. Today a post–Chalukya-period Chāmuṇḍā is kept inside this subshrine along with a Chalukya period image of a goat-headed sentry (Fig. 47b) carved in high relief. Another such goat-headed image that seems to be a pair with this one (Fig. 47a) is now kept in the Alampur site museum.[70] The Saptamātṛkās may have originally been kept in this broad hall, guarded as at Siddhanakolla, by the goat-headed figures by the door.

Opposite this subshrine is another that has a three-tiered spire (Bhūmiprāsāda *śikhara*) capped with a myrobalan-shaped stone (*āmalaka*) and a pot (*pūrṇa kumbha*). If the Bala Brahmā temple and subshrines had been laid out like those at the contemporary Siddhanakolla temple, then the image of the supine goddess would have originally been housed in the northeastern subshrine and she would not have been moved very far to her present location. At Alampur the goddess is called Reṇukā.[71]

NAGANATHAKOLLA

The third Early Chalukya temple where Lajjā Gaurī was found is at Naganathakolla. The Naganātha or Śiva temple stands in isolation outside the Chalukya capital, Badami (Bijapur District, Karnataka).[72] An excellent image of the goddess, found at this site, is now kept in the Badami Museum (B36) (Fig. 48). It is the finest of all Lajjā Gaurī images in its sensitive carving and details.[73] It is well preserved; in fact, its carving remains remarkably fresh as does the carving on the temple itself, both in red sandstone. The supervisor of excavations around the temple told me that to the northeast and southeast of the temple, that is, to the right and left of its entrance, are foundations, now reburied, of two subshrines. The Lajjā Gaurī image was found partially buried on the base of the southeastern subshrine. This repeats the location of the image at Siddhanakolla. No Saptamātṛkā set is known from this site, however, to complete the analogy to imagery at Siddanakolla and Alampur.

The Naganathakolla Lajjā Gaurī is nearly identical to that at Bala Brahmā temple, Alampur.[74] Two other images, though fragments, nearly duplicate the Naganātha image, one at Mahakuta (Fig. 50), the other at Chikkamahakuta (Fig. 51).[75] The intact Naganātha figure is carved in deep relief ($9\frac{1}{2}$ inches) and measures 38 inches in height and 28 inches in width (Fig. 48). The modeling of the female figure is supple and sensitive. The suggestion of soft, sagging stomach flesh like the slackening of a woman's abdomen after childbirth, is masterly. The breasts are firm with folds of flesh beneath them. The arms and shoulders are delicate and feminine. The legs, in *uttānapad,* are spread more naturally than in other images with the knees up, the feet are flexed with soles up, and the toes are tensed. The nude body is ornamented with necklace, *channavīra,* girdle, bracelets, and armlets that are like a vine tendril wrapping around the arms and actually ending in a leaf. Tassels of the anklets also seem plantlike. There is a cloth woven through the thighs. From the side view (Fig. 49) we see that the cloth touches the toes and then is joined to the back slab of the stone, serving as a sculptor's stone support.

The half-open lotus flower, sitting like a ruff on the shoulders, is turned three-quarters toward the viewer. The goddess holds, to either side of her lotus head a half open, smaller lotus flower, the stalk of which winds around her hand. The fingers themselves have a tendril-like quality. The fingers of the right hand seem to form a swastika, symbol of fortune and well-being. No doubt, the suggestion of her relation to vegetation is intended, as it is in the Paunar (Fig. 96) and other examples (Figs. 54, 67). This image is a masterpiece of fluid modeling and conscious symbol-making. It is no wonder that apparently three copies were made, at Bala Brahmā temple, Mahakuteśvara, and Chikkamahakuta.[76]

MAHAKUTEŚVARA

There is a large Lajjā Gaurī fragment at the site of Mahakuta, near Badami (Fig. 50). It is kept by a small shrine called Lakulīśa *mandira* on the southeast of the main temple at the site, the Makuteśvara (or Mahakuteśvara) temple, dedicated to Śiva. The Makuteśvara temple is Chalukya and dates to the late seventh century.[77] The Lakulīśa *mandira* and a second shrine of equal dimensions to the northeast of the main temple seem to form a pair of subshrines for the temple. The northeastern subshrine is empty and has lost its spire. The Lakulīśa *mandira* has a four-tier spire (Bhumiprasada *śikhara*). Although there are many other simple shrines at the site, these two, symmetrically located as they are before the temple, possibly were planned with the main temple. The southeastern subshrine may have once enshrined Lajjā Gaurī. This would repeat the organization of subshrines found at Alampur, Siddhanakolla, and Naganathakolla. The site of Mahakuta suggests, by the presence of several images of Lakulīśa on temple niches, its predominant dedication to the Pāśupata sect, as is also known to be the sectarian dedication of other sites with enshrined Lajjā Gaurī images.

John Faithful Fleet described this goddess, which he saw at Mahakuta before 1881, as a "somewhat notorious and very indecent headless stone figure." He recorded that the image was then kept inside a row of three small shrines on the west side of the compound.[78] Unfortunately, the directions Fleet recorded on this visit are inaccurate.[79] Possibly he reversed east and west. Lakulīśa *mandira* is one of a row of three small shrines on the east, and the broken image may now rest just outside its original subshrine.

The Mahakuteśvara image, now a fragment, was almost a twin of the Naganātha figure now in the Badami site museum, though an inch larger: 39 inches in height, by 38 inches in width, by 8 inches in depth. Like the Naganatha image the anklets are tasseled and the small lotus flowers held by the large lotus "head" are open, not buds. These figures must either have been made by one hand or copied one from the other.

Kudavelli

The goddess published as Aditi Uttānapad by Kramrisch (Fig. 52) came to the Alampur Museum from the site of Kudavelli where a Chalukya-period Śiva temple called Sangameśvara stood until 1984 at the confluence of the Krishna and Tungabhadra rivers.[80] At the southeast corner of the wall of this temple a *śala* element (rectangular decorative structure with a wagon-vaulted roof) of the wall is "expanded" into an actual rectangular wagon-vaulted *mātṛkā* subshrine. In the northeast corner of the wall there was a structure that has been lost. The inclusion of such subshrines in the plans of Chalukya temples was new in the late seventh century. Those temples, which seem to have had paired subshrines before the east entrance to the hall (*maṇḍapa*), also seem to have had Lajjā Gaurī images associated with them. Perhaps the subshrines were built specifically to house Lajjā Gaurī and the Saptamātṛkās.

The fine Kudavelli example Kramrisch published (Fig. 52) is probably Chalukya although its polished black stone is atypical of the red sandstone used almost exclusively for Chalukya sculpture. There are, however, several major eighth-century Chalukya *liṅgas* and Nandis carved in this stone, as for example those in the Virūpākṣa temple at Pattadakal. It measures 41 by 35 inches, or life-size. It is the most frequently published image of Lajjā Gaurī.[81] The female body is carved of a piece with the altar upon which it lies supine and there is an ablution drain (*nāla*) by the left knee. The lotus head has large petals. She holds a lotus bud in each hand and seems to proffer them onto her lotus head.[82] The elbows disappear behind the knees. The breasts are large and seem to flatten from their own weight as she lies on her back. The legs in *uttānapad* seem to bend impossibly backward, and the feet are flexed in an awkward manner. The leg pose would be more comfortable if the goddess's torso were facing the other way. In other words, her lower legs and feet seem to be on backward. The navel and the pudendum slit are included, as are tendril-like armlets, bracelets, and anklets, but there is no jeweled girdle around the hips, nor a cloth through the legs. This is a powerful figure indeed, described by Kramrisch as a "mighty female shape," a "majestic maternal body" with "surging modelling." This figure, when viewed "upside down" from the lotus head end reveals a lotus budlike phallus between the legs, the slit of the pudendum serving doubly as the slit of the phallus.

This image, now kept in the Alampur Museum, is nearly identical to one housed in a shrine on the side of a lotus pond about one mile from the Darasuram (Tamil Nadu) Airavateśvara (Bṛhadeśvara) temple and its major Ammaṇ shrine, which date to the Choḷa period, c. 1150–73 (Fig. 53). This is not to suggest that the Lajjā Gaurī is Choḷa. If it were Choḷa, it would be the only example known from the period. This may be a Chalukya figure and if it is Chalukya, then the image was moved here as other images were moved from other regions and installed in Choḷa temples.[83] The style is like Chalukya carving, and the figure is very similar to the Chalukya image in the Alampur Museum from Kudavelli.

The lotus head and the folds of flesh below the breasts (a conventional mark of female beauty) are more emphatically represented than they are on the similar figure at Alampur. The awkward "backward" leg pose and the clearly represented phallus are similar to these parts in the Alampur Museum figure (Fig. 52). The image wears no girdle or cloth. Here the lotus bracelets curl around the upper arm and into the hand that places a lotus bud, like an offering, onto the top of the lotus head.[84]

The modern shrine in which it is kept is called the Śrī Chakkrāyi Ammaṇ temple, and the image is locally called Kamalamukhi (Lotus-head) or Chakkrāyi. In the temple it is kept dressed, vertical; a wooden head of the goddess Kālī is balanced on top of the lotus head (Fig. 53).[85] Here the original function of Lajjā Gaurī seems to be forgotten.

A virtual copy of the life-size Kudavelli Lajjā Gaurī (Fig. 52), though only $12\frac{1}{2}$ by $14\frac{1}{2}$ inches and carved in white marble rather than polished black stone, was recently sold into a private London collection (Fig. 53). It was identified by the dealer as nineteenth century and from Rajasthan. This figure is likely to be a nineteenth- or twentieth-century copy of the Kudavelli image for several reasons. The figure is a very close repetition of the Kudavelli Form III image; in fact it is the most similar Lajjā Gaurī figure to another that is not actually a duplicate figure. Although white marble is the regional stone of Rajasthan and Gujarat carved actively in the medieval period, the dull style of carving of the lotus border is later. The border and the sunken tank in which the figure rests, though symbolically appropriate to the image-type, is not copied from the Kudavelli image, but must be the invention of the artist, whom we can believe was familiar with the meaning of the goddess and had seen other images. All indications are that there were no original images of Lajjā Gaurī made for worship after the twelfth century. The creation of this image was self-consciously motivated, for whatever unknown reason. The copy lacks the subtlety of the original, but is nonetheless an interesting image for the reasons just given.

I. K. Sarma reported in 1982 and 1987 the existence of an image of Lajjā Gaurī in the northwestern wall niche of the fouteenth-century Choḷa Kāmāksī temple in Kanchipuram in Tamil Nadu. He describes it as being post-Ikṣvāku and pre-Chalukya, that is, fourth to fifth century. He states that he believes this icon to be the original image for worship at this *śakti pīṭha*.[86] The figure, unfortunately is published without description or illustration. It is a rare image from Tamil Nadu, and of interest for the temple's history.

A number of other images of the Chalukya style are no longer in their original location and cannot be related to their original temple. Among these is the second image from Kudavelli, now also in the Alampur site museum (Fig. 55), which is Chalukya in style, but of a pedestrian quality.[87] It is similar to another image kept by the Pañchaliṅgala temple near Alampur (Fig. 56).[88] They are like the Kudavelli (Fig. 52) and Darasuram (Fig. 54) examples, but with a few differences: the lotus head is seen not from three-quarter view, but from the side, and they wear some clothing. Both hands hold lotus buds, but the buds incline away from the head in the Pañchaliṅgala image, whereas they are inclined toward the head in the Kudavelli image. The huge breasts and narrow waist of these two images and the insensitive modeling of the figure make them perfunctory carvings with a coarse form, rigid contours, and unexpressive details.

A figure from Yellala (Kurnool District, Andhra) (Fig. 57) is similar to the two examples just cited (Figs. 55 and 56), except that its carving is more refined. Like the other two, the legs are quite "backward," and the lotus buds are by the lotus head in profile. An interpretation of this detail of the backward froglike legs and feet is offered in chapter 3. The piece is now kept in the office of the Andhra Pradesh Department of Archaeology and Museums in Hyderabad. As on the Pañchaliṅgala and lesser-quality Kudavelli image, a triangle is created in the pudendum area by a double-ridged band, which may be either intended to represent a girdle or a loincloth, like that worn by the Keesaragutta figure (Fig. 103). The hole in this area of the Kudavelli Lajjā Gaurī is not original, but was worn by touching. These three examples—Kudavelli, Pañchaliṅgala, and Yellala—are probably late seventh century, judging by style, and made during the Early Chalukya period. Each is about 3 feet square.

Among lotus-headed Form III Lajjā Gaurīs there is some variation in the angle of the lotus head. Some are seen from three-quarter view, others from profile. A third type presents a full view of the lotus head like a wheel. Two such examples are at the minor Chalukya temple site near Pattadakal, Bhadranayika Jalihal (Figs. 58 and 59).[89] The goddess holds lotus buds in her hands. These images are stone as is a similar example from the Saṅgameśvara compound at Bhavanasi in Andhra (Fig. 60) where there are two Rashtrakuta (eighth-century) temples and a much later temple. Sivaramamurti dates the Bhavanasi image to sixth century, Viṣṇukundin dynasty.[90] Except for the tilt of the head this image is quite like the type found at Pañchaliṅgala and I would therefore prefer to date it later, c. seventh to eighth century.[91] A fourth example of a lotus wheel-headed figure is in worship at Belligamve (Shimoga District, Karnataka) (Fig. 61) next to the Later Chalukya period Kedareśvara temple of the twelfth century.[92] Her simple shrine is in front of the temple on the side of a lotus pond. The 28-inch-tall by 15-inch-wide figure is propped up vertically inside the small shrine, which has Gaja Lakṣmī carved in the center of its doorway lintel. The carving does not seem to be twelfth-century in style, but may be as early as eighth-century. Locally the goddess is called Kamalagaurīmā or Kamalagaṅgāmā, names that describe her as lotus-bearing.

A large ($23\frac{1}{2}$ inch) stone Form III Lajjā Gaurī from Miyapuram, Mahaboobnagar District, Andhra (Fig. 64) has been published by Bruno Dagens in his survey of the Srisailam area of Andhra that is to be submerged by a dam.[93] It was seen outside the Satyamma temple. The figure's lotus head is tilted slightly forward and a lotus is held in each hand. The goddess wears a necklace. This simple image is probably of the Chalukya period, c. seventh century, since it is comparable in style to several other Chalukya figures from Andhra state, such as Figures 54–56. The local name of the figure is Reṇukā, which is probably more a reflection of the popularity of the Paraśurāma myth in the area today and the headlessness of its female character, Reṇukā, than an accurate name of this image.

There are a number of Rashtrakuta-style Lajjā Gaurī images whose existence indicates that the dynasty that supplanted the Chalukyas continued her worship. Most important of these is a 41-inch-square Lajjā Gaurī found at the Galaganātha temple group at Aihole, now moved to the site museum. This life-size, red sandstone figure has a badly flaked surface (Fig. 61). Her lotus head is seen in profile with its petals resting down the "neck." I would date this piece not to the Early Chalukya period, but to the subsequent period of Rashtrakuta dominance at Aihole in the second half of the eighth century. The figure seems to be carved by the same hand as was the life-size *mātṛkā* set now displayed in the Aihole site museum. I have proposed elsewhere that this Lajjā Gaurī figure once may have been housed in a subshrine of a Rashtrakuta Śiva temple at Aihole paired to a parallel subshrine which housed the mentioned impressive (though fragmentary) *mātṛkā* set, thereby continuing the Early Chalukya tradition for her enshrinement in this situation as is evident at Siddhanakolla and at Alampur in the Bala Brahmā temple.[94]

Another lotus-headed Form III Lajjā Gaurī found at the Nageśvaraswami temple, Pratakota, Andhra, on the road to Kudavelli (now submerged), may also be Rashtrakuta or later, c. eighth to ninth century. Reassembled by splicing photos (Fig. 63), her body is quite like that of the Pañchaliṅgala figure (cf. Fig. 56), but the head is a pyramidal stack of three tiers of lotus petals seen in profile which occurs in no Early Chalukya figure. She holds lotus buds by her head. Here the goddess is called Belan Kallachema in Telegu.[95]

It is evident that the goddess Lajjā Gaurī was important to the Chalukya people because many large stone images were made and the temple plan was architecturally expanded to house the images. Inscriptional evidence to explain her importance is elusive. It seems that only hints at facts survive in regard to the identity of this goddess or her name or function, etc. For example, a corrupted copper-plate grant commences with "a mere farrago of vague tradition and Puranic myths of no authority" copied or created to join an authentic though copied later Eastern Chalukya inscription.[96] It alludes, in its vaguely traditional portion, to a prince of the Early Chalukya line whose father, Vijayāditya, had been killed in battle, leaving behind his queen pregnant with the prince. After he was safely born and was old enough, his mother sent him forth, and, "having worshiped Nanda, the holy Gaurī, on the Chalukya mountain . . . [he] ruled over the south." Although this inscription is a confusing compilation of facts and dates, this reference to a Gaurī, Nanda, a mother goddess otherwise worshiped in the form of Lajjā Gaurī (see Fig. 85 from Rajasthan, identified as Nanda and discussed, pages 42–43), is of interest. The "Chalukya mountain" near Aihole at Siddhanakolla preserves a seventh-century image of Lajjā Gaurī carved of the living mountain rock (Fig. 43). Other details referred to in the inscription seem datable to the late seventh century. This is the time of creation of the Siddhanakolla image, and the time of most active worship of the goddess by the Chalukyas. Though the inscription is a mishmash reconstructed at a later date, its references must have some grounding in fact, and the inscription may refer to our goddess as Gaurī.

A second mid-eighth-century Chalukya inscription exists on the Lakṣmī pillar at Pattadakal, which describes the goddess Gaurī in comparison to a lotus: "Victorious be that union of the god Hara with the goddess Gaurī in which the face and breasts of the goddess are passionately kissed by the left arm of the god; in which the fingers of the god separate themselves among the curled tresses of the goddess that imitate the quivering movements of a swarm of black bees and which resembles in beauty a fully expanded white lotus enhanced by the sweetness of a yellow lotus (the goddess) brought to maturity by the rays of the sun."[97] The language is suggestive of artistic associations visualized in Lajjā Gaurī images, while again, during the Chalukya period, the goddess so described is named Gaurī.

Gaurī is the female *śakti* of Śiva who is called Hara, and is considered to be the wife of Śiva or of Varuṇa, the waters. She is the oceans and the rains. She is the source of the world, the cosmic cow. The Gaurīs form a class of goddesses which includes Umā, Pārvatī, Rambhā, Totalā, Tripurā, but of which Śrī is considered Gaurī herself.[98] Evidently by the late seventh century this goddess, Gaurī, was associated to Śiva, and was specially revered by the Early Chalukyas. Relevant to this inscriptional description of Gaurī and Hara is the panel in Orissa on the Satrughneśvara temple which depicts Hara-Gaurī with lotus attributes (see pages 46–47 and Fig. 108)

The Lajjā Gaurī images of the Chalukya period are not from the earliest or the latest years of that dynasty but of the late seventh century. In A.D. 660 the line of kings switched from Vaiṣṇava to Śaiva devotion and began adding the *-aditya* (Son of Aditi) suffix to their coronation names. Whether or not the worship of the image and the king's assumption of this suffix implies her identification and worship by them as Aditi is unknown and probably unascertainable. The first two Śaiva kings, Vikramāditya (reign 654–81) and Vinayāditya (reign 681–96) ruled when the temples that were provided with images of Lajjā Gaurī and the Seven Mothers (and, as noted, in some instances goat-headed guards) were built.

The only hint of possible motivation of the renewal in this region of the by then ancient tradition of Lajjā Gaurī worship by the Early Chalukyas is given by a stone inscription discovered at Belligamve, where an eighth-century Lajjā Gaurī image is still worshiped by the side of the Kedareśvara temple (Fig. 61), recording that Early Chalukya King Vinayāditya (reign A.D. 681–96) imposed a tax on sonless couples.[99] The same inscription mentions a number of temples by name to which the king gave land grants but, unfortunately, none of the names corresponds to those of temples known today. It is speculative to suggest that Vinayāditya needed soldiers for his military campaigns, but perhaps the images of the fertility goddess were housed at special temples to serve as recourse for sonless women. This politico-religious motivation for readoption of this fertility goddess into the Hindu temple complex will be discussed in the conclusion to this study.

The final question of the presence of goat-headed guards by the Saptamātṛkā subshrines at two Chalukya temple sites is interesting, but their identity is problematic. The goat-headed Naigameṣa (or Naigameya) may accompany Skanda, whose foster mothers were the *mātṛkās,* as he does in earlier rock-cut temples at Ellora (21), Elephanta (I, east shrine), and Jogeśvari. He is either the son, brother, or playfellow of Skanda, or he may be Skanda himself. Naigameśa is considered injurious to children but nonetheless is connected with procreation in both Hindu and Jain myths.[100] But Skanda is not included with the Seven Mothers where the goat-headed guards are found at Siddhanakolla and Alampur.

Another possible identification of these problematic figures (Figs. 45, 47) is as the goat-headed

Dakṣa. Dakṣa was the father of Aditi, the mother of all, and Aditi was the mother of Dakṣa according to *Ṛg Veda* (x.72.2–4), paradoxically expressing the idea that existence sprang from nonexistence. Originally Dakṣa signified universal creative energy and embodied priestly skill ensuring the success of the sacrifice. Although Dakṣa's mind-born sons peopled the earth, they became ascetics and had no progeny. So Dakṣa, finding his mental creations futile, turned instead to sexual reproduction. This decision provides the occasion for a discourse on the importance of marriage and of begetting sons in the *Mahābhārata*, Adiparvan 74. Another daughter of Dakṣa is Gaurī: "Dakṣa prayed to Rudra to appease his anger and gave his daughter Gaurī in marriage to Rudra (a Vedic name of Śiva)."[101]

Whether these goat-headed sentries are to be identified as Naigameṣa or Dakṣa, either is associated with fertility. The Saptamātṛkās within the subshrine were considered nourishers to the Chalukya kings, as noted in their grant deeds. As a descriptive formula in their copperplate grant inscriptions, the Chalukya kings described themselves as "Beloved of Śrī, nourished by the Saptamātṛkās, and sons of the goddess Hārītī." The identification of Aditi with Lajjā Gaurī has been suggested by Kramrisch, but the present evidence does not adequately support their direct identification via Dakṣa.

FORM IV: ANTHROPOMORPHIC

Form IV Lajjā Gaurī figures are totally anthropomorphic, unlike Forms I, II and III, with a human female head and all parts, with legs in *uttānapad* pose, and the arms held up to the side of the head (Figs. 65–78, 81–90). This form of the goddess was especially popular in Gujarat and Rajasthan, although two examples are known from Maharashtra.

The majority of the Form IV anthropomorphic images have been dated sixth to seventh century by their style with two exceptions: one Form IV image from Amreli(?) (Amreli District, Gujarat) has been dated to the first to third century (Fig. 65), but should be dated as late as the sixth century by comparison to the Elephanta Lajjā Gaurī.[102] Second, Codrington suggested that the unique double-sided terra-cotta that bears a Form IV Lajjā Gaurī on one side and a frog on the other (Figs. 66–68) dates to Kuṣān period Mathura, c. second century.[103] His judgment was based on the fact that the Victoria and Albert Museum acquired the piece in a group of otherwise Kuṣān objects. Since the damaged piece would be the only example of Form IV not to date to the sixth to seventh century, some doubt is cast on Codrington's early dating, though due to the damage its style is difficult to assess and it cannot be dated later with certainty either. The human-headed Form IV Lajjā Gaurī predominated in the northwest region contemporaneously in the sixth and seventh centuries with the lotus-headed Forms II and III in the central and southern regions, although they seem not to have been made earlier, as were the images in Forms II and III.

Of twenty-three examples of Form IV human-headed figures documented, seventeen are carved on plaques in the company of other figures and will be discussed in chapter 2. Only six are individual icons. Form IV occurs most frequently in a group in contrast to the fact that Form I figures are all individual icons except one. All examples are stone except for the just mentioned unique double-sided terra-cotta frog/Lajjā Gaurī from Mathura. Form IV images are either about two inches square or quite large; for example, the Ellora rock-cut temple-21 relief image measures 50 inches tall by 77 inches wide. Three (possibly four) of the images in this group are carved with a halo clearly indicating divinity: that at Ellora (Fig. 75), the image in the Ajit Mookerjee collection from North India, site unknown (Fig. 69), and another from Tarsang (Fig. 86).[104]

The Elephanta Island surface find of a stone plaque with the Form IV human-headed goddess seems to have a devotee to her left and perhaps a bull to her right, but these details are now unclear (Fig. 76). This figure has been dated to the sixth century by S. Gorakshekar.[105] Its style is not akin to that of the panel figures of the Great Cave temple at Elephanta, which has been credited to the Kalachūri dynasty's patronage c. mid-sixth century and to the Pāśupata sect by Walter Spink and others.[106] The piece could be dated as early as c. A.D. 500.

The Central Indian human-headed figure now in the Mathura Museum (no. 15.597) seems to be a rare and excellent survivor of a medieval style, perhaps that of the Pratihāra dynasty of c. eighth century (Fig. 70), making it the latest Form IV example.[107] The figure is an unusual medium size: height 11 inches by width $5\frac{1}{2}$ inches. She held in each hand a lotus flower in bloom, and is carved against a curved stele with a ridged-edge pattern, with her knees protruding beyond this frame. Her earrings are like those worn by the Ellora 21 figure with large lotus flowers within the rings (Fig. 75). Her feet most emphatically are turned backward and her legs, like those of many of the images, seem to be pulled backward into the relief in an awkward manner (cf. Fig. 52). She wears her hair tied up in a bun on her head and standard jewelry. A halo may be intended around her head making this the possible fourth image bearing a halo.

A damaged, human-headed image in gray schist, measuring $1\frac{3}{4}$ by 2 inches from Kavi (Broach District, southern Gujarat) was a surface find, but may date c. sixth century (Fig. 84) by its style, though the piece is worn.[108] It is comparable to the Elephanta Lajjā Gaurī and to others from Amreli. It included a female figure to the right and perhaps a bull to the left of Lajjā Gaurī.

The Amreli (?) figure is carved in black schist or basalt. The goddess holds a lotus in her preserved hand. She wears a broad headdress and a necklace.[109] It was found in South Gujarat and resembles other images from Amreli, especially in the sharp segmental treatment of the body areas. While Margabandhu dated a similar Amreli figure to the third to fourth centuries, he dates this example first to third centuries by comparison to other figures from Amreli published by S. R. Rao. By comparison to other Amreli figures I would date both later, c. sixth century.

A rectangular light-green-schist plaque (5 inches tall by $3\frac{1}{2}$ inches wide) has recently been reported from Pavi-Jetpur (Baroda District, Gujarat) (Fig. 71). The figure of Lajjā Gaurī, which has no accompaniment of other figures, is slender with an elongated torso and is streamlined in detail. Her hands are empty (right broken). The image's face is broken off, but she wears a three-peaked headdress. This figure has been dated eighth to ninth century by V. H. Sonawane, who notes "Though the triple-peaked *makuṭa,* ornaments and style of depiction of the goddess are comparable with the figures of Akota hoard datable to 7th–8th centuries A.D. the modelling of the said image is slightly crude and hence it could be assigned to c. 8th–9th century A.D."[110] Because of the great preponderance of images of Form IV dating to the sixth and seventh centuries from this area the earlier dating may be more likely, that is, seventh century.

No human-headed images of Form IV Lajjā Gaurī are found in Andhra, to my knowledge, nor in Karnataka, except for the odd image that serves as part of a border decoration around a ceiling panel of Śiva (Fig. 72) in the Huchchapayya temple at Aihole, a Chalukya temple of the seventh century. Her leg pose and feet are completely backward in a manner suggesting a lack of understanding of this aspect.

Form IV is the latest iconographic type created. It is significant, and will be discussed in the conclusion, that all the images of this form are stone, except the unique terra-cotta, double-sided image from Mathura, and some are given a halo. Many more Form IV Lajjā Gaurī images are included in figure groups carved together on plaques. These will be discussed subsequently.

Notes

1. Kramrisch, 1956, 263, notes the conceptual similarity of the Alampur Lajjā Gaurī to the *pūrṇa ghaṭa*.
2. Dhere, 1978, 179.
3. Inglis, 1984, 184.
4. Tiwari, 1971, 282.
5. The Ter examples are previously unpublished.
6. Sankalia, 1960, fig. 9; Dhere, 1978, fig. 3; Tiwari, 1985, fig. 8.
7. Waheed Khan, 1963, mentioned without illustration, 46.
8. Pratapaditya Pal suggests that this cloth is used in Indian village births as an aid to delivery.
9. Ray, 1983, fig. 270, erroneously identified a Sannati example as being from Yellesvaram. Otherwise Sannati Lajjā Gaurī examples are previously unpublished. Other finds from Sannati were published by Seshadri, 1972, 160–70, and by M. S. Nagaraja Rao, *Progress of Archaeology in Karnataka 1956–1972* (Mysore, 1978), 29, 35–36.
10. The Early Chalukya stone images are quite similar, and two may be copies of the first. See pages 27–29.
11. Previously unpublished.
12. Kept in the Andhra Pradesh State Office of Archaeology and Museums, Hyderabad, no. 119, unpublished.
13. Dhere, 1978, fig. 2; Sankalia, 1960, fig. 4; Chapekar, 1969, fig. 27, no. 8; Tiwari, 1985, fig. 6. I did not find this example at Ter. I strongly suspect Dhere's line drawing errs in not including lotus petals on the mouth of the pot.
14. Dhere, 1978, fig. 4; Sankalia, 1960, fig. 10; Ray, 1983, fig. 269.
15. Narasimhaswami, 1952, 137–39; Dhere, 1978, fig. 9, republished the preconservation photo. For its postconservation state see Divakaran, 1981, pl. 112; Sarma, 1982, pl. 65; or Tiwari, 1985, fig. 11.
16. The clever combination of the phallus with the female body of fertility figurines is known from many ancient cultures. See, for example, Gimbutas, 1982, 216–20.
17. Gerow, 1971, 288, *śleṣa*. For an example of double-meaning poetry see Dhanamjaya, *Dvisandhanakavya*, an eighth-century simultaneous rendering of the *Mahabharata* and the *Rāmāyaṇa*.
18. Egnor, 1978, 140.
19. Kramrisch, 1981, 162–78, for an explanation of the *liṅga*.
20. Ter Museum RC 7.219 terra-cotta, $2\frac{1}{4}$ inches square; RC 7.220 terra-cotta $2\frac{1}{2}$ inches square; Bhita example, Allahabad Museum no. 299, S. C. Kala, 1957, not illustrated, stone, $5\frac{7}{10}$ by $5\frac{1}{2}$ inches.
21. Now kept in the Shri Bhavani Museum and Library, Aundh, Satara District, Maharashtra, 3 by 4 inches, stone, published Dhere, 1978, fig. 13; Sankalia, 1960, fig. 8; Tiwari, 1985, fig. 9.
22. Dhere, 1978, 172. Allchin, 1985, discusses a unique Indus seal representing intercourse between a bull and a figure he identifies as an antecedent of Aditi of the Ṛg Veda.
23. No. 3.80, previously unpublished.
24. C. Gupta, 1987, reported the Maharashtrian images. Misra, 1985, fig. XLVIII, 140, reported the four images from Madhya Pradesh that he dates as ninth to tenth century.
25. Kala, 1980, 66, no illustration, Allahabad Museum no. 3904, $1\frac{1}{4}$ inches square.
26. Barrett, 1960, 9, fig. 13, British Museum no. 1958.10–17.2, $2\frac{1}{4}$ inches square; also published by Desai, 1984, fig. 12, 49; Dhere, 1978, fig. 12; Sankalia, 1960, fig. 3, 113–14; Sankalia and Dhavalikar, 1969, fig. 18, 49; and Arts Council of Great Britain, 1982, no. 52, 109.
27. Mukhopadhyay, 1972, pl. 8, height 5 inches, width $4\frac{1}{2}$ inches.
28. Deo, 1974, pl. 39, no. 4. The more intact example, now kept at Nagpur University, was a stratified find and measures $2\frac{1}{4}$ by $2\frac{1}{2}$ inches. The actual find spot was Alapur for both. The second is now in Marathwada University. It was a surface find. Deo, 1974, pl. 39, no. 3.
29. Unpublished examples in red sandstone, 2 by $2\frac{1}{4}$ inches, Ter Museum RC 9.168 and British Museum 1958.10–17.2, just cited.
30. Indian Museum A12088, published by Mukhopadhyay, 1972, 76–77, pl. 8, and Allahabad Museum 3904, terra-cotta, published by Kala, 1980, 66, no illustration.
31. C. Gupta, 1987, $4\frac{1}{2}$ inches square and $4\frac{1}{4}$ by 3 inches, both stone.
32. Sanchi site museum, stone, about 3 inches by $3\frac{1}{4}$. Kala, 1980 refers to this example, 64.
33. Ter Museum 9.148, stone fragment, $2\frac{1}{4}$ inches square, unpublished.
34. Deo, 1974, pl. 39.
35. British Museum 1976.4–5.2, stone, $2\frac{5}{8}$ by 3 inches, previously unpublished. Nagpur Central Museum has a plaster cast of this example.
36. Muley, 1979, 187–89. Also published by Tiwari, 1985, fig. 13. Another plaque of this sort with tanks is from Surera, Nagpur, and is in the Maharashtra Department of Antiquities.
37. Jamkhedkar, 1985, 18, mentions it, red sandstone.

38. Paunar published by C. Gupta, 1987, 48.

39. The Mansar stone image is in Nagpur Central Museum, no. C203, and measures 4 by $3\frac{1}{4}$ inches.

40. Dhere, 1978, fig. 7; Deo, 1973, pl. II, 3; Hunter, 1933, 30–35; Tiwari, 1985, fig. 12.

41. Misra, 1985.

42. Private collection, Nagpur. C. Gupta, 1987, fig. 1, 47; The Paunar Lajjā Gaurī supports Kramrisch's idea that the Sanchi lotiform lady is related to the Alampur figure; Kramrisch, 1956, 260.

43. Unpublished. Kept in the Andhra Pradesh State Department of Archaeology and Museums Office, no. 31, 2 inches × $1\frac{3}{4}$ inches.

44. Bhita, Allahabad District, U.P., published: Marshall, Archaeological Survey of India, Annual Report 1927–28 (ASIAR) 1911–12, pl. 23, no. 40, 75, Kushan-Gupta dating: Marshall, ASIAR 1927–28, 67; Dhavalikar, 1977, pl. 56, 58, reasons for his c. first- to second-century dating given; Banerjea, 1974, 168; Sankalia, 1960, pl. 5, 114, cites Marshall's Kushan-Gupta dating but prefers Kushan because the piece was found with a red polished ware vessel of second-century type and because the Lajjā Gaurī bears a consecutive number in Marshall's report. All subsequent authors repeat Sankalia's dating. C. C. Dasgupta, 1961, fig. 106, 300; Tiwari, 1985, fig. 1, 270.

45. The Kausambi examples in this Form include four fragments published by Kala, 1980: Allahabad Museum no. 3894, 66, no illustration, measures $4\frac{3}{8}$ by $2\frac{3}{4}$ inches; no. 5214, $3\frac{1}{2}$ by $3\frac{1}{4}$ inches, 66; Allahabad Museum no. 5034, $6\frac{1}{4}$ by $4\frac{1}{4}$ inches, 66; and Allahabad Museum no. 3849, $3\frac{1}{2}$ by $4\frac{1}{4}$ inches, 65, also illustrated in Kala, 1950, pl. III, 14. Kala has identified these as second century though reasons are not provided.

46. Shere, 1961; P. L. Gupta, 1965, pl. L, 307, entry 145; Tiwari, 1985, fig. 10, 280. Again no reasons are provided for the Kushan dating.

47. The figure is damaged, 2 inches square, published by Margabandhu, 1975–76, fig. 5.

48. Dikshit, 1957, pl. XVIA, 30. In the museum it is misidentified as Uṣas or Sūrya.

49. Mookerjee and Kala have dated it about second century, but Sivaramamurti, 1982, fig. 55, dated it first century B.C.

50. Mookerjee, 1971, pl. 40, called Adi Sakti; Dhere, 1978, fig. 16; Kala, 1980, fig. 164, 64, Kala, 1958–60, pl. 7A, 7; Sivaramamurti, 1982, fig. 55; Poster, 1986, fig. 55.

51. Harle, 1986, fig. 24, 39–40 (Gaja Lakṣmī from Kausambi).

52. P. L. Gupta, 1965, 27, dates it Kushan-Gupta, first to fifth century.

53. Narasimhaswami, 1952, 137–39.

54. Discussed by Sircar, 1980. He suggests that the image was made for worship as a testament to the fortunate character of the queen, or to fulfill a vow promised to the goddess in prayer for cure of illness of her husband or sons.

55. K. V. Soundara Rajan, "Andhra Ikshavaku Chronology and its Significance for Early History of Gujarat," *Journal of the Gujarat Research Society* 25, 1963, 285–94; Sarkar in Asher, 1985, 29.

56. Sarkar and Misra, 1972, 25–26.

57. It has been partially restored since it was first published, as previously noted. Unrestored photos have been published by Rawson, 1968, 46, fig. 15, and by P. K. Agrawala, 1983a, wherein fig. 99 is described, xviii, thus: "Lotus headed Nude Goddess with her legs apart. She is the Earth Mother Prithvi or Ultimate Nature presiding at the head of creation as Adi-Sakti or Primordial Femininity. She is the 'origin ground' or birth-place of all creation who poses to receive 'seed' or 'drop' of the Absolute Male Sky as making life to pour from Her Inexhaustible Womb."

58. Narasimhaswami, 1952, 138; Coomaraswamy, 1971, 61, discusses the relation of the goddess and the *kumbha*.

59. Settar, 1979, 19, has commented on the tradition of Lajjā Gaurī images in the Deccan.

60. Eliade, 1973, 110.

61. These may be the earliest surviving instances of the addition of subshrines to the temple compound in South India.

62. Chapgar's inaccurate diary sketch (omitting the lotus head) was reproduced by Sankalia, 1960, fig. 6, 114; and Dhere, 1978, fig. 6; photo published by Divakaran, 1981, 59, pl. 113.

63. Unobserved by Chapgar.

64. Sundara Rajan 1981, 114, reports the same.

65. Radcliffe, 1981, 304–8. A second temple stands at the site. It is Later Chalukya.

66. Kosambi, 1962, 91, 95, suggests an explanation for placement of temples of the goddess outside the village boundary or at a crossroads. A non-Brahmanic mother goddess may only be worshiped outside the village, unless specially brought to the temple for convenience. Furthermore, the crossroads would be the ancient location for meeting and performing barter and fertility rituals. Not all temples with Lajjā Gaurī are outside the village, and several are clearly not at an ancient crossroads, being on top of a mountain, for instance. Isolation for fertility rituals may be the proper explanation in these instances.

67. Sonawane, 1986, suggests that Lajjā Gaurī is located in a tank because of her power to ward off droughts, as also suggested by Dhavalikar. Sonawane further believes this association explains her lotus head.

68. Radcliffe, 1981, 191, and references therein.

69. de Lippe, 1978, figs. 135–37.

70. Waheed Khan, 1973, fig. 1, "Daksha 1.40 × .45 m."

71. For the myth of Renukā see Ramesan, 1969, 35–38, or Gopinatha Rao, 1968, vol. 1, pt. 1, 184–85, cited from *Mahābhārata*, III.115, *Bhagavata Purāṇa* and *Vishnu Purāṇa*. The switching of heads of a Brahmin and Sūdra woman does not explain the lotus head of this image.

72. Radcliffe, 1981, 296; Harle, 1969, 53–83, for description of the temple.

73. Published by Annigere, 1978; Sivaramamurti, 1982, fig. 46; Nagaswamy, 1978, 135, called Kamalamukhi; P. K. Agrawala, 1983a, xvii, fig. 6, described her thus: "Great Nude Earth Goddess with a lotus head posing in the act of creation. Her arch attribute is the Lotus, also held in Her hands. Incumbent upon her is the Invisible Sky God." Lal, 1980, 1a, 273, misattributed the image to Badami cave number IV.

74. Despite the 200 miles separating the sites, it is possible that one workshop of artists was responsible for producing images enshrined at Alampur and in the Badami area. At Alampur there are a few *mātṛkā* images which duplicate some of the Bala Brahmā set.

75. Only the thigh, left arm, and a bit of the lotus head of the Chikkamahakuta image survive (Fig. 51). The back slab measures $39\frac{1}{2}$ inches in height. What remains as far as size and details is identical to the Naganātha and Mahakuta images. The presence of this fragment at Chikkamahakuta may confirm a theory of Dhere, 1978, 1–21, about the old Mahakuta being the same as Nandikeśvara and originally Langeśvara.

76. Radcliffe, 1981, 305–8, 485; The apsidal temple at Chikkamahakuta is the main temple aligned to the tank of c. 660. The other temple there may date c. 710. See Bolon in Meister, 1986, 61–64.

77. The date is debated. See Bolon, 1985, 153–60.

78. Fleet, 1881, 103. Published by Kramrisch, 1956, fig. 3, and Dhere, 1978, fig. 5.

79. Tartakov, 1980, 39–99, discusses Fleet's confused directions.

80. Kramrisch, 1956; Bolon, 1985; Dagens, 1984, 376–387.

81. Kramrisch, 1956, figs. 1–2; Sankalia, 1960, fig. 10a, 114–21; Waheed Khan, 1973, fig. 52; Tiwari, 1971, 273; Mookerjee, 1967, pl. 58, called Adya Śakti; Mookerjee and Khanna, 1977, 181; Rawson, n.d., 100, no. 15, called eleventh-century "goddess displaying vulva"; Rawson, 1978, fig. 33, 55; Arts Council of Great Britain, 1982, no. 55, 110; Sivaramamurti, 1982, fig. 45; Desai, 1984, fig. 13, 49; Tiwari, 1985, fig. 4.

82. Kramrisch, 1956, 267, describes the buds bent toward the head-flower as like a "rite of insemination."

83. As for example the inscribed Later Western Chalukya *dvārapāla* installed on the Choḷa Airavateśvara temple at Darasuram now in the Tanjore Art Gallery, de Lippe, 1978, 183–84, pl. 298. See L'Hernault, 1987, 3–5, pl. 1 goddess and pl. 2 her wooden head, and map II for location of the shrine. L'Hernault states that the Lajjā Gaurī is not Choḷa but Chalukya.

84. Nagaswamy, 1978, illustrated, describes her as holding a lock of hair in either hand; these are lotus buds.

85. Published by Sivaramamurti, 1982, fig. 52, called later Pallava, eighth to ninth century. Lal, 1980, fig. 1c, 275. Nagaswamy, 1978, believes the sculpture is Choḷa, twelfth century, by its proximity to the late Choḷa temple and that it is Śakta, and discusses Choḷa Śakta poetry. He identifies the image as the Tantric goddess Kāmakalā, or Cakra raji (locally corrupted to Cakrayi). In 1981 Nagaswamy read a paper identifying the image as Kāmakalā or Mahākuṇḍalinī by reference to the commentary on verses 34–40 of the *Lalitāsahasranāma*. The *Lalitāsahasranāma* is a medieval *stotra* (hymn of praise) of the goddess. Its commentary, the *Saubhagyabhaskara*, was written in 1728 by Bhaskaraya. See Sastry, 1951, lines 34–40 (text lines 84–90) with commentary on pages 89–93 translated into English; Sanskrit in back of volume, 10. This eighteenth-century interpretation and Nagaswamy's additional interpretation are possible, but not incontrovertible, arguments of explanation of the Lajjā Gaurī images. His argument is based on the local, modern name of the goddess which he feels is a corruption of Cakra Raji, referring to the yogic Mahākuṇḍalinī. Like other local names, this name may tell us more about recent associations with the image than about ancient, original associations. Nagaswamy, 1986, relates the image of Lajjā Gaurī to anthropomorphic *visirikkal* (fan-stones) of the megalithic period (c. 500 B.C.) in south India found set up in the middle of a circle of stones. The stone is headless and with curled "legs." Nagaswamy relates the form of this cult object to that of Śrīvatsa and to the Vedic concept of Aditi which gave rise to the later Hindu conceptions of the principal goddesses: Durgā, Lakṣmī, and Saraswatī, and to Lajjā Gaurī and Kāmākṣī. He believes she is a Tantric form representing Mahākuṇḍalinī śakti. The *Lalitāsahasranāma* states that her worship will bestow all prayers and she is the embodiment of grace and dispeller of ignorance.

86. Sarma, 1982, 171; 187, 239.

87. Published Donaldson, 1975, fig. 3, 75; Waheed Khan, 1973, fig. 53, measures $2\frac{1}{2}$ by $2\frac{1}{4}$ feet.

88. About 3 feet square; published Dagens, 1984, fig. 435, Renuka. The second Kudavelli image and the Pañchaliṅgala image may date to the late seventh century.

89. The larger of the two is 34 by 24 inches, the other is 23 by 13 inches.

90. Sivaramamurti, 1982, fig. 50.

91. Dagens, 1984, Pañchaliṅgala, fig. 435, 394–401; Bhanavasi, fig. 774, 533; Pratakota, 545.

92. Cousens, 1926, 105, misidentified the site as Hoysala, pl. CXII.

93. Dagens, 1984, fig. 271, 327–30.

94. Bolon, 1986.

95. Dagens, 1984, fig. 721, 545; for figure illustration see Sivaramamurti, 1982, fig. 51.

96. *Indian Antiquary* 2, 1878, 241–51.

97. *Epigraphia Indica*, 3, 1894–95, 1.

98. Stutley and Stutley, 1977, 96; Banerjea, 1974, 502.

99. *Indian Antiquary* 19, no. 186, 1890, 142–64.

100. Coomaraswamy, 1971, 12.

101. Gopinatha Rao, 1968, vol. 2, pt. 1, 185, from *Varāhapurāṇa*.

102. Amreli: Margabandhu, 1975–76, 208, fig. 3, 2 inches square, stone; mentioned by Sonawane, 1986.

103. Codrington, 1935, 65–66.

104. Ellora, Dhere, 1978, fig. 17; Mookerjee Collection, Rawson, 1978, fig. 32, 55; Tarsang, Sonawane, 1986.

105. Gorakshekar, 1982, 2–3, see Form IV multifigured representations.

106. Spink, 1967, 1983.

107. Codrington, 1926, pl. 21c.

108. Margabandhu, 1976, 208, fig. 2, now in the collection of U. P. Shah.

109. Margabandhu, 1976, 28, fig. 3; S. R. Rao, 1966.

110. Sonawane, 1986.

II

Lajjā Gaurī in Multifigured Plaques

ALL ICONOGRAPHIC FORMS OF Lajjā Gaurī (I–IV) are found carved on plaques in combination with other figures: humans, animals, and gods. Such multifigured plaques are known from Andhra, Karnataka, Maharashtra, and Gujarat, but none are known from Uttar Pradesh. They will be described individually in this chapter. By the analysis of repetitions in choices of figures to accompany Lajjā Gaurī light is shed on her meaning.

There is only one Form I *uttānapad* pot Lajjā Gaurī combined with another figure: a couchant bull to her side. It is from Jayaramaswami Vadgaon (Satara District, Maharashtra) (Fig. 73). Although this is the only *uttānapad* pot Form I goddess combined with another figure, Lajjā Gaurī in the lotus-headed Forms II and III and anthropomorphic Form IV is frequently combined with either a bull and a devotee (Fig. 77); a bull, a devotee, and a *liṅga* (Fig. 81); a bull, a devotee, a *liṅga,* and a lion face (Fig. 99); or, in one example, bull, devotee, a *liṅga,* lion face, and conch (Fig. 102). Except possibly for the Vadgaon example that may date c. fourth century or earlier (Fig. 73) judged by its style and relation to several other similar pieces (Figs. 1–4), these are not early plaques but date between approximately the fifth and eighth centuries. A number of group plaques bear figures arranged in a consistent order. The meaning and cult use of these group plaques has not been determined although observations can be made.

FORM IV: ANTHROPOMORPHIC LAJJĀ GAURĪ IN MULTIFIGURED PLAQUES

ELLORA LAJJĀ GAURĪ

In the courtyard before the Hindu rock cut temple 21, known as Rameśvara, at Ellora, is a monolithic platform with a couchant Nandi, Śiva's bull, on top that faces into the temple toward the enshrined Śivaliṅga (Fig. 74). On the southwestern face of the solid platform, prominent on approach to the "cave" temple, is carved an anthropomorphic Form IV Lajjā Gaurī (Fig. 75). The goddess is located below the hind of the couchant bull atop the platform. The large, vertically carved, relief figure of Lajjā Gaurī in the center of the panel is damaged, but the *uttānapad* pose of the legs is clear. She seems to be squatting, but this may be the artist's compromise of the supine position proper for the goddess adjusted to a vertical format, as seen only in Form IV figures. The goddess and her two flanking female attendants who bear fly whisks are carved into the rock between relief pilasters. The panel measures 50 inches in height by 77 inches wide. The goddess's head is haloed, her arms are held up, but are damaged, her hair is tied up in a large bun and she wears a jeweled headband, lotus earrings, necklace, girdle, and anklets. The other three sides of the Nandi platform are damaged, but each panel seems to have had a *gaṇa* or several *gaṇas* carved beneath an arch that spans pilasters at each corner. On the panel adjacent to the goddess moving toward the right (east) a *gaṇa* was seated with a pot.[1] These *gaṇas*, which resemble fat children, are commonly associated with Śiva as an expression of his boundless creative energy.

Since the bull on the Nandi *maṇḍapa* platform faces the Śivaliṅga of rock-cut temple 21, the goddess is clearly associated with Śiva and Nandi. One explanation of this association depends on the identification of Lajjā Gaurī as Gaurī, who is a form of Śiva's consort Pārvatī and a form of Śrī.[2] All modern or traditional explanations of the lotus-headed goddess bear some association to Pārvatī, and such evidence must be at least entered into the argument supporting this Śaivite association, though it cannot be depended upon for historic accuracy. By the mid-sixth century the early auspicious *uttānapad* pot goddess in a new anthropomorphic form seems to have become identified as a *śakti* of Śiva, possibly known as Gaurī.

In his study, *Lajjā Gaurī,* Dhere notes that the name of this famous site, Ellora or Elura, may be derived from Elapura and Ellama and that Ellama is a name of the goddess otherwise called Lajjā Gaurī. Today, he records, this figure in front of Ellora 21 is called Sang.[3] Burgess recorded another ancient name of Ellora—Verul[4] upon which he does not elaborate, but Dhere explains that a *verul,* or pot, in South India was worshiped from ancient times as a symbol of the *yoni,* or womb, which later came to be the form of the goddess, and that the *verul* is a symbol of Renuka (a name applied to Lajjā Gaurī images), who is the *yoni* of Pṛthvī (Earth).[5] The river that flows past Ellora is the Verul River (also called Yelgaṇga). These name associations suggest symbolic interrelation of the pot, womb, and the Ellora 21 Lajjā Gaurī figure.[6] Although the name applied to Lajjā Gaurī over the centuries changed it never lost its allusion to fertility.

Furthermore, it should be noted that the iconographic depictions of the panels within Ellora 21 are unusual in that more than other Hindu cave temples of Western India they seem to elaborate the theme of the courtship, marriage, and the marital relationship of Śiva and Pārvatī as a divine example of the ideal behavior in the "householder" stage of life. This cave temple may have been the earliest at the site of Ellora, where more than thirty were eventually made. It is near the waterfall, which elsewhere is the prime location for temple placement; water is essentially associated to fertility worship and Lajjā Gaurī as previously discussed. Perhaps Rameśvara temple once stood alone as a fertility worship center like the later Chalukya temple at Siddhanakolla near Aihole. Both are dedicated to the Pāśupata sect of Śaivite worship. Lakulīśa, the Pāśupata saint iconographically distinguished by his erect phallus and the attribute of the club, is located at the center of the entrance lintel of Ellora temple 21, defining its sect. We also note the inclusion within the Ellora temple 21 program of imagery of the Saptamātṛkās, which group of goddesses seems to become standardly associated with Lajjā Gaurī, as for example at Siddhanakolla and elsewhere.

It is interesting to note that there are historic links between the Chalukya dynasty and the site of Ellora, though evidence for the Chalukya overlordship of the area is scant. There are also stylistic and iconographic links between figures found in Ellora cave temple 21 and the early images in cave temples of the Chalukyas at Badami and Aihole that date to the second half of the sixth century also. But there are no Chalukya images of Lajjā Gaurī carved until the late seventh century, and their iconography (Form III) is distinct from that of the image before Ellora 21 (Form IV).

Other Form IV Multifigured Plaques

The form of the goddess at Ellora 21 is like that most often found in Gujarat, anthropomorphic Form IV, and is also like the small (3 inch by $2\frac{1}{4}$ inch) human-headed figure found on Elephanta Island (Fig. 76). Both rock-cut temples, Ellora 21 and Elephanta 1, have been attributed to the Kalachūri period, c. 550.[7] This apparent regional domination by this iconographic Form IV and similar style in carving is only one of many evidences of a regional cohesion of the western coastal area from Karnataka to Gujarat at this time. In a smaller format and different arrangement, the Elephanta schist plaque includes the elements associated with the goddess at Ellora 21: the bull and the attending figure or devotee. The hands of the Elephanta figure seem to be merely held up to the sides of the head without lotus buds. This surface find has been dated by style to the sixth century, which seems correct.[8] The goddess wears a distinctive kind of cap with side crests. Her legs, as in many examples, clearly slant toward the back plane of the plaque.

These two images from western Maharashtra, the Ellora and Elephanta figures, are similar to a number of multifigured plaques from Gujarat of Form IV, anthropomorphic or human-headed. For example, a Form IV multifigured plaque from Gujarat, now in the Kutch Museum in Bhuj, carved in a dark stone, has the same arrangement of the bull to the left, goddess at center, and devotee to the right with hands in adoration (fig. 77).[9] The hands of the human- (or animal-?) headed goddess are also held up by the sides of the head and are empty. This example may date from the fourth to fifth century. The bull in all such examples is seen from above, the devotee is seen frontally, while Lajjā Gaurī is supine in relation to the bull, but vertical like the devotee. This spatial disjunction has good reason and will be discussed shortly.

A stone Form IV multifigured plaque from Bhinmal (Jalor District, Rajasthan), dated c. seventh century by U. P. Shah judging the style of a group of figures from the area, includes a human-headed goddess in the center with lotus buds in the upheld hands (Fig. 78).[10] To her proper right is a Śivaliṅga above a bull that is differently presented, that is, from a side view. Over the bull is a shrine with a curved eave. The proper left area is lost where, judging by analogous organization on many other multifigured plaques, a devotee may have been carved.

A terra-cotta plaque of the lotus-headed Form III goddess is from Kanad (Surat District, Gujarat) (Fig. 79). It is the only terra-cotta plaque of Lajjā Gaurī from Gujarat. It bears a group including a female attendant or devotee who carries a pot standing to the right of Lajjā Gaurī and perhaps a bull couchant to the left. Lajjā Gaurī reclines upon an open lotus. The moldmade plaque is 2 inches tall by 3 inches wide and has a red slip. I would date this plaque to about the sixth century by its assured style, while others have dated it earlier, reasoning that all known images of Lajjā Gaurī in terra-cotta are earlier, which I find not to be true. If this later dating is correct this piece demonstrates that, although the Form IV Lajjā Gaurī with a human head is most common in Gujarat, the Form III lotus-headed Lajjā Gaurī was contemporary with it there.[11] In fact, a second Gujarati Form III lotus-headed Lajjā Gaurī has been reported by V. H. Sonawane (Fig. 80).[12] It was found at Bavaka (Panchmahals District, Gujarat). The large lotus-headed female is accompanied in the light-green-schist plaque by a couchant bull on the right and a kneeling female making a gesture of adoration on the left. The goddess wears the standard jewelry and holds lotus flowers in her hands. The rectangular plaque measures $3\frac{3}{4}$ inches tall by 5 inches wide. Sonawane dates the piece to the tenth to eleventh century, but suggests it may have been made elsewhere, since Bavaka has only existed since the twelfth century. I would date it by style to the ninth to tenth century, by comparison to the images from Malhar.

It is interesting to note that in the Kanad, Bavaka, and Ellora Form IV Lajjā Gaurīs the attendants are clearly female, while in examples from other areas and of other Forms they seem to be male. Perhaps this difference points toward a distinction in their ritual use of some unknown sort.

Several Lajjā Gaurī images are found on walls of tanks. There are two such examples from Gujarat and another from Aihole in Karnataka. On the wall of a stepwell, or tank, at Dhank (Rajkot District, Gujarat) a human-headed Form IV Lajjā Gaurī, much worn, holds lotus flowers in her hands and is adored by a kneeling figure to her left (Fig. 81).[13] A *liṅga* and a bull, seen from above, are to the right. It is unanimously dated to c. seventh century on the basis of style. Regarding this type of figure, U.P. Shah wrote that "the two lotuses show she was regarded as a form of Gaurī, the bull *vāhana* further suggesting that she was regarded in this age as a Śiva Śakti."[14] Shah's observation would also apply to the Ellora 21 figure and others. The third constant presence in these multifigured plaques, the devotee, indicates Lajjā Gaurī's status as a goddess to be worshiped.

A second stone panel is carved in the wall of a stepwell (Mañjuśrī *vapi*) at Dhank. It is also of the Form IV anthropomorphic type and may also be dated to c. seventh century (Fig. 82).[15] The goddess holds lotus flowers to either side of her head. Her coiffure is richly elaborated and she wears beaded ornaments. This image includes a lotus base beneath the goddess and an eave with *chaitya* arches overhead. If anything was to her right it is now lost, but to her left is a kneeling female devotee and a new presence is added: the god Gaṇeśa is above the devotee. His addition here is in accordance with Śaivite fortune imagery. Gaṇeśa, as he became formulated from a diverse origin, is "an embodiment of success in life and its accompaniments of good-living, prosperity and peace."[16] Mythically his dominant association is as a son of Śiva and Pārvatī.

Such images as this Dhank Lajjā Gaurī installed in a vertical position have been described as "squatting" but since the vast majority of images represent the goddess supine, we may suppose these are also meant to be supine but their location required an upright position.

A small damaged sandstone plaque about 2 inches tall by 4 inches wide, probably from Variavi (Surat District, Gujarat) or Kavi (Broach District, Gujarat), similarly includes the human-headed goddess flanked by Gaṇeśa and human figures (Fig. 83). Another damaged figure from Kavi in schist seems to have had a female devotee to the right and a bull to the left of the central figure of Lajjā Gaurī (Fig. 84). This was a surface find. It is $1\frac{3}{4}$ inches tall by 2 inches wide. It is in the collection of U. P. Shah, Baroda.[17] Despite damage both plaques may be datable by their style to c. sixth century.

Carved on a rock near the temple of the goddess Nanda, who is, significantly, a form of Pārvatī and one of the five Gaurīs, at Arna, Rajasthan, is a 16-inch figure of a Form IV anthropomorphic clothed Lajjā Gaurī holding lotuses in her hands by her head (Fig. 85). Separately carved to her right side is an image of Gaṇeśa. The association of Lajjā Gaurī with Gaṇeśa in these images is more common in Andhra plaques (yet to be discussed) than in those from anywhere else, but is, as mentioned, not a surprising addition in that Gaṇeśa, Remover of Obstacles, is a son of Śiva and Pārvatī. The association of Lajjā Gaurī with Gaṇeśa further supports other Śaivite associations of this goddess. The Arna figure is clothed on her lower body, as are Lajjā Gaurī images found in Andhra plaques. A snake (?) is carved directly below the goddess. R. C. Agrawala has published this figure and the Gaṇeśa to her side, and has dated it to the ninth century (Pratihāra period) by comparison to the Lajjā Gaurī from Bhinmal (Fig. 78).[18] I would date the Arna and Bhinmal figures earlier, c. seventh century by comparison to the Dhank figures (Figs. 81 and 82).

Compared to Lajjā Gaurī images there is a striking similarity of the headdress, pose, and lotus buds held in the upraised hands of a Gaṇeśa carved in wood in Kerala in the seventeenth century.[19] The four-armed figure has his vehicle, the rat, below his feet, and a lamp to his right side. He holds his tusk for writing in the book he holds opposite, while the upper two hands each hold a lotus bud, the stalk of which grows out of his trunk. This late form of Gaṇeśa seems to be given some aspects of iconography of Lajjā Gaurī including, most important, her *uttānapad* pose.[20]

An interesting stone relief plaque with a grouping of figures around Lajjā Gaurī comes from Tarsang (Panchmahals District, Gujarat) (Fig. 86).[21] The damaged gray-schist plaque preserves the Form IV human-headed Lajjā Gaurī in the center, flanked on the proper upper right by a *liṅga* and on the lower left (damaged) by a devotee who may have been kneeling and praying to her with his hands held in *añjalimudrā*. The lower-right portion is missing but may have had a bull facing toward the *liṅga*. The upper right has a trident above *śrīpada* (sacred feet), symbols of faith. To my knowledge the inclusion of the trident and *śrīpada* in this example is unique. The trident is always Śaivite in association. The upraised hands of the goddess are empty and turned inward. She has a halo incised about her head. She wears a plant necklace and a jeweled girdle. A cloth is woven through her legs. The plaque measures $3\frac{1}{2}$ inches square, and is kept at the Department of Archaeology and Ancient History of M. S. University of Baroda. The plaque may date to c. sixth century as suggested by Sonawane, comparing it to a figure of Ardhanāriśvara from the same site that is similar in modeling to the figure of this Lajjā Gaurī, and by comparison to the Elephanta Lajjā Gaurī, which seems stylistically of the sixth century. The Tarsang image, like the Elephanta goddess, was a surface find.

A Form IV Lajjā Gaurī from Valabhipur (Bhavnagar District, Gujarat) (Fig. 87) is also kept at the Department of Archaeology of M. S. University, Baroda. The dark-green-schist plaque measures $2\frac{1}{2}$ inches tall by $4\frac{1}{2}$ inches wide. The human-headed goddess holds long stalks with lotus buds that curve emphatically toward her shoulders by her head. To her right is a bull and to her left a kneeling figure in a pose of adoration. The goddess is obviously meant to be supine between the bull (seen from above) and the devotee (seen from the side). The artists of these Lajjā Gaurī plaques that include the kneeling devotee to the side never coordinated the perspective space of the upright devotee to that of the crouching bull and the supine goddess, probably so that the recognizability of the devotee would be maintained and because if the kneeling figure were properly carved upright, no doubt in every case the figure would have broken off. In this example the goddess's facial features are almost worn smooth. The piece has been dated c. seventh century by comparison to the previously discussed piece from Tarsang and because this date would place its creation during the time Valabhipur was the Maitraka capital.[22]

Sonawane has also reported three other Form IV Lajjā Gaurīs from Randelia (Bhavnagar District, Gujarat) (Fig. 88) (very worn and pierced fragment); Gadhali (Bhavnagar District, Gujarat) (Fig. 89) with bull and devotee; and Sathal (Ahmedabad District, Gujarat) (Fig. 90), also with bull and devotee. These are all kept at the Department of Archaeology, M. S. University, Baroda.

Form IV Lajjā Gaurī figures occur most frequently in a group of figures rather than singly whereas Form I figures are almost always unaccompanied, with only the exception of the example from Vadgaon wherein she is paired with a bull.

Form II: Lotus-Headed Lajjā Gaurī in Multifigured Plaques

While Form IV multifigured plaques occur in western Maharashtra, Gujarat, and western Rajasthan, several Form II (lotus-headed, armless) Lajjā Gaurīs are found represented on such plaques from the area around Nagpur in central Maharashtra. An interesting plaque of this type from Mandhal, Nagpur District, is now in the Central Museum, Nagpur (Fig. 91).[23] In this grouping above Lajjā Gaurī's bent knees and to the left is the small face of a lion, to the right a side view of a small couchant bull, and to the far right (the opposite side from the typical Gujarati organization) a large kneeling devotee of indeterminate gender with hands in adoration. This schist plaque measures $3\frac{3}{4}$ inches tall by 4 inches wide. It may date fourth to fifth century. The lion face, the lotus head, and the bull read in a line and are of equal size, like a script of symbols.

Also from the Nagpur area town of Mahurjhari is another Lajjā Gaurī in stone of the Maharashtrian lotus-headed Form II. She is accompanied to her right by a bull, to her left by a small devotee, and above and to the side of her large lotus head are lotus flowers (Fig. 92). The lower portion is damaged.[24]

A better preserved and quite handsomely carved sixth- to seventh-century example of the same arrangement is the Form II Lajjā Gaurī plaque reported in a Sotheby catalogue to have been brought from Seoni District of Madhya Pradesh.[25] This 4-inch square stone plaque (Fig. 98) presents a slender Lajjā Gaurī with lotus flowers turned from either side (right one lost) toward the lotus head. To the right of her *uttānapad* legs is a bull, turned head down (toward her feet) and to her left a kneeling, praying devotee. She wears a necklace between her breasts that looks like the stalk of the lotus flower/head above. She is further adorned with anklets and a jeweled girdle.

Another armless, lotus-headed Form II Lajjā Gaurī from Mansar (Nagpur District) has a bull to her right side but no devotee to the left. This piece is kept in the Central Museum, Nagpur (no. C 203). It is red sandstone and measures $3\frac{1}{4}$ inches tall by 4 inches wide (Fig. 93). Two other stone examples that are quite similar to the Mansar relief in that a bull is placed to the right of Lajjā Gaurī and lotuses to the right and left of her head, but there is no devotee, are from Paunar (Wardha District, Maharashtra) (Figs. 94 and 95). They are in a private collection in Nagpur; photographs of them have been published by C. Gupta.[26] The repeated presence of the bull and the devotee seems to indicate Śaivite association as a constant, and that this is a goddess to whom *pūjā* is to be offered.

A damaged multifigured plaque from Ter (Fig. 97) (Ter Museum no. 9.168) was probably originally like the Keesaragutta example (Form II, to be described) except that the goddess is of Form II: armless and lotus-headed. The bull faces the *liṅga* on the right edge, and the devotee and lion face are badly damaged on the left edge. This previously unpublished red sandstone image of Lajjā Gaurī measures 2 inches tall by $2\frac{1}{4}$ inches wide. She wears anklets, a girdle, and a lotus necklace and she has a cloth woven through her legs.

Form III: Lotus-Headed Lajjā Gaurī in Multifigured Plaques

Several southern examples have an arrangement similar to that of the Mandhal (Form II) plaque just described (Fig. 91) but with a Form III Lajjā Gaurī. For example, a similar organization recurs four times with variations in plaques from Ter in southern Maharashtra, and once from Majati in Hukkeri Taluk of Belgaum District, Karnataka (Figs. 99–102). Sundara dates the Majati example to the seventh to eighth centuries by particular stylistic features which are pre-Rashtrakuta, and by evidence of religious activity at the site at this time.[27] I prefer an earlier dating of fourth to sixth century. In the lower-right area of these four similar stone plaques is the Form III goddess with lotus head and arms holding a leaf rather than a lotus. She wears bracelets, necklace, anklets, armlets, girdle, and a cloth through her legs. She is narrow-waisted and may not be unclothed. Her lotus head is seen in three-quarter view. To her left is a three-quarter view of a kneeling, adoring devotee of indeterminate sex who, in three of the four examples, is set apart from the goddess by a border or a stick that he holds in one hand. In one Ter image (no. RC 8192) (Fig. 99) this division is clearly made by a stick or staff held in the hand of the human figure.[28] Across the top of all four images from left to right there is, or was, a *liṅga,* bull, and a lion's face. The Majati plaque, which is larger than the others (five inches square), adds a conch to the series on the upper right (Fig. 102). The significance of the lion face is ambiguous. It could represent a *kīrttimukha,* the lion vehicle (*vāhana*) of the goddess, or Narasiṁha Viṣṇu. I think it most likely represents the vehicle of the goddess.[29] The conch, likewise, can represent Viṣṇu or may be an emblem of the goddess as symbolic of water and thereby fertility. I do not believe that the conch and lion face can be interpreted as associations with Viṣṇu, since this is the only instance among all Lajjā Gaurī images of such an association. Lajjā Gaurī is related to Śiva in all other examples. One Ter example (no. 9.166) is damaged in the upper right and may have also originally included a conch (Fig. 100). This Ter example is not compartmentalized by lines as the others are. The third Ter example is a fragment (no. 9.154) (Fig. 101), and the goddess clearly holds a leaf, not a lotus, in either hand. The leaf in hand may suggest a relation of the goddess to Śakambhari iconography, Śakambhari being a vegetation goddess popular today in Bengal, but otherwise not similar to the image of Lajjā Gaurī.[30] The three smaller plaques are about $2\frac{3}{4}$ inches by $2\frac{1}{2}$ inches.

I. K. Sarma has reported a most interesting discovery in regard to Lajjā Gaurī; a $4\frac{3}{4}$-inch square stone plaque with Lajjā Gaurī (Form III) and other figures (Fig. 103) found in the excavation of a c. fourth-century brick Śiva temple at Keesaragutta in Andhra. Specifically, it was found buried under the base of the altar, and an earthen pot bearing six female figures and a human skeleton were found buried nearby.[31] This association suggests the use of the small stone plaques as an auspicious ritual item, buried to consecrate the land for sacred use as according to Vedic ritual. This is the only instance discovered of this location and apparent use of an image. In this plaque, rather than a lotus, the goddess holds in either hand a *liṅga* (right) and a lion face (left), while below to either side are the bull (right) facing the *liṅga* and presented as seen from above, and (left) facing the goddess is a kneeling devotee with a bowl of food as an offering. The lotus head of the goddess is aligned with the lion face and the *liṅga*. The goddess wears a *kaupīna* (loincloth) and her feet rest on lotus flowers. The goddess here holds emblems of Śiva and Śakti balanced in her hands: the *vāhana* (vehicle) of Śiva, the bull, and her own vehicle, the lion. The Keesaragutta example is compositionally like one from Ter (Fig. 97), but in the Ter example Lajjā Gaurī is armless.

Other Multifigured Representations of Unusual Types

There are a number of long rectangular plaques from Andhra that are similar to the square plaques just described in that they include some of the same figures although they are arranged differently, in a single row rather than being placed above or to the side of Lajjā Gaurī in compartments. For example, two plaques from Darsi (Figs. 104 and 105) include the lotus-headed goddess in Form II, the typically Maharashtrian armless Form, at the center.[32] She wears a lower garment and is seated in *uttānapad* pose above the bust of a *yakṣi,* or female demiurge or nature spirit. She seems to be enthroned, like the figure from Kausambi now in the Indian Museum, Calcutta (Fig. 21). To her left stands a male figure with a trident and to his left is a lion whose seated pose is like that of the goddess. To her right is the Śiva *liṅga* with couchant bull on its shaft. Next to the *liṅga* sits Brahmā. The same arrangement of figures is found on two other stone plaques. One is from Kunidane (Fig. 106), c. fourth to fifth century and the other is from Uppalapadu (Fig. 107), third to fourth century.[33] In the Kunidane and Uppalapadu reliefs the standing male holds not a trident but a stick or spear like the male figure in the Majati plaque (Fig. 102).

The seated lion in the examples from Darsi, Uppalapadu, and Kunidane calls to mind the well-known fourth-century rectangular limestone plaque from Kondamotu (now in the Andhra Pradesh State Department of Archaeology and Museums, Hyderabad), in which the central figure is a similarly seated man—lion form of Narasiṁha Viṣṇu. In fact, the plaques including Lajjā Gaurī from Darsi, Uppalapadu, and Kunidane are dated c. fourth century by their similarity to the Kondamotu figure by Sarma and Sivaramamurti.[34] This earliest depiction of Narasiṁha from Kondamotu is flanked by five male figures identified as the Pañchaviras. To assume that Narasiṁha is also depicted in the Lajjā Gaurī plaques because of the similar sitting pose, style, and naiveté of the form of the man-lion figure would ignore the facts that the Kondamotu plaque is clearly Vaiṣṇava and that, unlike the lion in the Lajjā Gaurī plaques, the Kondamotu man-lion has four human arms holding Viṣṇu's implements, a *śrīvatsa* on his chest, and an erect phallus (which is most atypical of Viṣṇu). The lion in the Darsi, Kunidane, and Uppalapadu plaques is totally animal. He may, therefore, merely represent the Śakti *vāhana,* as in the instances of a lion's face carved on other plaques previously discussed (Ter and Majati).

These plaques seem to be cult images that give the goddess prominence by her central location. She is equal in size (an indication of status) to Śiva, Brahmā, and either the man-lion form of Viṣṇu as Narasiṁha or the Śakti *vāhana*. The goddess consistently forms a couple with the Śivaliṅga, which implies that the male to her left could be the son of Śiva and Pārvatī, Kārttikeya. However, the male figure seems to be the same in location and proportion to the goddess as the kneeling Gujarati figure; therefore, it is equally likely that he may here, as there, be a Śaivite devotee, attendant, or a guard. Here he is clearly male, whereas the gender of the kneeling adoring figures in northern plaques was not discernible except for three instances where they may be female. Only in the Ellora temple 21 panel are the standing attendants, who wave fly whisks, clearly female.

In the plaques, which present a line-up of gods, logic would suggest that the young male holding a lance or trident should be identified as the god Kārttikeya, but the identity of the male figure as Kārttikeya or as a devotee remains unresolved since he sometimes holds a trident (as Kārttikeya never does). However, evidence of imagery carved on a temple in Orissa, which seems relevant, is persuasive that he is a devotee or guard rather than Kārttikeya. On the architrave of the doorway of the sixth- to seventh-century Satrugneśvara temple in Bhuvaneshvara, Orissa, are carved Śiva and Pārvatī, or Hara and Gaurī (Fig. 108).[35] Areas around these two main figures are divided or compartmentalized, like the Ter plaques described earlier (Figs. 99–101). There is, significantly in relation to Lajjā Gaurī, a lotus above Pārvatī's human head and she wears lotus earrings. Śiva holds a lotus flower, and a snake appears over his right shoulder. Pārvatī is attended by a female maid, and to either side of the couple a male attendant stands at ease holding a trident. Below Pārvatī a lion mask is worshiped by two figures and below Śiva a bull is similarly worshiped. In this context the lion face would seem not to suggest Narasiṁha Viṣṇu or *kīrttimukha* (the lionlike face of glory) but instead the lion vehicle of the goddess as counterpart to Śiva's vehicle represented opposite. Whether or not this verifies that the other occurrences of the lion mask should be identified as a lion *vāhana* of the goddess is not certain, although Donaldson interprets these, the lion and the bull, as the mounts of the deities Hara and Pārvatī.[36] In pavilions outside the central plaquelike arrangement are single ladies on each side. One admires herself in a mirror, the other holds her hand over her pubis suggesting vanity and modesty, the two natures of the Lajjā form of Gaurī. Donaldson, in fact, states that the dominant theme of the panel is "the conjunction of opposites, i.e., the union of male and female principles."[37] Beyond these two ladies to either side are shrines with a *liṅga* (left) and the head of Śiva (right). This representation, because of its location on the temple architrave suggests that the temple is dedicated to the worship of Hara and Gaurī, forms of Śiva and Pārvatī. This plaque-format lintel on the Satrughneśvara temple, which seems to be a unique occurrence and location for the plaque elements otherwise so similar to those found in small multifigured plaques of Lajjā Gaurī from Andhra and Maharashtra, is an important relative to them. The union of Śiva and Pārvatī in Lajjā Gaurī reliefs, *liṅga* and *yoni,* or Hara and Gaurī, seems to be depicted on this Orissan temple, with the two deities represented separately and in anthropomorphic forms. Apparently none of the four Forms of Lajjā Gaurī described in this study exist in Orissa, but it seems this single temple architrave depiction does represent her. There are examples of a self-exposing mortal Tantric practitioner on this and other temples including, at Bhuvaneshvara: Parasurameśvara, Tangi, Sisireśvara, and Rajarani temples, published by Thomas Donaldson.[38] They are not images of Lajjā Gaurī.

Other stone plaques with groups of gods in a row that are similar to those discussed are found in Andhra, especially from Peddamudiam. In these a similar, but more elaborate, line-up of deities includes (left to right): Gaṇeśa, Brahmā, Narasiṁha, *liṅga,* Devī, Viṣṇu, Umamaheśvara with Nandi, Lakṣmī as human-headed Śrīvatsa or as aniconic Śrīvatsa, Mahiṣāsuramardinī, and two severed arms held up like those of a devotee in prayer or as found on Satī stones where typically they appear severed. These have been variously dated between the fourth and seventh century (Figs. 126 and 127). These plaques, which include Śrīvatsa instead of Lajjā Gaurī, will be discussed in chapter 3.

One final odd example of a grouping of figures including Lajjā Gaurī does not seem related to any of those discussed. It comes from the rim of the tank by Huchchimalli temple built by the Chalukyas at Aihole in Karnataka in the early eighth century. It is a large stone piece (16 inches in height by 51 inches long) with a lotus-headed Form III Lajjā Gaurī in a series including from left to right: a mongoose, a monkey in a tree, the goddess, a man riding forward on a bull or buffalo, and an umbrella bearer leading the procession (Fig. 109). The tank was an addition to the Early Chalukya temple (c. A.D. 700) made by the Rashtrakutas in about the late eighth century, which is evident by its style and the site's history. I can offer no explanation of the association of these figures. It may illustrate a local story concerning Lajjā Gaurī. The piece is now kept in the Aihole site museum. Like several other representations of Lajjā Gaurī it was originally a part of a temple tank, in this case serving as a part of the tank's rim. If this narrative relief could be deciphered it might yield valuable information about Lajjā Gaurī.

The associations of figures provided by the multifigured plaques described in this chapter provide evidence of recurring patterns of arrangement of certain figures around Lajjā Gaurī. Most standard of these are the bull, lion, *liṅga,* and adoring devotee or guardian. These recurring figures, although their locations in various plaques change, are all Śaivite. Even the less frequent associations of Gaṇeśa, or the trident are Śaivite. This is not unsuspected, given other contextual information such as the fact that all in situ images of Lajjā Gaurī are in Śaivite temples. There is no doubt that at least by the fourth century Lajjā Gaurī had become accepted into the Hindu pantheon as a *Śakti* of Śiva.

Furthermore, it is evident from the group of large multifigured panels from Andhra that in the fourth to seventh century in this area, and to a lesser extent elsewhere in India, Lajjā Gaurī became an adjunct to the triad of Brahmā, Viṣṇu, and Śiva, specifically coupled to Śiva as elsewhere. Her head is either lotus or human, her *uttānapad* pose is less stressed in some images (she seems to sit), and she is sometimes clothed by a loin cloth or a skirt. She is represented as an equal to the other gods by her equal size. From these plaques it is evident to us that Lajjā Gaurī has undergone an elevation in status and has entered the Hindu pantheon at least in South India.

This occurrence of apparent absorption of an erstwhile village goddess, perhaps a *grāmadevatā,* into the Hindu pantheon is not surprising as a process; it has occurred many times.[39] Nor is it surprising that her high status was short-lived. It is of interest that for two centuries—the second to the fourth—Lajjā Gaurī (perhaps not known as Lajjā Gaurī, but by another name) existed independently.

Images of Lajjā Gaurī were rarely made after the eighth century and apparently were not made later than the twelfth century anywhere in India (except for the copy cited earlier) although worship of some of the ancient images has been maintained.

Notes

1. The Ellora goddess has been published by Sankalia, 1960, fig. 7.
2. Stutley and Stutley, 1977, 96; Gopinatha Rao, 1968, 502.
3. Dhere, 1978, 206–8.
4. Burgess, 1981 reprint.
5. Dhere, 1978, 55.
6. The earliest mention of the name Elapura is made in a Chalukya copperplate grant of A.D. 704, Haran Chandra Chakladar, "Elapura Grant of Western Calukya Vijayāditya Śaka Samvat 626," *Indian Historical Quarterly* 4, 1928, 425–30. The iconographic program of Ellora temple 21 and its implications is under study by Shantanu Phukan. His ideas have stimulated my own in regard to this unusual cave temple.
7. Spink, 1967, 11–22, and 1983, 235–84.
8. Gorakshekar, 1982, 2–3. It is kept in the Prince of Wales Museum, no. 81.7/1.
9. Previously unpublished.
10. Shah, 1955–56, pl. 41, fig. 10.
11. Margabandhu, 1976, 206, fig. 1, and 1981, pl. 28c, 105–6. Also mentioned by Sarma, 1982, 148, and Sonawane, 1986. It has been dated either first to second century or fourth. I would tend toward a fourth- to sixth-century date for it. The piece is in the Western Circle Office, Archaeological Survey of India, Baroda.
12. Sonawane, 1986.
13. Vora and Palan, 1971, 357–58, fig. 10.
14. Shah, 1955–56, 55–56.
15. Schastok, 1980, fig. 171, discussed in relation to the pose of the female on an Indus seal and the female as source of all being, 128; Sonawane, 1986; Vora and Palan, 1971, fig. 5. All date it by style to the seventh century.
16. Stutley and Stutley, 1977, 92.
17. Margabandhu, 1976, 208–9, figs. 4 and 2. Collection of U. P. Shah. No dating of these two figures is proposed by Margabandhu.
18. R. C. Agrawala, 1972, 351.
19. Illustrated as an advertisement in *Marg* 1978, vol. 32, no. 2.
20. Louise Cort described to me a form of Gaṇeśa in Orissa made by placing a coconut on top of a pot and adding the stem of a green coconut as the trunk. This would seem to be another ramification of Fortune-associated pot imagery.
21. Sonawane, 1986.
22. Ibid.
23. Muley, 1979, 187–89. Also *Indian Archaeology: A Review 1969–70,* pl. 64, no. B. Muley refers to the lion face as *kīrttimukh*. It seems more likely to be the *śakti vāhana*. Also C. Gupta, 1981, 145; Tiwari, 1985, fig. 14.

24. Dhere, 1978, fig. 8; Deo, 1973, fig. 27, no. 23. The relief is in the collection of Brahmananda Deshpande of Sarasvatī Bhavan Mahāvidhyalaya, in Aurangabad.

25. Sotheby Parke Bernet, "Khmer, Thai, Indian and Himalayan Works of Art," London, 15 June 1987, lot 244, now Eilenberg Collection, London.

26. C. Gupta, 1987. In this article Gupta cites thirty-four images, many lost to dealers, from the central Maharashtra region. He dates the Paunar images to the Sātavāhana-Vākāṭaka period and describes four of them. He prefers to distinguish Lajjā Gaurī with a bull as Lajjā Gaurī or Koṭvī, and without a bull as simply Lajjā.

27. A. Sundara, 1979.

28. Ter figure published here for the first time.

29. C. Gupta, 1987, in reference to a plaque from Mandhal, believes it is not *kīrttimukh,* but a lion or tiger head.

30. Concerning Śākambharī see Shetti, 1971, 46–53, especially 48–50; Hopkins, 1968, 11–12; Larson, 1980, 41, Fig. 2.; B. Srivastava, 1978, 10, identifies the class of terra-cotta lotus-headed figures as Śākambharī, but makes no explanation. He illustrates the Bhita (Fig. 33) Lajjā Gaurī and another from Agiavira in line drawings. Dhavalikar, 1986, identified the Mahakuta Lajjā Gaurī as Śākambharī basing his argument on the *Śākambharīmahātmya* that says that she resided at Mahakuta. He discusses the Mahakuta fragment. He erroneously identifies Mahakuta as the same as Banashankari (=Śākambharī) though these are two separate temple sites. He also states that all Lajjā Gaurī images are headless and nude, and he assumes that all have marked pudenda. He states that the latest such figure is sixth-century, although he mentions one as being seventh-century.

31. Sarma, 1987.

32. Unpublished. Darsi is in Prakasam District of Andhra Pradesh. One example measures 12½ by 5 inches in the Nellore Museum, green limestone, c. fourth to fifth century; second image measuring 10½ by 5 inches is kept in Director's Office, Andhra Pradesh State Directorate of Archaeology and Museums, Hyderabad, also green limestone.

33. Kunidane plaque measures 10½ by 7½ inches. Published: Sivaramamurti, 1957, 1979, fig. 41, 1982, fig. 48; Sastri, 1967–68, 16–22; Prasad, 1980, 68–69. Uppalapadu published: Sivaramamurti, 1979, fig. 41, 1982, fig. 48.

34. Sarma, 1987, Sivaramamurti, 1979.

35. Donaldson, 1985, figs. 12, 17, described 36.

36. Donaldson, 1985, 36.

37. Ibid.

38. Donaldson, 1975, fig. 20, 5; 1976, fig. 1, 44, 208.

39. Eschmann, 1978.

III

Related Forms

ALTHOUGH IMAGES OF LAJJĀ GAURĪ were not made, in my opinion, before the second century A.D., some more ancient images have been cited by various scholars as conceptual antecedents to Lajjā Gaurī: for example, Lajjā Gaurī has been related to an Indus Valley seal of c. 1500 B.C. which depicts a woman with a plant issuing from her vagina, and to another image of a similar type from Chandraketugarh of the second century B.C. through the shared feature of plant parts and the birth pose, which seem to express the conception of the female as the source of all life. Scholars have also compared Lajjā Gaurī images to the Inamgaon stub-headed female figure with spread legs and a bull of c. 1200 B.C. sharing the similarity of the headless female associated with the bull as emblematic of the fertile earth and fertilizing rain (the bull as symbol of virility).[1]

But other more direct antecedents to Lajjā Gaurī may be recognized in the actual incorporation of auspicious symbols as parts of the images. These hold the key to understanding the nature of this goddess and to perceiving the artistic process behind creation and elaboration of her images into their four forms. By the first century B.C. a vocabulary of symbolism was established in Indian art including three paramount symbols: the lotus, the brimming pot, and the mark of fortune (*śrīvatsa*). Each of these symbols is obviously or subtly incorporated into images of Lajjā Gaurī. Also, though less obviously, related to her images by their form and symbolism are the *yakṣa* and the frog. In this chapter the meanings of the symbolic forms of lotus, pot, *yakṣa, śrīvatsa* and frog in relation to Lajjā Gaurī will be discussed. These seem to be the true artistic antecedents of Lajjā Gaurī that came together, given the conceptual environment that admitted of the boundless life-giving power of the mother goddess. The four forms of Lajjā Gaurī seem to have grown out of the artists' imaginations without a text through "resemblance-elaboration," to use Bosch's term (discussed in the introduction), that is, incorporation of certain forms that have a traditional meaning in Indian art into her form.[2]

LOTUS

The concept of fortune underlies the meaning of the forms of the goddess Lajjā Gaurī, and specifically the fortune of fertility and reproduction. In Indian art the lotus is the symbol par excellence of fortune, fertility, and reproduction. An appreciation of the symbolism accrued to this flower, which extends well beyond the meanings just listed, is essential to an understanding of Lajjā Gaurī's nature. Surprisingly, a satisfying essay on this subject does not exist.[3]

The lotus, *padmā* or *kamala*, is the sacred flower of India. It is found in Indian art associated with all deities of Buddhism, Hinduism, and Jainism. The lotus is *devī,* the goddess, *padmā śrī lakṣmī*. Her nature is beauty, purity, and good fortune. On the microcosmic level the flowering of the lotus is symbolic of the opening of an individual's consciousness to its full potential. With its roots in the mud of the pond, the stalk traverses the water and the plant blooms on top of the water, opening to the light in full and perfect beauty. Thus, purity is distilled from base impurity, as one's consciousness may also become pure through spiritual devotion. Macrocosmically the lotus symbolizes cosmic consciousness or the idea of perfect wisdom.

The lotus floats upon the water; as it was conceived by Indian mythologists, the earth floats upon the waters and thereby the lotus is also a symbol of the earth, source of all life and fortune. All life originates from the waters and the earth is the absolute upon which all depends. The lotus symbolizes, thereby, both the potency of life-giving water and the earth.

In association with ideas of the lotus's purity, ideal of consciousness, perfect wisdom, and relation to earth and fortune, gods and goddesses have the lotus as their abode, that is their seat or throne. The temple, as the perfect home of the deity, may be carved all around its base with lotus petals. The gods wear lotuses as ornaments or hold them in their hands.

In many Hindu myths, after the devastating flood and between creations (of which there have been many), the first life of a new age arises from the ocean floor in the form of a lotus. In Hinduism, therefore, the lotus is a symbol of creation. In one myth the lotus grows from the navel of Viṣṇu to begin a new creation, as Viṣṇu dreams it while he sleeps floating on the waters. Out of the lotus that grows from his navel as he sleeps, emerges Brahmā, Lord of Creation.

The botanical characteristics of the lotus plant give rise to further meanings. Because of the means of reproduction of the lotus plant from a seed that matures within the pod, or calyx, of the plant and then bursts out as a new plant, the analogy to human reproduction is made. Thus the lotus is seen as a plant carrying the potential for future generations and is given meanings of cyclic renewal of life, of regeneration of life, or reincarnations. Similar in meaning is the frequent depiction by Indian artists of a bouquet of lotuses issuing from a pot with each flower in a different stage of its life-cycle: buds, half-open flowers, fully open flowers, and wilting flowers, suggesting infancy, maturity, and old age and death. These represent stages in the life or lives of a seeker of full consciousness. The lotus is associated with the goddess Lajjā Gaurī as a fully mature, open flower as her head and as new buds held in her hands as appropriate symbols of generation suggesting adult and child, and womb and phallus, or the potential for new life.

All of these meanings charge the images of Lajjā Gaurī, all of which bear lotus parts. Forms I, II and III culminate in a lotus flower. All forms incorporate the lotus into the iconography of the image as an attribute, a seat, ornament, etc. The plant parts of Lajjā Gaurī express the irrepressible reproductive force of nature and are related to human and divine creation by visual metaphor.

In Indian poetry all parts and aspects of the ideal human or divine body are described by comparing them to lotuses: lotuslike eyes, lotuslike feet, limbs, face, fragrance, etc. It may be that every part of the Lajjā Gaurī image, not only the lotus head, is meant in some images to bear resemblance to a plant form. The lithe female arms are adorned by bangles that are like entwining tendrils, the breasts are like ripe fruit or flower buds, the fingers flex unnaturally but as a vine would naturally bend. At Sanchi in the *stūpa* II railing medallion cited by Kramrisch, the female form is implied in the shapes of the lotus plant.[4] Kramrisch discusses its form and details as a "sculptural synonym" to Aditi (Lajjā Gaurī), or as the result of "cognate conceptions." This remarkable medallion is an optical illusion operating doubly as a lotus-headed female figure and a lotus plant. The lotus calyx forms the head, the petals form a rufflike necklace, and there even seem to be hands held up to the side of the head holding buds, as in images of Lajjā Gaurī. Over the "head" of this image is hung a garland, which undoubtedly honors a deity, the lotus goddess, represented below. A unique and remarkable sculpture of Padmādevī in the Mathura Museum represents much the same conception. In this large image ($3\frac{3}{4}$ feet in height) Padmādevī is represented in her plant form but with visual analogy to a female human form. The undulating, rising stalk of the lotus suggests the curves of a female body, a lotus head tops the stalk, and a lotus bud on a stalk grows to either side below the lotus head. Sheltering the lotus goddess is a canopy of serpent hoods, which, like the garland in the Sanchi image, indicates that the figure represents a goddess. In other images (Figs. 8 and 9) of Lajjā Gaurī the feet rest on lotuses. At Darasuram, and elsewhere, the image wears a creeper bracelet (Figs. 52, 54). In several examples the necklace is vegetation (Figs. 67, 96).

If the lotus culmination of Lajjā Gaurī images began as the flower in the brimming vase of Form I, certainly there are other associations that have relevance to its continuation in place of a head in examples of Forms II and III. Sivaramamurti wrote that the lotus is mentioned in *Viṣṇudharmottara* (III.882.8–9) as the face of Lakṣmī, and its presence there is explained as expressing her *saubhagya,* or good fortune.[5] Based on this literary description Sivaramamurti identified images of the lotus-headed goddess as Śrī Lakṣmī. This identification does not take into consideration the fact that the earliest goddesses of this type (Form I) did not have a lotus head, but only a lotus on top of the pot/abdomen.

The *śiraścakra,* or nimbus, around the head of Indian gods and goddesses is often figured with a lotus design, the lotus being a flower that symbolizes pure consciousness and one that opens and closes in response to the presence or absence of the sun's rays. The open lotus behind the head is an indication of special consciousness, and light or radiance is implied by its presence to be emitted from the deity's center of consciousness. The lotus is also sometimes worn like a crown by a god, as seen, for example, on top of the head of Narasiṁha in Badami rock-cut temple III.[6] Replacing the normal head on the human body of this goddess with this flower is a purposeful allusion to the extensive meanings and associations with the lotus in Indian art and symbolism.[7] It is also interesting, in this regard, that only Form IV human-headed Lajjā Gaurīs are provided with halos, suggesting to us that the lotus head of the goddess in other forms adequately denotes her divinity.

In a group of Form I images (Figs. 1–5) it has been noted that the centering of the sex parts of the female figure where the seed pod of the lotus flower incised on the background plaque would occur is clearly meant to draw the analogy of their generative aspects. In these images the legs, to some observers, seem like lotus petals. A further sort of double-entendre involving lotus imagery and cultural associations was described earlier (pages 15–16) as it is visible in most Lajjā Gaurī images; that is, the fact that if inverted the potform belly area of Lajjā Gaurī is either the form of a closed bud or a phallus with the slit serving as the opening of the womb and of the penis or lotus bud. Within the womb of Lajjā Gaurī, this suggests, is a phallus, or within the pot is a lotus bud. Certain cultural and literary metaphors, described previously, make it clear that the visual illusion is intended to express union and generation: a metaphor for the womb may be an open flower or a ripe fruit. The womb is described as a lotus flower that opens and closes rhythmically (responding to the sun's rays), and the womb, the *yoni,* is the vessel that receives. The penis is called a closed bud, or a green fruit. All such associations find visual expression in Lajjā Gaurī images.

POT

Associations of form and meaning give rise to alternate or interchangeable symbols in Indian art. The language that describes the female body metaphorically in terms of lotuses, and the association of both the female body and the lotus plant with generation and auspiciousness, gave the artist license to suggest that the female vessel itself—the womb (*yoni*)—is like a pot (*kumbha*) brimming with lotus flowers. In the *uttānapad* pot Form I the artist sat the pot-abdomen with flowers coming from its mouth, on the stand of the *uttānapad* legs.

The extension of the torso to include breasts, flanking buds, and a full flowering lotus in the location of the head may have taken some inspiration from a *pūrṇa kumbha* association as well, in which the round full breasts were suggested by the standard inclusion of two more round, open lotuses growing out of the pot in a cognate location. This can be seen by comparing the Amaravati relief of a *pūrṇa kumbha* (Fig. 113) with the Lajjā Gaurī from Paunar (Fig. 96).

The formal and symbolic similarity of the *pūrṇa kumbha* and the *uttānapad*-pot (Form 1) figure cannot be missed. Not only is the womb and abdomen area of Lajjā Gaurī often shaped like a *pūrṇa kumbha,* but the configuration of the *pūrṇa kumbha,* as an auspicious motif, one of the *aṣṭamaṅgala,* at Nagarjunakonda, Amaravati, Aihole, and many other sites (Figs. 112–117), is only a degree more abstract than the representation of the anthropomorphized lotus-headed goddess; the "shoulder" portion of the pot has the shape of the raised knees of the goddess, as can be seen in the pot pattern of the Aihole Huchchimalli temple's porch railing (Fig. 114). Both are crowned with a lotus and have a lotus bud or flower to either side of the crowning lotus. The *channavīra* and the necklace are included on the *pūrṇa kumbha* as adornment of the "neck" and "shoulder" just as they are found on the body of images of the goddess Lajjā Gaurī. A *pūrṇa kumbha* carved on an ivory piece found at Begram and many other examples has a cloth around its girth, as Lajjā Gaurī often does. In literature this is called a *mekhalī-ghaṭa* (girdled vase).[8] The symbolic meaning of *pūrṇa kumbha* is equivalent to that of Lajjā Gaurī; in Form I figures their shapes and details are similar as well.[9]

The repeating pot motif is seen on the third-century *stūpa* casing slabs in the south at Nagarjunakonda and Amaravati, and is also part of the decoration of *stūpas* at Sanchi, Mathura, Bharhut, and Sarnath. In the later periods the pot is held by the river goddess to underline her meaning as source of life-giving water; it is appropriate beneath the feet of the goddess Lakṣmī carved on a pillar from Mathura as her source, the source of fortune. Repeated in a series of the porch railing of a seventh-century Hindu temple at Aihole in Karnataka (Fig. 114) and on many other temples there, a swastika (sign of well-being) is carved on the central lotus flower growing from the pot. The pot is often included as a part of the auspicious doorjamb imagery of temples, too. At Bharhut in a railing medallion a pot issues not only lotus flowers, but an entire lotus rhizome that winds around the pot (Fig. 116). The pot in this example serves as a source of life or as a "root device," others of which will be discussed subsequently. Like the lotus, the pot symbolizes well-being, fertility, and the power of water as the source of life. Throughout India a traditional wedding gift to the bride is a water pot, symbolic of the wish for success in producing offspring. The underlying idea is that nothing grows without water, including the embryo, which is surrounded in a life-supporting fluid in the womb.[10]

The potent metaphor of the pot as womb brimming with life is given visual expression in Form I images of Lajjā Gaurī, the earliest form of her images. The primal power of this phoneme, however, is dropped in other Forms, some of which are contemporary with it, in favor of a more fully female anthropomorphic representation of the same idea.

YAKṢA

Yakṣas were nature deities in India, worshiped since Vedic times, and associated with fertility and well-being of the community and the land.[11] Their most frequent site of worship was beneath a tree, and *yakṣīs* (the female form) were considered to embody the life-sap of the tree. Hence it was believed that barren women could be made fertile by *yakṣīs*. The *yakṣa* cult was assimilated by Hinduism, Buddhism and Jainism.

At the major Buddhist *stūpa* site of Bharhut the symbolic function of the pot as the source of all life, carved on some *vedikā* medallions, is interchanged on some others with the figure of a male *yakṣa* in the *uttānapad* pose, from whose navel or mouth issue lotus plants representing the irrepressible force of life (Figs. 118–120). The *yakṣa* in these different relief representations is not only in *uttānapad* pose like Lajjā Gaurī, but also has the elbows behind the knees and each hand holding a stalk of a lotus bud, just as Lajjā Gaurī does. The use of the *uttānapad* pose for the male *yakṣa* makes it evident that birth-giving is only metaphorically associated with the pose.

In relation to the pose of these early *yakṣa* figures, it is interesting to recall the multifigured plaques from Andhra Pradesh (Figs. 104–7) discussed on page 46 in which a *yakṣi* carved beneath Lajjā Gaurī seems to serve as her vehicle (*vāhana*). Such representations, whose original religious explanation is lost, date from the third to fourth centuries, whereas the Buddhist figures mentioned here are earlier, between the first century B.C. and the first century A.D. In other images of *yakṣas* from Bharhut, the *vāhana* of the *yakṣa* is a smaller *yakṣa*.

Beyond observing this apparent interchangeability of aspects of form of the pot, *yakṣa*, and Lajjā Gaurī it is difficult to draw conclusions regarding the process of formal sharing that obviously occurred. However, it is the common ground of conceptual expression of these images that allows one to read the images of Lajjā Gaurī. Coomaraswamy (1971), in fact, believed that the *yakṣa's* nature served as the model after which that of the Hindu god Śiva was formed. It is therefore not surprising that a goddess who came to be considered a counterpart of Śiva should be given attributes and powers earlier owned by *yakṣis*, such as the *uttānapad* pose, the lotus in hand, and the role as source of life.

ŚRIVATSA

Where artists, their patrons, or the priest perceived a conceptual affinity of meanings between deities or aniconic symbols of deities, it seems, aspects of their forms were interchanged readily. As another alternative symbol of the life-force, besides the *pūrṇa kumbha* or *yakṣa*, the *śrīvatsa*, the mark or sign of fortune, served as a symbol of the source of life, as in a Buddhist shrine doorstep from Kesanapalli (Guntur District, Andhra Pradesh) dated by the paleography of its inscription to the third century A.D. (Fig. 121). In the same manner as in pot and *yakṣa* depictions described, a frenzy of lotus life issues from the "root device" of the *śrīvatsa* seen here. A chain of association of visual imagery links these "source symbols" to Lajjā Gaurī. Kindred antecedents to Lajjā Gaurī may be recognized in assemblages of auspicious motifs, such as the curious and abundant designs that combine lotuses and *śrīvatsas* into a shape similar in outline to parts of the later Lajjā Gaurī images, as, for example, those seen ornamenting *stūpa* rails of Sanchi II and Bharhut (c. 100 B.C.) (Figs. 110–11, 122). In these I find generally analogous artistic abstractions compared to images of Lajjā Gaurī, for instance, in Figure 110 a nub-headed form with lotus buds to each side and anthropomorphic curled "arms" and "legs." In Figure 111, from Sanchi II, with the same outline, a lotus flower serves as a "head," with lotus stalk arms and budding flower "hands" while the lower "body" is the abstracted form of the lower *śrīvatsa*. The same design recurs many times at Sanchi. Some conjunction of the forms represented here with *śrīvatsa* parts and the form of Lajjā Gaurī seems apparent.[12]

In another example from Bharhut (Satna District, Madhya Pradesh) a second-century B.C. crossbar medallion of the *stūpa* railing has the same outline as a *śrīvatsa* but is composed of plant parts issuing from a lotus (Fig. 122). The outline suggests a head, arms held up, and legs spread out in positions typical of Lajjā Gaurī, with the addition of griffinlike animals leaping out of its center to the sides.[13]

There seems to be a relationship in meaning as well as form of Lajjā Gaurī and *śrīvatsa,* and thereby kinship with Śrī, Śrī Lakṣmī, and Gaja Lakṣmī—all goddesses of well-being.[14] The outline of *śrīvatsa* is similar to that of Lajjā Gaurī, and their meanings are also shared. Lakṣmī is said to be within *śrīvatsa,* or *śrīvatsa* is the sign of Lakṣmī. In her aniconic form as *śrīvatsa* Śrī is represented on top of the *toraṇas* (gateways) of the Buddhist *stūpa* I at Sanchi and at the apex of the doorway of the Jain rock-cut temple, Annantagumpha, at Udayagiri-Khandagiri (second century B.C.). At Bharhut, as mentioned, the form of *śrīvatsa* is created with plant parts (Fig. 122), the upturned arms and legs made of leaves rising from a lotus base. At Amaravati the same shape is more formally rendered in a form that is quasi-anthropomorphic. There it sits on an altar (Fig. 112). Within its belly area is a lotus medallion.

Śrīvatsa is often translated as "beloved of Fortune." Another translation of the term, which lends itself to multiple translations, is "babe of Śrī," the goddess of fortune.[15] Artistically, *śrīvatsa* also has many forms. Later examples are rendered like a whorl of hair, a triangle, or a cruciform flower, but in its early form *śrīvatsa* has four upwardly curved "limbs" symmetrically paired, which form has been described as "shield-shaped." The derivation of the early sign, Agrawala asserts, is from that of a crudely rendered baby, an abstraction of a human figure with upreaching arms and spread legs reduced to nubs, and the head likewise a nub at the center top.[16] To support the identification of *śrīvatsa* with a baby, Agrawala points to a type of bronze anthropomorph (Fig. 128) that has nub arms and legs and is similar to a *śrīvatsa*-shaped ornament worn by the female of a loving couple on a terra-cotta plaque from Ahichchatra. It seems significant that this Ahichchatra *śrīvatsa* ornament, which hangs at the center of a long necklace, rests just over her womb. Agrawala believes the object represents a fertility amulet. He further suggests a relation between *śrīvatsa* and anthropomorphic copper objects found in the Gangetic valley, dated c. 1500 B.C. These objects, whose original function is not known, he suggests, may have been used as a token of the mother goddess.[17]

Śrīvatsa appears throughout Indian art in the art of the *yakṣa* cult and in Buddhism, Hinduism, and Jainism. It is fashioned on coins, clay seals, *stūpa* parts, *āyāgapaṭas,* and as individual bronzes. It is one of the eight auspicious symbols, as is the pot. It appears on the chest of Jain, Buddhist, Vaiṣṇava, and Śaiva gods, and even on the chest of Garuḍa, the vehicle of Viṣṇu. Interestingly, it does not appear on goddesses except as a part of an ornament. Śrī, "Fortune" or "well-being," is worn as the mark of great beings.

Śrīvatsa represents a family of meanings. It symbolizes human and vegetal fecundity, uniting the two through the broader concept of Fortune—fertility, prosperity, abundance—and using forms analogous to either animals or plants. The same concept is expressed on stone disks (ring stones) of the third century B.C. on which the *nāgapuṣpā* is alternated with a female figure (Fig. 123).[18] This female figure standing in a rigid frontal pose is identified as Śrī Lakṣmī, the sign of, or goddess of, Fortune. The alternation of her figure with the *nāgapuṣpā* may be understood as a repetition of two interchangeable symbols of fertility—one plant, the other animal.

The interchangeability of *śrīvatsa* and Lakṣmī is made evident by three stone relief sculptures and a bronze from Andhra. In a multifigured stone plaque from Peddamudiyam the lotus-headed goddess, present in otherwise similar plaques, is substituted by a *śrīvatsa* (Fig. 126). The *śrīvatsa,* seen on the right side, is personified with a head, but the head has no facial features, just as Lajjā Gaurī often has no face other than the lotus. Her outline with upturned "arms" and "legs" is like that of Lajjā Gaurī with her arms held up and her legs spread and turned up though somewhat differently than the *uttānapad* pose. In this plaque she wears a crown like the other gods who are (left to right): Gaṇeśa, Brahmā, Narasiṁha, the *liṅga* form of Śiva, Viṣṇu and Devī, Umāmaheśvara over Nandi, Mahiṣāsuramardinī defeating Mahiṣa. *Śrīvatsa* is located above Mahiṣāsuramardinī on the right end. On the far right are two severed arms.[19]

A small (2 by $1\frac{1}{2}$ inch) bronze *śrīvatsa* from Enadi (Tanjore District, Tamil Nadu) of the ninth century (Fig. 125) (Government Museum, Madras 39/35) similarly represents *śrīvatsa* with a head but no facial features. This *śrīvatsa* wears a *channavīra*. The legs and arms are foliate and she sits on the lotus throne.[20]

Also in the Government Museum, Madras (112/38–39) is a relief from Kaveripakkam (North Arcot District, Tamil Nadu) representing Gaja Lakṣmī with a *śrīvatsa* body, bathed by two elephants; it is carved in the Pallava style of the eighth to ninth century in grey granite (Fig. 124). Again, she has no facial features. The elephant on the left holds a lotus in his trunk over her head. A lamp is on each side of the lotus throne, below the lamp on the left is a lotus while below that on the right is a conch. A *channavīra* crosses the torso, which has upcurved nub arms and legs; the goddess also wears a necklace, earrings, and a crown or cap. In this example Lakṣmī is identified with the *śrīvatsa* symbol.[21]

Possibly Lajjā Gaurī should be identified with the chief of the six Gaurīs, Śrī, as the form associations discussed suggest. She may trace a part of her symbolic ancestry back to such images as two bronze *śrīvatsa* dating to c. 1000 B.C. The first of these, found in Sri Lanka and now in the British Museum (1898.7–2.102), measures $5\frac{1}{2}$ inches in height.[22] Its outline and nub head are relevant to the later *uttānapad* goddess with upturned arms and nonhuman head (Fig. 128). The second bronze is from Manbhum in Dhanbad District, Bihar, and is now kept in the Patna Museum (Arch 240).[23]

FROG

A unique image in the Victoria and Albert Museum offers another possible source for the outline and some details of Lajjā Gaurī figures. This is perhaps the most curious of all Lajjā Gaurī figures

(Figs. 66–68). It is a solid, double-sided terra-cotta that exactly fits into the palm of the hand (height $3\frac{4}{5}$ inches) and weighs about one pound. One side represents the goddess in anthropomorphic Form IV, in the *uttānapad* pose. The unique feature of this example is that she is in a pose not only similar to that of a frog but she is also conjoined to a figure of a frog on the other side. Although there are many other examples like the Lajjā Gaurī side of the Victoria and Albert Museum's image, no other Indian image of Lajjā Gaurī is double-sided, and no other has a frog on its reverse.

Codrington reported the provenance of reddish terra-cotta frog/goddess as Mathura because it was acquired by the museum as part of a group of images from Mathura, and he thought it should be dated, like the others in the group, to the second century A.D.[24] The frog is difficult to date by style, and the female's nose and breasts are somewhat crushed. Nonetheless, a Mathura provenance and a Kuṣāṇ period date of the second century are possible, although this would be the only early Form IV Lajjā Gaurī. Otherwise Form IV dates, at the earliest, to the sixth century.

The frog side is slightly larger than the female side. The crouched frog figure has emphasized bulbous eyes on top, and the backbone is indicated as an incised ridge.

The piece has been published several times with photos of the front and back. Those two views do not reveal an interesting aspect of the figurine seen from the side: the upraised arms of the woman are the frog's forelegs, and her legs are conjoined to the frog's back legs in such a manner that her feet are flexed, soles up, in an odd way (Fig. 68) of great relevance to Lajjā Gaurī images in general. Furthermore, the pointed cap worn by the female is the lower jaw of the frog. The face is only roughly indicated with a large nose and eyes and ears, but *no* mouth. This is interesting because of the featureless faces of humanized *śrīvatsas* as discussed. The raised hands are damaged, and it cannot be distinguished whether anything was held in them. Her hair is drawn smoothly back from her forehead and tied up on her head and fanned out above in a topknot. She wears a necklace ridged like the hair pattern and the hair and the necklace together frame her head like the filaments of a flower. The pudendum area of the nude figure is stippled with two patterns.

The Victoria and Albert terra-cotta has been identified as a fertility amulet, which is likely since the frog and a female in this position with emphasized pudendum both suggest the idea of fertility. The joining of the two in this manner is unique, but in Indian art composite beings with shared body parts and double-sided images are common.[25] The artist depicted the froglike pose of this female literally and graphically. We recognize in this artistic merging of human, animal, and plant parts a philosophical suggestion that all forms of life share a life-force that is continuous, and that is basic not only to Hindu but also to Buddhist philosophy.

The frog image resembles in its outline and ridged back the early form of *śrīvatsa* seen, for example, in a first-century B.C. rail post from Sarnath (Fig. 129). The outline of the female is also that of *śrīvatsa,* the Favorite of Śrī, the symbol of that goddess of Fortune. The same pointed cap is seen on the head of the Victoria and Albert Lajjā Gaurī, on the *śrīvatsa* from Enadi and Gaja Lakṣmī from Kaveripakkam (Figs. 124 and 125), another *śrīvatsa* from Peddamudiyam (Fig. 126), and a *śrīvatsa* on the chest of a Jain Tirthankara from Kankali Tila, Mathura, dated by inscription A.D. 165.[26] In fact a very similar lotuslike cap is seen in the elemental Form I *uttānapad* pot figures of Lajjā Gaurī from Sannati in Karnataka (Fig. 7). The coincidence of these iconographic elements suggests that the various forms used to represent the idea of Fortune, whether as Śrī Lakṣmī, Padmā Śrī Lakṣmī, Śrīvatsa, or Lajjā Gaurī, draw from one pool of forms. Although the different forms of the goddess of Fortune retain individual associations, in the realm of artistic representation they share many features.

The association of the frog (or toad) with fertility is an ancient and universal symbolism. Examples of toad-goddess images dating to the seventh and sixth millennia B.C. from the Balkans and northern Greece are published by Marija Gimbutas. These stone and terra-cotta figures are schematized with spread legs in an *M*-shaped pose, with accentuated pubic triangle and no head or just a cone head. One figure from northern Greece (Nea Nikomedeia) very much resembles an Indian Lajjā Gaurī figure, but has a hole into which, Gimbutas speculates, a human head may have been inserted.[27] Perhaps, instead, a lotus might have been inserted there originally. In pre-Indo-European mythology the toad was connected, she says, with birth, pregnancy, or the womb.[28]

The frog as a fertility charm surely is derived from a universal observance of its fertility and its apparently miraculous regeneration from the earth in response to the rain. In Egyptian hieroglyphs the sign of the tadpole serves as the number 100,000, a clear reference to the frog's amazing powers of procreation. It is thought that it was the frog's fertility and apparently spontaneous reappearance out of the mudbanks of the Nile River each rainy season that gave to the frog-form goddess Heqat the role of patroness of childbirth.[29] Votive figures like an early dynastic (c. 3100–2700 B.C.) frog-form Heqat, now in the Cleveland Museum, are still offered by women desiring fertility or successful childbirth at such sites as Abydos. In later Egyptian art the goddess Heqat was presented with a frog head joined to a human body. "The frog came to symbolize the cycle of rebirth, the hieroglyph being used as an abbreviation for the phrase 'repeating births.' "[30]

A composite toad-goddess dating to c. 1000 B.C. from Maissau in lower Austria has been published by Gulder.[31] One side of this very crude double-sided figure is a toad, whereas the reverse has female features. This is quite like the Mathura frog-goddess in conception, though the Mathura image is much more artistically refined. Gulder hypothesizes that the reason for the association of the toad to the woman and fertility is that ancient man, seeing the one- or two-month-old fetus, thought that it was a toad and that pregnancy was caused by toads.

The closest relative to the Victoria and Albert frog-goddess in Indian art is found on a medallion of a *stūpa* rail-post from Mathura now in the State Museum, Lucknow.[32] On one side is a figure with a frog body and a human head, apparently male, seen as if we are looking down at the frog and he is looking up at us. The hair is ridged, like that of the Victoria and Albert female figure. On the opposite side of the composite frog-man is a lotus medallion; a possible visual interpretation is that the viewer is looking down on a frog-man seated on a lotus pad. This *stūpa* medallion may be dated to the Kuṣāṇ period, c. second century, that is, perhaps contemporary with the Victoria and Albert terra-cotta.

Frogs did not gain enduring popularity in Indian art as a symbol of fertility or rebirth, but a detail of the frog-fertility symbolism may have been retained in figures of Lajjā Gaurī; that is, the froglike crouching pose of the Lajjā Gaurī images, with its froglike outline and "backward"angle of the legs and feet.[33] Looking again at the lotus-headed Kudavelli goddess (Fig. 52), as one of many examples, we notice that the feet are peculiarly flexed and the soles turned up unnaturally (see also Figs. 48, 52–54, 69, 70). This detail may suggest that the feet are tensed in the strain of childbirth. Whether the artist intended to suggest this idea or not we do not know. Childbirth is not literally represented, of course. Indian goddesses do not give birth like mortals. It is a frog pose. Not all the images have this detail of upturned feet, but the legs are more often than not angled like frog legs. (Figs. 18, 42)

In another *stūpa* rail medallion from Sarnath of the first century B.C. a female image seems to bear some artistic and perhaps symbolic affinity to the Victoria and Albert terra-cotta's female side.[34] The similarities are most apparent in the lotus filamentlike treatment of the hair, the protruding ears, and the generally similar outline of the female figure. In the medallion she is clearly a plant woman, a lotus woman. Her torso, like a pericarp, emerges from a lotus leaf and her head bursts into bloom. Her lower limbs curl like a stylization of the legs of the Victoria and Albert female figure, and her shawl ends fly up like fishtails. The flying shawl ends resemble the raised hands of the Victoria and Albert Museum Lajjā Gaurī. Here the natural hands rest on the curled "legs." Some scholars see in images like this Sarṇath figure a form related to *śrīvatsa*.[35]

The origin and identity of the Victoria and Albert Lajjā Gaurī image and others has been discussed in articles by Codrington and Sankalia. Is her conception Indian or foreign? Is she derived from an imported type or does she derive from Indian ideas and iconography with ancestry traceable to the Indus Valley, or to Ṛg Vedic descriptions of the goddess Aditi? Murray, Codrington, and Sankalia have related this figure to Roman Baubo fertility goddess figurines in a so-called phryne (froglike) pose.[36]

Referring to the Victoria and Albert terra-cotta female, Codrington concluded that "if this little figure is accepted as Baubo, it is one of very few, indeed possibly the only, directly borrowed Classical icon known to Indian archaeology."[37] Sankalia linked these Baubo-like figures to Egypto-Roman sources. These scholars considered only the female side of the terra-cotta, not making the other possible argument for a frog-deity of foreign ancestry from the reverse frog side. Nor have these scholars mentioned any relation of the figure to the well-known Indus image of a woman bearing a plant (?) from her womb or other Indian figures cited earlier, or to literary descriptions of the similar goddess concept discussed by Kramrisch.[38] The presence of Romans in India in the early centuries A.D. is weak evidence from which to conclude that it was a Roman impetus that resulted in the creation of such images. When the Roman Baubo image is compared to the Indian Lajjā Gaurī, it is obvious that the emphasis is quite different (Fig. 130). Baubo is typically represented either in a pose with legs spread as if seated in a saddle, with her hands holding up food, or seated with legs spread and her hands spreading her genitals, the latter being called the Baubo-phryne pose.[39] There are depictions of the same gesture in Indian art, but these are not figures of Lajjā Gaurī. They are mortals, not a goddess.[40] In many images, as previously described, Lajjā Gaurī is dressed and in others she is enthroned. The primary message of images of Lajjā Gaurī is not, as I have argued, a sexual display.

The question of foreign or indigenous origin of the double-sided frog-female fertility image (Figs. 66–68) seems a moot point given the existence of the similar figure from Maissau. The idea of the association of female human and frog is ancient. A similar, older image may yet be discovered in India. A headless female figure was reported by H. D. Sankalia himself, dating to c. 1200 B.C. found at Inamgaon in the river inside a clay box. The head of a bull was also found there, and the two fit together. This would seem to be a fertility figure but her legs are not in the *M*-pose. Sankalia cites the figure as a precursor to the Lajjā Gaurī type, which suggests that he changed his mind about the Roman origin of Lajjā Gaurī.[41] It seems, however, that foreign influence is likely in regard to the frog side of the figure. Frogs in Indian art are not common, though some frog amulets have been found made of precious stones, shell, and metal.[42] This is the only known frog-related image of Lajjā Gaurī. It cannot be said that Lajjā Gaurī images in India are the result of foreign influence, however, because their earliest form incorporates a basic Indian fortune symbol, the pot. A specific influence, however, on Form IV human-headed figures, may be possible.

A tiny amulet was described to me, though it is unpublished, that bears *śrīvatsa* on the reverse of a frog with parts joined back to back, like the Victoria and Albert Museum's female figure and the frog.[43] Such a piece would be convincing evidence of the interrelations of the figures of *śrīvatsa*, frog, and Lajjā Gaurī discussed in this chapter.

Notes

1. Dhere, 1978; *Illustrated London News*, 1971; Desai, 1984.

2. Bosch, 1960, suggests that this idea lies behind the formation of the *makara* through the artist's imaginative elaboration of a lotus node, 27.

3. See discussions of lotus symbolism in Coomaraswamy, 1971, vol. 2, 56ff., Liebert, 1976, 202–4, and Roşu, 1966.

4. Kramrisch, 1956, fig. 4, cites an example from Sanchi of a female figure formed by subtly combined lotus parts in relation to her identification of the goddess with the lotus head as Aditi.

5. Sivaramamurti, 1982, 23; Kramrisch, 1928, 106, provides a different translation of this passage.

6. Illustrated in *Marg*, 1979, *In Praise of Aihole, Badami, Mahakuta, Pattadakal*, fig. 25, 45.

7. Liebert, 1976, 202–4.

8. V. S. Agrawala, 1951, 26.

9. Coomaraswamy, 1971, 61.

10. V. S. Agrawala, 1951, 27: "At the time of child-birth the mother holds a *pūrṇa ghaṭa* and walks with it to the nearest well, reservoir or pool of water to offer worship, as the latter represents the bigger source of the same fecundating waters of creative life."

11. *Yakṣas* are discussed by Coomaraswamy, 1971, R. N. Misra, 1981, and Gail Hinich Sutherland, "The Demon and His Disguises: the Yakṣa in Hindu and Buddhist Art and Literature," Ph.D. diss., University of Chicago, 1987.

12. A. L. Srivastava, 1979, 51, believes the *śrīvatsa* to be derived from a human figure.

13. The griffin occurs often in an early Buddhist context, and it may be an imported image, but its significance in an Indian Buddhist context has not been interpreted. Kramrisch, 1956, cites this example as a "cognate conception" to Lajjā Gaurī. She notes that Lajjā Gaurī is not Lakṣmī.

14. S. P. Gupta, 1980, 325.

15. P. K. Agrawala, 1974.

16. Ibid.

17. For a Gangetic copper anthropomorph, see Martin Lerner, "The Sword and the Lotus," Metropolitan Museum of Art, New York, 1984, pl. 1. A *yakṣa* image has been reported which holds *śrīvatsa* in his hand, like such an object: C. Lin-Bodien, "An Early Yakṣa from Aktha near Sarnath . . . ," in *Chhavi II*, ed. Anand Krishna, Banaras, 1981, 294–97. In another carving a *śrīvatsa* is an ornament on the rigging of a horse.

18. Examples have been published by P. Chandra, 1971, 139–48.

19. The human-headed *śrīvatsa* is included in a large stone relief ($16\frac{1}{2}$ by 10 inches) in the Government Museum, Madras, no. 17, from Peddamudiyam (Cuddapah District, Andrha) of c. fourth century (Fig. 122), published by Sivaramamurti, 1957, vol. 7, pl. 1a, 12, dated Vishnukundin or early Pallava, also 1950, pl. XVa, 21–63, and 1982, fig. 47; Sarma, 1972, fig. 6, and 1982, figs. 86a–f, 155, where examples of the same iconography are called "trimurti plaques"; A. L. Srivastava, 1979, fig. 3; and Banerjea [1956] 1974, pl. XLVII 1, 545, where an incorrect provenance is given for the Peddamudiyam plaque. A previously unpublished example of the same iconography is kept in the Government Museum, Madras, no 18, fragment 10 by 9 inches in schist from Peddamudiyam of c. eighth century (fig. 127). The portion on the right, which would bear *śrīvatsa*, is missing. While these multifigured plaques with Lajjā Gaurī were being made in the south c. fourth to seventh century, groupings of emblems of the deities were made in the north on clay seals, each figure placed on an altar or pedestal. Many of these represent *śrīvatsa* alone. Others, as for example that from Bhita, represent *śrīvatsa* flanked by Viṣṇu's conch and wheel, or *śrīvatsa* with Nandi and the wheel. In these glyptics *śrīvatsa* stands for the goddess and is given equal status to the two other main gods. Many other seals represent Lakṣmī and Gaja Lakṣmī (Archaeological Survey of India, *Annual Report 1911–12*, 19, 44). These are official seals for letters, parcels, or identification of the bearer. The above-mentioned seal is inscribed as that of the chief of police. The emblems indicate the personal devotion of the owner.

20. Published drawings include facial features, but there actually are none: Sivaramamurti, 1954, pl. Ia, 12; 1941, pl. 1, fig. 4, 24; Sivaramamurti, *South Indian Bronzes*, 1963, fig. 31, 42; Sarma, 1972; A. L. Srivastava, 1979, line drawing 3; Banerjea, 1974, pl. XIX, 376; photo published by Sivaramamurti 1982, pl. 68, identified by Pallava, ninth century.

21. Kiran Kumar Thaplyal, *Studies in Ancient Indian Seals*, Lucknow, 1972, 188 n. 4, remarks. "The elephants, symbolic of glory and royalty, might have even once represented the goddess theriomorphically and the *śrīvatsa* aniconically, as can be inferred from the three Madras Museum statues depicting the figures of the goddess within the framework of the *śrīvatsa* [illegible] and both might have been retained as accessories in her anthropomorphic representation." Sivaramamurti, 1982, 32, notes that the outline of the goddess Lajjā Gaurī is that of *śrīvatsa*.

22. von Schroeder, 1981, 62, 1B.

23. P. K. Agrawala, *Early Indian Bronzes*, 1977, fig. 44, and von Schroeder, 1981, 62, 1a. Nagaswamy, 1986, also relates Lajjā Gaurī to *śrīvatsa* and to even more ancient (sixth century B.C.) south Indian colossal stone *visirikkal*.

24. Codrington, 1935, 65; also published by Tiwari, 1971 and 1985, figs. 2 and 3.

25. For example, Pratapaditya Pal discusses many in "An

Addorsed Saiva Image from Kashmir and its Cultural Significance," *Art International* 24, 5–6 (January–February 1981): 46–52.

26. Reproduced enlarged by Agrawala, 1974 as the frontispiece.

27. Gimbutas, 1982, 175, fig. 171. Kala, 1980, 64, refers to these images.

28. Gimbutas, 1982, 178.

29. The role of goddess of childbirth is distinct from that of fertility goddess.

30. John D. Cooney and William Kelly Simpson, "An Early Dynastic Statuette of the Goddess Heqat," *Cleveland Museum Bulletin* (September 1976): 202–9.

31. Gulder, 1960–62.

32. R. N. Misra, 1981, pl. 76, 132.

33. The froglike outline of Lajjā Gaurī has been remarked upon by Tiwari, 1971, chap. 4, and Sisodia, 1969, 411.

34. Srivastava, 1979, fig. 2, no. 3.

35. Sivaramamurti, 1982, 28.

36. Murray, 1934, 93–100; Codrington, 1935, 65–66; Sankalia, 1960, 111–23; Tiwari, 1971, chap. 4.

37. Codrington, 1935, 66.

38. H. Heras, "A Proto-Indian Representation of the Fertility God," *D. R. Bhandarkar Volume*, ed. B. C. Law (Calcutta, 1940), 121–30, argues that this is not a plant at all, but is a scarab; Kramrisch, 1956.

39. The former "saddle-posed" female finds its counterpart in terra-cottas like one example from Sannati and many from Ter and Kondapur, of the second century, in which the pose is duplicated in an Indian context. Figurines in this pose are called the "Divine Woman."

40. Donaldson, 1975, 75–100.

41. *Illustrated London News*, August 1971, 42; Sarma, 1982, fig. 3, 15; 1978, 4 illustrated.

42. Margabandhu, 1975–76, 86–90; Gaur, 1983, see two copper frogs of c. 200–250 B.C. illustrated pl. CXXXIIb, 445, 447, from Etah District, U.P.

43. Professor Chandrasekhara Gupta of Nagpur University mentioned it to me.

IV

Names

Names used by villagers or scholars for the images I call Lajjā Gaurī include:

Ananti devī	Belan Kallachema	Jogulamba
Nagnamātā	Nagna kabamdha	Matangi
Kumkana	Verul	Marai
Kolambika	Kamalamukhī	Mahurama
Aditi	Kamalagaurīmā	Ekavira
Reṇukā	Kamalagaṅgāmā	Yamabai
Elamba	Kāmakalā	Yamai
Yellama	Mahākuṇḍalinī	Vyagreśvari
Kotvī	Chakrayī	Sang
Pṛthvī	Adya Śakti	Sākambharī

Many of these are descriptive of her physical aspects, for example, the name Nagna Kabamdha means "nude, headless body." *Nagna* means nude in Kannada, *kabamdha* means a headless torso. *Kabamdha* is also identified with *rasa,* cloud and water. *Ka* means head, water, and pleasure. *Bunda* means a clubbing of two parts, an embankment. This may be a descriptive name applied to an image whose identity was otherwise lost. Such descriptive names are probably local inventions of no great antiquity. Many of her names refer, similarly, to her lotus head: Kamalāmukhī, Kamalāgaurīmā, Kamalagaṅgāmā.

Others are names of known goddesses that share a similar feature, such as Śākambharī, who is a fertility goddess, though specifically associated with the harvest. The name is not likely to have anything to do with the ancient icon studied here, which is not to say that the same confusion may not have existed in ancient times and even crept into the iconography of some of the images, such as Figure 98, which, as discussed, holds a leaf in either hand rather than a lotus bud or flower. Such names have been applied to Lajjā Gaurī by scholars for lack of a more informed ancient name.

It should be noted that the names of many sites where images of Lajjā Gaurī have been found are derivatives from one name of the goddess, Ellama (Goddess of the Boundary), for example, Yellala, Yelleśvara, Elapura, Alapuri, Alampur, and Hamlapuri. This may be significant in that it suggests the goddess's original function as a *grāmadevatā* or village goddess implored (especially by women) to grant family well-being and children. However, such rural mother goddesses, called *grāmadevatās,* are tutelary, meant to protect a place or a house and I have found no evidence that Lajjā

Gaurī functioned in this way. This does not rule out the possibility, however, that she originally was a *grāmadevatā*. But, by the fourth century such evidence of her constant association with Śiva as has been presented, proves that she had become elevated in status. In fact, there are many *grāmadevatās* and they are often associated with the waterpot, as Lajjā Gaurī is in her earliest images (Form I), indicating a close association with the cult of fertility.[1] Another indication of these place names, which seem to derive from the name of one such tutelary *grāmadevatā,* Ellama, is that these ancient sites were fertility worship centers where Lajjā Gaurī was the presiding goddess. This is especially interesting in regard to the site of Ellora where a major image of Lajjā Gaurī survives from the sixth century before the Rāmeśvara temple (cave 21).

The linguistic analysis of Indian names applied to Lajjā Gaurī images has been well executed by Dhere, and I defer to his erudition on the topic for the explanation of other names.[2]

In his article "The Nude Goddess or 'Shameless Woman' in Western Asia, India and South-Eastern Asia," Sankalia interpreted the name "Lajjā Gaurī," which was reported to him by C. Chapgar as being used for the *uttānapad* goddess, as "Shameless Woman."[3] The sensational suggestion is that her indecent display is shameless behavior, that this female has no sense of shame, no modesty. In Sanskrit *lajjā* does not mean shameless, but derives from the root *lajj,* meaning to be ashamed, to blush.[4] It means shame in the sense of modesty, or embarrassment. To right the wrong translation, D. C. Sircar inserted Lajjā*hina* Gaurī, which would mean Shameless Gaurī.[5]

The *Viṣṇu Purāṇa* explains that the goddess Lajjā is Modesty, personified as one of Dakṣa's daughters. Lajjā became the wife of Dharma and the mother of a son named Vināya. Vināya is the personification of good behavior. Gaurī means the brilliant one or the golden one, the wife of Śiva or of Varuṇa, the waters, the source of the world, the cosmic cow, the undifferentiated form before creation. The waters, the oceans, and the fertilizing rains flow from her. She is the very source of life-giving water and of fertility.[6]

Gaurī, as the wife of Śiva, is a form of Pārvatī, and Gaurī is the name of a class of goddesses called Gaurīs that includes Pārvatī, Umā, Rambhā, Totalā, Tripurā, and Śrī. Śrī, as one of the six varieties of Gaurī, is sometimes called Gaurī herself.[7] Gaurī is the aspect in which the gods contemplate Śrī.[8] Each form of Gaurī grants fortune to her worshiper. Gaurī cannot be translated as "woman" since she is a goddess, nor is the goddess always represented as nude as Sankalia's title suggests. Taken together, something akin to modest or innocent creatrix, wife of Śiva, is more nearly the meaning of the name Lajjā Gaurī.

The traditional explanation of the headless lotus goddess at Mahakuta was reported by Fleet.[9] This story or variants of it are still told. Basically, it is the story of Pārvatī being tested and embarrassed by Śiva as a result of which her head either sinks into her shoulders, or is chopped off. Traditionally, then, the image is explained as a form of Pārvatī, who is embarrassed, ashamed, and modest.[10]

Another traditional explanation, however, is told in the Andhra Telegu areas, where the figures are identified as Reṇukā. In myth Reṇukā is the daughter of King Prasenajit, and she became the wife of Jamadagni and mother of Paraśurāma.[11] She brought water from the Tungabhadra every day in a clay pot she made. One day she glanced at a king and queen who were bathing in the river. This disturbed her and she was not able to make a pot that day and came back home without water. Her husband understood what had happened and ordered his sons to kill her. Paraśurāma did so. Jamadagni was pleased and when he asked Paraśurāma what boon he wished, the son replied that he wished his mother be brought back to life. "Jamadagni told him that her head could not be attached to her body as it fell in some impure place, but he gave the boon that the head would be worshiped by all classes of people under the name of Yellamma, and the body would be equally renowned in the name of Bhūdevī."[12] In other accounts Pārvatī was born from an anthill in the form of Reṇukā or she was born to a pious, daughterless king.[13] Reṇukā is Pārvatī in the form of Śakti. She multiplied into 101 Śaktis and became the wives of Śiva. The *Skanda Purāṇa* implies that Reṇukā is an avatar of Aditi.[14] Reṇu translates as the pollen of flowers, or dust of anything, a head of dust, or of flowers, or of pollen, while the name Reṇukā, in Yogic terminology, refers to semen.[15]

Is Lajjā Gaurī the same goddess as the Vedic Aditi? The conception of Aditi must be considered to foster, philosophically, the idea of Lajjā Gaurī, though the artist may have been unaware of Aditi. He was carving a goddess of fortune and fertility whose original name we do not know. The form of the goddess most widely known today as Lajjā Gaurī fits the Vedic descriptions of the mother of the gods, Aditi, as Kramrisch published in detail.[16] A study of the *Ṛg Vedic* Ādityas by Joel Brereton makes a strong argument that Aditi means Innocence (as does Lajjā), and that Aditi is, in the *Ṛg Veda,* the personification of Innocence, the Goddess of Innocence.[17] Brereton notes that in her earliest meaning in the *Ṛg Veda* Aditi was the Goddess of Innocence whereas by the late *Ṛg Veda* and *Atharva Veda* her motherhood (of the gods and the Ādityas) changes from being subsidiary to being paramount. She is an ideal of innocence. Aditi is the unbound, in the sense of the unfettered. If sin results in fettering then her creativity is unchecked because it is innocent. The inclusion of a cloth "woven" between the legs of the Lajjā Gaurī, as seen in the Naganātha example (Fig. 42) and many others, left free on each end, could be related to the idea of this goddess as the "unbound" or "unfettered."[18] M. C. P. Srivastava remarks, "in later Hinduism Aditi is almost forgotten and is not worshiped; no image is found probably because no clear anthropomorphic form was evolved for her and no clear geographic phenomenon was personified by her. The conception of the Supreme Mother Goddess was in an incipient stage as denoted in the *Ṛg Veda* by Aditi, but it is remarkable that while the idea became a major part of later Hinduism, Aditi herself did not assume that position."[19]

Aditi, the Vedic goddess, is the boundless one, identified as Earth and Nature in the *Ṛg Veda.*[20] Gonda considers her name to mean "Freedom" and her nature to be manifested in any expansion of phenomenal life.[21] *Ṛg Veda* 1.89.10 declares her to be all that has been, and is yet to be, in whom all the gods are comprised. She was born of Dakṣa and Dakṣa of her according to *Ṛg Veda* x.72.5. She is the mother of the thirty-three gods in *Ṛg Veda.*[22]

Aditi represents cosmic energy. The Ādityas, her seven or eight sons (*Ṛg Veda* x.72), collectively represent the whole range of phenomenal manifestation. Aditi is the mother of kings, the mother of excellent sons, especially the gods Mitra and Varuṇa. Monier Williams defines Aditi as "not tied, free, boundless, unbroken, entire, unimpaired, happy, boundlessness, inexhaustible abundance, creative power."[23] In *Ṛg Veda* she is the sinless one, one who removes sin; the earth's center (the altar); the one invoked for prosperity; she is luminous, bounteous, spacious. The Earth is the lap of Aditi.

As Dhere wrote, the ideas embodied in the textual descriptions of Aditi seem to correspond to the appearance of the image of Lajjā Gaurī.[24] The images made between the second and twelfth centuries A.D. seem quickly to have been drawn into a Śaivite association that redefined her as Gaurī.

I believe that the name Gaurī is correct in the sense of probably being ancient because of the associations of *pūrṇa kumbha,* bulls, deities paired with her, her shrines placed by lotus ponds or springs, her association with Śaiva temples, and the Pattadakal inscription, which seems to describe Gaurī with lotuslike tresses, as the wife of Hara or Śiva. *Lajjā* was possibly an explanatory term added, not in great antiquity, to replace the original lost meaning of the lotus culmination of most forms of this goddess. Her importance lies in her role as goddess of creative power, which is the primary symbolic association of the lotus. Her *uttānapad* pose, her *pūrṇa kumbha* ancestry, and her lotus head suggest this meaning.

Notes

1. Stutley and Stutley, 1977, 104.
2. Dhere, 1978.
3. Sankalia, 1960.
4. Monier-Williams, 1976, 895.
5. Sircar, 1980.
6. Stutley and Stutley, 1977, 96.
7. Banerjea, 1974, 502.
8. Stutley and Stutley, 1977.
9. Fleet, 1881.
10. Ramesan, 1969, 35.
11. Brubaker, 1978; Ramesan, 1969; Jayakar, 1981, 31–33.
12. Ramesan, 1969, 36.
13. Elmore, 1925, 78–79.
14. *Ṛg Veda* I.14.17.
15. Monier-Williams, 1976, 887.
16. Kramrisch, 1956 and 1975; see also P. K. Agrawala, 1983a: 56–60.
17. Brereton, 1981.
18. P. Pal has suggested that this cloth is used by villagers as an aid to birth.
19. Srivastava, 1979, 41.
20. F. Max Müller, ed. *Vedic Hymns, Sacred Books of the East,* vol. 32, 1962–66, rpt. of 1879–1910 edition, 248ff.
21. Gonda, 1970, 7.
22. Monier-Williams, 1976, 18.
23. *Ṛg Veda* IX.71.5, IX.74.5, VII.88.7, X.70.6–7.
24. Review summary in English by Dhavalikar, 1979–80.

Conclusion

An image of a Hindu deity is usually identified by its description in an ancient iconographic text. If it is not found in a text, then a priest familiar with the gods in worship may provide an identification, or villagers may do the same. In this case only the later two resources are available for identification of Lajjā Gaurī images, but they cannot be relied upon—especially given the corruption by Victorian attitudes, which led to an outcast status for Lajjā Gaurī, resulting in destruction of her images, confinement of others in storerooms of museums, loss of her worship tradition (except in a few locations), and her oversight by modern scholars.

Instead, to reconstruct her lost meaning, various other approaches of the types Panofsky gathered into his idea of "iconology" must be employed:[1] identification of in situ evidence of her context to ascertain her meaning and use; identification of the symbolism of her iconographic parts, surveying of current myths, names, legends, and rituals of worship. Cumulatively from such information a consistent, uncontradictory, profile has emerged for Lajjā Gaurī.

It has been found that recurring features of Lajjā Gaurī images and even unique features are not contradictory within the Hindu system of symbolism; that is to say, all evidence points toward the identification of Lajjā Gaurī images as symbolic of fertility, as belonging within the Hindu religion and Śaiva sect, and that Lajjā Gaurī was considered, by the sixth century, to be a *Śakti* of Śiva.

Four distinct iconographic forms of Lajjā Gaurī, each with a broad but clearly defined correspondence to a period and area of India, have been uncovered. What is the significance of this discovery? Why are there four forms and what does their regional and chronologic association indicate? What were the socioreligious processes affecting them; to what extent does their iconographic variety reflect artistic license or inventiveness or other forces? What does the physical evidence of the images studied tell us about iconographic formation or change in Indian art? Can this image-type, Lajjā Gaurī, inform us in any general or substantive way about the process of formulation of iconography for images of other Indian deities? What are the factors, contexts, and contingencies that shape the metamorphosis in form and meaning of a symbolic icon in Indian art?

The change in form of this goddess from a personified symbol, the brimming vase, to an incomplete female form with plant parts, to a fully female form with a human, not a lotus, head through a period of at least four centuries is a change for which a rationale can be identified. Research findings in the field of anthropology published by the South Asia Interdisciplinary Regional Research Programme, Orissa Research Project of Heidelberg University, lend some guidance to our understanding of this apparent process of iconographic change in the absence of a descriptive text for the image.[2] Anncharlott Eschmann, in a study relevant to the project of study of the Jagannātha cult in Orissa, explains the process of Hinduization of tribal or village deities in Orissa, and her findings have larger applicability in Indian art history. "Hinduism," she remarks, as have many others, "has an extraordinary capacity to incorporate and amalgamate [assimilate] other religions and alien cults" because in Hinduism Brahman is considered to be within everything. In tribal India, anthropomorphic images of the gods are rare.[3] Tribal shrines usually contain aniconic symbols in the form of stones, sticks, pots, etc. In village communities where tribal groups may live together with caste Hindus an aboriginal cult may become a village cult and may eventually become incorporated into a Hindu temple. The motivation for this assimilation is discussed by Herman Kulke:[4] "Such a Hindu temple is distinguished from the village cult by three characteristics: daily performance of *pūjā,* recognition by all castes, and more than local importance." In this context a Hinduized *grāmadevī,*[5] for example, may have attained subregional importance and later may attain importance within a regional area. "A temple cult of regional importance might become an integral part of the highest level of Hinduism valid for all of India"; Eschmann refers to this as the end result of the process she labels "Brahminization." This might occur as a result of royal patronage.[6] She further observes that, "Most of the tribal cults in Orissa, which are important enough to be Hinduized, are related to a female deity."

In contrast to tribal aniconic imagery, worship at the temple level concentrates on *mūrti* or anthropomorphic images, considered proper Hindu images. The original symbol may be changed to look like an image when it is introduced into a Hindu temple, or the symbol may be identified with another image of a goddess, such as Durga; one whose nature is similar.

Royal patronage of a deity of a local cult may have induced the anthropomorphization of the symbol. In regard to Lajjā Gaurī the first instance of known royal patronage occurs at Nagarjunakonda where the fragmentary state of the life-size stone image of the fourth century A.D. leaves its form type unascertainable, though, as argued it was probably not the pot-type, Form I, but more likely was Form III, fully human except for the lotus head. Form III was the form also chosen for images created with royal patronage, I believe, during the Early Chalukya period of the late seventh century, when more than a dozen life-size images were enshrined in major Śaiva temples. As Lajjā Gaurī became Hinduized and admitted into the Hindu temple, she also became Hinduized mythologically in that she became considered as (assimilated to be) a consort of Śiva.

Interestingly, Eschmann emphasizes the point that "the first requirement of an anthropomorphic image is certainly a head," so that a natural stone serving as an aniconic image, may first be given a pair of painted-on eyes or applied silver eyes. The importance of the head, which may serve alone as the image of the goddess, corresponds to—or has originated from—a particular popular iconography of Devī, obviously associated with the idea of a sacrifice.[7] In the case of Lajjā Gaurī the original form of the goddess was a pot. Then, not eyes, but legs in *uttānapad* pose were added because of her particular function as a fertility goddess. The pot clearly was meant to symbolize her womb. The fact that the first three forms of the goddess bear no head, but a lotus flower, distinguishes this goddess from the major trend of goddess images that consist of heads only, described by Eschmann. The explanation again, may be the very distinct function of fertility worship served by the images of Lajjā Gaurī. She is also therefore sometimes armless, the focus of her power being the distinct female parts, womb and breasts.

Lajjā Gaurī may have originated on either a tribal or local village level as a *grāmadevī* with a pot serving as her original aniconic form. Her fully anthropomorphized and haloed form (IV), formulated by about A.D. 500 as in the Elephanta example (Fig. 76), and found in situ at Ellora 21 by about A.D. 550 (Fig. 75), and persisting throughout Gujarat in the sixth and seventh centuries (Figs. 77, 82, 86, etc.), marks the completion of the process of Brahminization, wherein she has reached the status of a pan-Indian Hindu goddess, consort of Śiva. Forms I, II, and III are stages with regional associations, along the path to this elevated status and form, but, for this image the path is not linear by any means. While Lajjā Gaurī seems to have reached pan-Indian Brahmanical status by the sixth century, as evidenced by, for example, the Ellora 21 image, there persist regional and distinct developments. Most interesting of these are the plaques from Andhra (Figs. 104–7), which form a distinct subgroup of imagery by their portrayal of Lajjā Gaurī in a plaque-format and in association with a fixed line-up of other deities including Brahmā, Śiva as *liṅga,* Lajjā Gaurī, Kārttikeya or a guard, and a lion, probably the *śakti vāhana.*

The political motivation for admission of tribal or local deities into the Hindu structure and temple proper is of great interest. Like the assimilative expertise of the Hindu religion, and actually operating hand in hand with it, is the king's strategy for gaining the loyalty of his diverse subjects. In fact a standard process for gaining the loyalty of diverse village and tribal populations within the realm and thereby uniting the region into a functioning entity ready to defend itself, was either to patronize the temples of the tribals or villagers, or to bring their deities into the royal sphere, that is, into the royal temple complex, thereby assimilating them into Hinduism.[8] This practice and its function of ensuring loyalty so that the kingdom will be defended helps the interpretation of an inscription cited earlier in this study. The inscription records that Chalukya King Vinayāditya (reigned A.D. 681–96) imposed a tax on sonless couples. This may be evidence of such a strategy in operation: the king, needing soldiers, may have found it necessary to provide his great temples with images of the popular village fertility deity Lajjā Gaurī as recourse for sonless couples.[9] This inscription was found at Belligamve, a site where a Lajjā Gaurī image is still worshiped (Fig. 61).

The only certain instance of royal patronage of an image of Lajjā Gaurī is that by the Ikṣvāku Queen Mahādevī Khaṁḍuvula at Nagarjunakonda (Fig. 42) in the fourth century A.D., recorded in an inscription on the lower rim of the stone figure; I believe this figure originally conformed to Form III. But, even without inscriptional verification, royal patronage is almost certain for some of the outstandingly well-carved Chalukya images, which are also Form III, of the seventh century, and for the in-situ image before Ellora temple 21, Form IV, of the sixth century, whatever royal line that monument owes its existence to (perhaps the Kalachūris). It seems very likely that the dynamic described by Eschmann, Kulke and others was operative in these more ancient periods.

The original village goddess worshiped for fertility in the form of a pot was elaborated in the second century to include legs (Form I). In the third century in South India the goddess was elaborated into Form III and was royally patronized. In the mid-sixth century a fully anthropomorphic Form IV goddess, was royally patronized, I believe, at Ellora (cave 21, Rameśvara temple) in Maharashtra; in the late seventh century in Andhra and Karnataka, several Form III images were royally patronized by the Early Chalukya kings or, more likely, queens. This meager evidence suggests that regional allegiances determined the Form of the goddess Lajjā Gaurī chosen for worship. That is to say that even though the Form IV type already existed at Ellora in the sixth century, rather than imitating the northern form-type, the Chalukyas turned to a southern model at Nagarjunakonda (or others then suviving of this type) as their model.

It is also apparent that royal impetus to the Brahminization of this goddess occurs at different times and regions under different rulers. The process of Brahminization of the Early Chalukya, seventh-century Lajjā Gaurī image is special because its context survives more thoroughly and visibly than others. The subshrines built as part of the temple complex to house her image before major Śaiva Pāśupata temples, and the inscription discussed from Belligamve seem to support the identification of the religio-political motivation for reintroduction of the image of this fertility goddess to the temple at this time.

Such examples as the Nagarjunakonda Lajjā Gaurī with its royal inscription and the Darsi plaque in which Lajjā Gaurī is in the company of major Hindu deities attest that in the Andhra area Lajjā Gaurī had already been Brahminized by the fourth century.

No doubt the Early Chalukyas were aware of that area's Brahminization as legitimization of Lajjā Gaurī when they adopted her for their use. They are known to have felt cultural ties to the Ikṣvākus. It is therefore less surprising that the Early Chalukyas chose to use the same form of iconography (III) for the goddess as the Ikṣvākus had.

Although the enshrined aniconic pot in village worship was, in certain regions and times, elevated to temple status as Lajjā Gaurī, its ancient worship in that setting has endured continually. Such an enshrined pot can be seen in the main square of Bhaktapur in Nepal.

The imperially patronized images of Lajjā Gaurī are life-size and stone. The smaller images come in clusters from several sites but also exist singly from many sites. Does this suggest anything about their function? The largest number have been preserved at Ter where about thirty images, including fragments, are kept at the site museum. Images are found in quantity in several districts around Nagpur in Maharashtra. Concentrations of small images have also been found at Kondapur, Kausambi, and Sannati. At Ter small images of the goddess were made of both stone and terra-cotta, and seem to have been made from the second to at least the sixth century. Nagpur images are stone and date c. fifth to sixth century. Kondapur, Kausambi, and Sannati images are terra-cotta and c. third century. Perhaps these places were fertility pilgrimage sites and the small stone or terra-cotta images served as votive offerings, resulting in large numbers remaining at certain sites, while others were carried away from the centers for worship at a home shrine, resulting in the disbursed pattern of their occurrence. It is curious that in the seventh century the Chalukyas made only life-size stone images of Lajjā Gaurī. There are no small or terra-cotta Chalukya images of Lajjā Gaurī.

Lajjā Gaurī entered the Hindu pantheon with minor status, "through the back door." Her early image was simply an elaboration of a pan-Indian symbol (the brimming pot) of auspicious fertility known since Vedic times and indeed imbedded with its meaning into the language itself. The small images were a part of the popular culture. By the second century, however, this local goddess became "Brahminized"; that is, she became identified with a proper Hindu goddess, actually with both Śrī and Pārvatī in the form of Gaurī and she was drawn into Śaivism as a consort of Śiva. She was represented with Śiva's bull and *liṅga,* and was given her own *vāhana,* the lion of *śakti.* In Andhra she was represented as equal in status to the great Hindu gods in several plaques depicting groups of deities (Figs. 104–7). To explain the curious headless image, villagers created various stories. Her names proliferated and the same image-type was given different names in different localities. As a mother goddess Lajjā Gaurī was worshiped for fertility in isolated locations, outside of town, but as she was Brahminized she was given special housing in a subshrine of major Śiva temples at least in the Early Chalukya domain in the late seventh century. At about the same time in northwestern India, Lajjā Gaurī was represented with a human head with a halo and thereby became an even more "legitimate" or proper Hindu goddess, though she thereby lost her most distinctive and potent feature, the lotus culmination.

We recognize the social and political motivations behind the changing forms of the icon as her importance for fertility worship was exploited within intersecting religious and political spheres. We see equally the effect of regional identification or cultural definition on coherence of form-types within a region. We see also that the artists within each region created form by drawing from a vast, pan-Indian shared pool of imagery with consciousness of the essential features of this goddess, their imagination governed by these bounds even for unique resemblance elaborations. But, finally within each image the artist has displayed either an abundance or a lack of personal inventiveness visible in small details, and great skill or ineptitude at carving form.

Does the coexistence of forms within a region indicate that each form had a specific meaning? There is apparent temporal and spatial coexistence of Forms II and III in central and northern India from the fourth to sixth century. Forms I, II, and III coexist at Ter during one century, the fourth century, though the types assume regional dominations too. No answer to this question is currently apparent.

Form III is the most nearly pan-Indian form of the goddess, existing from the fourth to the tenth century in Gujarat and Madhya Pradesh, Andhra and Karnataka. Although Form II is as long-lived, it was made only in Maharashtra and Madhya Pradesh, never gaining popularity in the south. Form IV was made and found only in the north in Maharashtra and Gujarat. Twice as many figures are known from later centuries than earlier, and in later periods the combination of Lajjā Gaurī with other images of gods is much more common than it was in early centuries. This trend merely underlines the fact of the entry of the goddess into the Hindu fold after her early individual existence as a village goddess.

It should be noted that Lajjā Gaurī images were never worshiped throughout all of India; at least they are not known from all areas. They are known from the "core" area of India, but not from Bihar, Bengal, the far northern states of Punjab, Himachal Pradesh, and Kashmir, nor from the southern state of Kerala, and only one odd example is found in Orissa. I would suspect this lack of cultural dissemination in at least some of the areas that do not render Lajjā Gaurī images has to do with patterns of ancient population density.

The single most important site for creation and history of this icon is Ter. Ter was both an important Hindu and Buddhist center as well as a trade center with connections to the west, as documented in the *Periplus of the Erythraen Sea,* a first- or second-century manual of sea travel and trade along the western coast of India, written by an anonymous Greek merchant.[10] The site is well known as an early Buddhist center, but it is less known that contemporary with early Buddhist *stūpas* and their art from Ter, is evidence of equally early Hindu temples and sculptures.[11] The large quantity of small images of Lajjā Gaurī in three different forms from Ter is unique and requires further investigation at the site.

The latest figure of Lajjā Gaurī reported by Dhere is eleventh century and is from Karnataka. More likely than the advance of Islam on Hinduism as a cause for the demise of creation of her images is the functional replacement of them by linear abstract Tantric symbols of the *yoni* later worshiped for fertility. The symbolism specific to the Lajjā Gaurī image may have been lost to general comprehension as early as the eleventh century.

Notes

1. Panofsky, 1955.
2. Eschmann, Kulke, and Tripathi, 1978, chapters 4 and 7.
3. Ibid., 81.
4. Ibid., 125ff.

5. Ibid., 83.
6. Ibid.
7. Ibid., 91.
8. Ibid., discussed by Kulke, 132.
9. See discussion on page 32.
10. W. H. Schoff, trans. *The Periplus of the Erythraen Sea*, New Delhi, 1974.
11. Cousens, 1926.

Appendix of Known Figures

Figure number, district, state, current location, size (inches, height precedes width), material, approximate date.

Form I

1. Ter, Osmanabad District, Maharashtra, Ter Museum unnumbered, $3\frac{3}{4} \times 5$, stone, third–fourth century
2. Ter, Osmanabad District, Maharashtra, Ter Museum 9.144, $2 \times 2\frac{1}{4}$, stone, third–fourth century
3. Ter, Osmanabad District, Maharashtra, Ter Museum RC 9.120, $4\frac{5}{8} \times 5$, stone, third–fourth century
4. Nevase, Ahmadnagar District, Maharashtra, Deccan College Museum, Poona, $2\frac{1}{2} \times 2\frac{1}{2}$, stone, third–fourth century
5. Yellesvaram, Nalgonda District, Andhra Pradesh, Andhra Directorate of Archaeology and Museums 1718, $7 \times 6\frac{1}{2}$, stone, third–fourth century
6. Ter, Osmanabad District, Maharashtra, Ter Museum RC 9.119, 5×6, stone, third–fourth century
7. Sannati, Gulbarga District, Karnataka, Karnataka Directorate of Archaeology and Museums, 2×2, terra-cotta, third–fourth century
8. Kondapur, Khammam District, Andhra, Andhra Directorate of Archaeology and Museums 119, $3\frac{1}{2} \times 3$, terra-cotta, third–fourth century
9. Ter, Osmanabad District, Maharashtra, Ter Museum RC 1.258, $3\frac{1}{2} \times 2$, terra-cotta, third century
10. Ter, Osmanabad District, Maharashtra, Ter Museum 785.C2, size?, terra-cotta, third–fourth century
11. Nagarjunakonda (a), Guntur District, Andhra, Archaeological Museum, Nagarjunakonda, 2×2, terra-cotta, third–fourth century
12. Site unknown, Andhra Pradesh, Victoria Jubilee Museum, Vijayawada, 10×10, stone, third–fourth century
13. Ter, Osmanabad District, Maharashtra, Ter Museum 7.219, $2\frac{1}{4} \times 2\frac{1}{4}$, terra-cotta, third–fourth century
14. Ter, Osmanabad District, Maharashtra, Ter Museum RC 7.220, $2\frac{1}{2} \times 2\frac{1}{2}$, terra-cotta, third–fourth century
15. Bhita, Allahabad District, Uttar Pradesh, Allahabad Municipal Museum 299, $5\frac{7}{10} \times 5\frac{1}{2}$, stone, third–fourth century
16. Kausambi, Allahabad District, Uttar Pradesh, Allahabad Municipal Museum K5053, $1\frac{1}{4} \times 2$, terra-cotta, third century
17. Ter, Osmanabad District, Maharashtra, Ter Museum 3.80, $\frac{7}{8} \times \frac{7}{8}$, faience, third century

Form II

18. Ter, Osmanabad District, Maharashtra, British Museum 1958.10–17.2, $2\frac{1}{2} \times 2\frac{1}{2}$, terra-cotta, second–third century
19. Kausambi, Allahabad District, Uttar Pradesh, Allahabad Museum K3904, $1\frac{1}{4} \times 1\frac{1}{4}$, terra-cotta, fourth–fifth century
20. Site unknown, Uttar Pradesh, Kanoria Collection, Patna (Bihar), 1-inch diameter, terra-cotta, fourth–fifth century
21. Kausambi, Allahabad District, Uttar Pradesh, Indian Museum, Calcutta A12688, $5 \times 4\frac{1}{2}$, stone, fourth–fifth century
22. Alapur (a), Aurangabad District, Maharashtra, Marathwada University Museum, 4×4, stone, fourth–sixth century
23. Alapur (b), Aurangabad District, Maharashtra, Nagpur University Museum, $2\frac{1}{4} \times 2\frac{1}{2}$, stone, fourth–sixth century
24. Paunar (a), Wardha District, Maharashtra, private collection, Nagpur, $4\frac{1}{2} \times 4\frac{1}{2}$, stone, fourth century

25. Paunar (b), Wardha District, Maharashtra, private collection, Nagpur, $4\frac{1}{4}$ × 3, stone, fourth century
26. Sanchi, Raisen District, Madhya Pradesh, Archaeological Museum, Sanchi 387, 2 × 2, stone, fourth century
27. Ter, Osmanabad District, Maharashtra, Ter Museum 9.148, $2\frac{1}{4}$ × $2\frac{1}{4}$, stone, fourth century
28. Pauni, Nagpur District, Maharashtra, British Museum 1976.4–5.2, $2\frac{5}{8}$ × 3, stone, fourth–fifth century
29. Ramatola (a), Bhandara District, Maharashtra, Central Museum, Nagpur, 6 × $8\frac{3}{4}$, stone, fourth–sixth century
30. Ramatola (b), Bhandara District, Maharashtra, Central Museum, Nagpur, 5 × $7\frac{3}{4}$, stone, fourth–sixth century
31. Mahurjhari (a), Nagpur District, Maharashtra, Sharadasrama, Yeotmal, size?, stone, seventh century

[no fig.] Hamlapuri, Ramtek, Nagpur District, Maharashtra, size?, stone, fourth–fifth century

[no figs.] four images. Site unknown, Madhya Pradesh, Archaeological Survey of India reserve collection Malhar, Bilaspur District, Madhya Pradesh, sizes? stone, ninth–tenth century

[no fig.] Surera, Nagpur District, Maharashtra, Antiquities Dept., size?, stone, fourth–fifth century

Form III

32. Yellesvaram, Nalgonda District, Andhra Pradesh, Andhra Directorate of Archaeology and Museums 31, 2 × $1\frac{3}{4}$, terra-cotta, third century
33. Bhita, Allahabad District, Uttar Pradesh, Indian Museum, Calcutta A10431, $4\frac{5}{8}$ diameter, terracotta, fourth–sixth century
34. Kausambi, Allahabad District, Uttar Pradesh, Patna Museum Arch 7716, $7\frac{1}{2}$ × $6\frac{7}{8}$, terra-cotta, third–fourth century
35. Bilagi, Siddheśvara temple, Bijapur District, Karnataka, c. 4 feet, stone, twentieth century
36. Bundelkhand, Rewa District, Madhya Pradesh, State Museum, Dhubela, M.P., 5 × 5, stone, third–fourth century
37. Kausambi, Allahabad District, Uttar Pradesh, Allahabad Municipal Museum 5034, $6\frac{1}{4}$ × $4\frac{1}{4}$, terra-cotta, third–fourth century
38. Jhusi, Allahabad District, Uttar Pradesh, Allahabad Municipal Museum 4617, 5 × $5\frac{1}{2}$, terracotta, fourth century
39. Kausambi, Allahabad District, Uttar Pradesh, State Museum, Lucknow 79.15.6, height 8, fragment, terra-cotta, fourth century
40. Kausambi, Allahabad District, Uttar Pradesh, Patna Museum 7606, 5 × $5\frac{1}{2}$, stone, date?
41. Ter, Osmanabad District, Maharashtra, Ter Museum 9.147, $2\frac{3}{4}$ × $2\frac{3}{4}$, stone, fourth century
42. Nagarjunakonda (b), Guntur District, Andhra Pradesh, Archaeological Museum, Nagarjunakonda, 3–4 feet square, stone, late third–early fourth century

[no fig.] Kausambi, Allahabad District, Uttar Pradesh, Allahabad Municipal Museum 5039, $4\frac{1}{2}$ × $4\frac{2}{3}$, stone fragment

[no fig.] Kausambi, Allahabad District, Uttar Pradesh, Allahabad Municipal Museum 3849, $3\frac{1}{2}$ × $4\frac{1}{4}$, terra-cotta fragment

[no fig.] Kausambi, Allahabad District, Uttar Pradesh, Allahabad Municipal Museum 5214, $3\frac{1}{2}$ × $3\frac{1}{4}$, terra-cotta fragment

[no fig.] Kausambi, Allahabad District, Uttar Pradesh, Allahabad Municipal Museum 3894, $4\frac{3}{8}$ × $2\frac{3}{4}$, terra-cotta

[no fig.] Amreli, Amreli District, Gujarat, current location? 2 × 2, stone

[no fig.] Agiavira (no information given)

[no fig.] Mandanapuri, Nagpur District, Maharashtra

[no fig.] Valad, Bhandara District, Maharashtra

[no fig.] Nagara, Bhandara District, Maharashtra

[no fig.] Supala, Amaravati District, Maharashtra

[no fig.] Buldahana, Buldahana District, Maharashtra

[no fig.] Chandrapur, Chandrapur District, Maharashtra

[no fig.] Bhambragarh, Chandrapur District, Maharashtra

[no fig.] Kanchipuram, Chingleput District, Tamil Nadu, Kamakshi temple, northwest niche, stone, fourth–fifth century

Form III Early Western Chalukya Images

43. Siddhanakolla, Lakulīśa temple, Bijapur District, Karnataka, 32 × 39, stone, late seventh century

44. Siddhanakolla, path marker
46. Alampur, Bala Brahmā temple, Kurnool District, Andhra Pradesh, 3–4 feet square, stone, late seventh century
48. Naganathakolla, Nāganātha temple, Bijapur District, Karnataka, Badami Museum B36, 38 × 28, stone, late seventh century
50. Mahakuta, Mahakuteśvara temple, Bijapur District, Karnataka, 39 × 38, stone, late seventh century
51. Chikkamahakuta, Bijapur District, Karnataka, $39\frac{1}{2}$ × $16\frac{1}{2}$ fragment, stone, late seventh century
52. Kudavelli (a), Saṅgameśvara temple, Kurnool District, Andhra Pradesh, Alampur Museum, 35 × 41, stone, late seventh century
53. copy after Kudavelli (a) late seventh–eighth century, made in Rajasthan, nineteenth–twentieth century, private collection, United Kingdom, $12\frac{1}{2}$ × $14\frac{1}{2}$, marble
54. Darasuram, Chakrayi temple, Tanjore District, Tamil Nadu, 45 × 33, stone, late seventh century
55. Kudavelli (b), Saṅgameśvara temple, Kurnool District, Andhra Pradesh, Alampur Museum, $2\frac{1}{2}$ × $2\frac{1}{4}$, stone, late seventh century
56. Panchalingala, Pañchalingeśvara temple, Kurnool District, Andhra Pradesh, c. 3 feet square, stone, late seventh century
57. Yellala, Kurnool District, Andhra Pradesh, Andhra Directorate of Archaeology and Museums, 36 × 36, stone, late seventh century
58. Bhadranayika Jalihal (a), Hulligamakolla, Bijapur District, Karnataka, 34 × 24, stone, late seventh century
59. Bhadranayika Jalihal (b), Hulligamakolla, Bijapur District, Karnataka, 23 × 13, stone, late seventh century
60. Bhavanasi, Nivrittisaṅgameśvara temple, Kurnool District, Andhra Pradesh, height 41, stone, seventh–eighth century
61. Belligamve, Kedareśvara temple, Shimoga District, Karnataka, 28 × 15, stone, eighth century
62. Aihole, Galaganātha temple area, Bijapur District, Karnataka, 41 × 41, stone, eighth century
63. Pratakota, Nageśvaraswami temple, Kurnool District, Andhra Pradesh, height c. 3–4 feet, stone, eighth–ninth century
64. Miyapuram, Satyamma temple, Mahaboobnagar District, Andhra Pradesh, height $23\frac{1}{2}$, stone, late seventh century

Form IV

65. Amreli, Amreli District, Gujarat, Collection of U. P. Shah, Baroda, 2 × 2, stone, sixth century
66. Mathura, Mathura District, Uttar Pradesh, Victoria and Albert Museum 177, height $3\frac{4}{5}$, terracotta, second century?
69. Site unknown, North India, Gulbenkian Museum, University of Durham (England), Collection of Ajit Mookerjee, height 4, stone, sixth century
70. Site unknown, Central India, Archaeological Museum, Mathura 15.597, 11 × $5\frac{1}{2}$, stone, eighth century
71. Pavi-Jetpur, Baroda District, Gujarat, Department of Archaeology and Ancient History, M. S. University of Baroda, 5 × $3\frac{1}{2}$, stone, seventh century
72. Aihole, Huchchapayya temple ceiling border, Bijapur District, Karnataka, stone, c. 700

Form I Multifigured Representations

73. Vadgaon, Satara District, Maharashtra, Shri Bhavani Museum and Library, Aundh, Satara District, Maharashtra, 3 × 4, stone, fourth century

Form IV Multifigured Representations

75. Ellora, Rāmeśvara temple (21), Aurangabad District, Maharashtra, 50 × 77, stone, sixth century
76. Elephanta, Bombay District, Maharashtra, Prince of Wales Museum, 81.7/1, 3 × 2, stone, sixth century
77. Bhuj, Kutch District, Gujarat, Kutch Museum, Bhuj, size?, stone, fourth–fifth century
78. Bhinmal, Jalor District, Rajasthan, size?, stone, seventh century
81. Dhank (a), Rajkot District, Gujarat, size?, stone, seventh century
82. Dhank (b), Manjusri *vapi,* Rajkot District, Gujarat, size?, stone, seventh century
83. Variavi, Surat District, Gujarat, Collection of U. P. Shah, 2 × 4, stone, sixth century
84. Kavi, Broach District, Gujarat, Collection of U. P. Shah, $1\frac{3}{4}$ × 2, stone, sixth century
85. Arna, Jodhpur District, Rajasthan, height 16, stone, seventh century

86. Tarsang, Panchmahals District, Gujarat, Department of Archaeology and Ancient History, M. S. University of Baroda, $3\frac{1}{2} \times 3\frac{1}{2}$, stone, sixth century
87. Valabhipur, Bhavanagar District, Gujarat, Department of Archaeology and Ancient History, M. S. University of Baroda, $2\frac{1}{2} \times 4\frac{1}{2}$, stone, seventh century
88. Randelia, Bhavanagar District, Gujarat, Department of Archaeology and Ancient History, M. S. University of Baroda, height 2 (fragment), stone, date?
89. Gadhali, Bhavanagar District, Gujarat, Department of Archaeology and Ancient History, M. S. University of Baroda, $2 \times 2\frac{1}{2}$, stone, seventh century
90. Sathal, Ahmedabad District, Gujarat, Department of Archaeology and Ancient History, M. S. University of Baroda, $3 \times 4\frac{1}{2}$, stone, fourth–fifth century

Form II Multifigured Representations

91. Mandhal, Nagpur District, Maharashtra, Central Museum, Nagpur, $3\frac{1}{4} \times 4$, stone, fourth–fifth century
92. Mahurjhari (b), Nagpur District, Maharashtra, Sarasvatī Bhavan Mahavidyalaya (College), Aurangabad, size?, stone, seventh century
93. Mansar, Nagpur District, Maharashtra, Central Museum, Nagpur C 203, $4 \times 3\frac{1}{4}$, stone, fourth–sixth century
94. Paunar (a), Wardha District, Maharashtra, private collection, $3\frac{1}{4} \times 2\frac{3}{4}$ (fragment), stone, fourth–sixth century
95. Paunar (b), Wardha District, Maharashtra, private collection, $7 \times 5\frac{1}{4}$, stone, fourth–sixth century
96. Paunar (c), Wardha District, Maharashtra, private collection, $5\frac{1}{4} \times 7$, stone, fourth–fifth century
97. Ter, Osmanabad District, Maharashtra, Ter Museum 9.168, $2 \times 2\frac{1}{4}$, stone, fourth–sixth century
98. Site unknown, Seoni District, Madhya Pradesh, Eilenberg Collection, London, 4×4, stone, sixth–seventh century

[no fig.] Surera, Nagpur District, Maharashtra, Maharashtra Antiquities Department, $5\frac{4}{5} \times 5\frac{4}{5}$, stone, fourth–sixth century

Form III Multifigured Representations

79. Kanad, Surat District, Gugjarat, Western Circle Office, Archaeological Survey of India, Baroda, 2×3, terra-cotta, sixth century
80. Bavaka, Panchmahals District, Gujarat, Museum of Gujarat Vidyapith, Ahmedabad, $3\frac{3}{4} \times 5$, stone, ninth–tenth century
99. Ter, Osmanabad District, Maharashtra, Ter Museum RC 8192, $2\frac{1}{2} \times 2\frac{3}{4}$, stone, fourth–sixth century
100. Ter, Osmanabad District, Maharashtra, Ter Museum 9.166, $2\frac{1}{2} \times 2\frac{3}{4}$, stone, fourth–sixth century
101. Ter, Osmanabad District, Maharashtra, Ter Museum 9.154, width $3\frac{1}{2}$ (fragment), stone, fourth–sixth century
102. Majati, Belgaum District, Karnataka, Karnatak University, 5×5, stone, fourth–sixth century
103. Keesaragutta, Hyderabad District, Andhra Pradesh, Andhra Directorate of Archaeology and Museums, $4\frac{3}{4} \times 4\frac{3}{4}$, stone, fourth century

Other Multifigured Representations of Unusual Types

104. Darsi (a), Prakasam District, Andhra Pradesh, Andhra Directorate of Archaeology and Museums, $5 \times 10\frac{1}{2}$, stone, third–fourth century
105. Darsi (b), Prakasam District, Andhra Pradesh, Nellore Museum, $5 \times 12\frac{1}{2}$, stone, third–fourth century
106. Kunidane, Guntur District, Andhra Pradesh, current location unknown, $10\frac{1}{2} \times 7\frac{1}{2}$, stone, fourth–fifth century
107. Uppalapadu, Guntur District, Andhra Pradesh, current location unknown, size?, stone, third–fourth century
108. Bhuvanesvara, Puri District, Orissa, Satrugneśvara temple, lintel, stone, sixth–seventh century
109. Aihole, Bijapur District, Karnataka, Huchchapayya temple tank rim, Aihole Museum, 16×51, stone, eighth–ninth century

Fragments: Ter 12, Ter Museum; Kausambi 1, Allahabad Municipal Museum 4865; Nandapur 1, private collection, Nagpur; Kolhapur 1

Glossary

Aditi: "boundless; the primordial vastness"; one of the names sometimes associated with Lajjā Gaurī images.

āgama: tradition, a traditional doctrine, a collection of such doctrines.

āmalaka: crowning architectural part shaped like a round, ribbed cushion.

amman̠: "great mother," the primeval mother of all living things.

añjalimudrā: prayerful gesture; a hand gesture of respectful salutation and adoration; both hands are placed together, palms touching, and held near the chest.

aṣṭamaṅgala: eight auspicious things, used as art motifs, such as *pūrṇa kumbha, svastika, triratna, matsya yugma* (couple of fishes), etc.

avatāra: "descent" form of a deity; a divine incarnation, the birth into the world of a divine being, in order to save the world from a peril and to restore world order.

āyāgapaṭas: votive tablets.

bhadrāsana: pose of some of the *mātṛkās* (mothers), who sometimes are represented seated with the legs spread.

Bhūdevī: goddess Earth, consort of Viṣṇu.

bhūmiprasada śikhara: style of temple superstructure, pyramidal in outline, composed of a broad curved eave on a vertical riser repeated in diminishing tiers, capped by an *āmalaka* (crowning part shaped like a round, ribbed cushion).

Brahmā: one of the three chief gods of the Hindu triad (with Śiva and Viṣṇu); in early times, the god of sacrifice and worship symbolizing the yearning for god; in later times, regarded as the god of creation.

brahman: in Hinduism, the ultimate divine principle, which cannot be perceived by the senses and is formless, but which abstraction can assume many forms, the three principal being Brahmā, the creator, Viṣṇu, the preserver, and Śiva, the creator-destroyer.

Buddha: a title ("enlightened") of the founder of Buddhism.

chaitya: a Buddhist prayer and temple hall that enshrines a *stūpa;* its arched, open-windowed façade is used as a motif in art.

Chalukya: name of a dynasty and a school or period of art flourishing between the fifth and seventh centuries A.D. (c. 550–750) in the Deccan.

Chāmuṇḍā: name of a form of Durgā.

channavīra: body-encompassing jewelry that hangs from the neck, crosses between the breasts, passes around the waist and up the back.

Choḷa: name of a south Indian Tamil dynasty and a period or school of art flourishing between the ninth and fourteenth centuries A.D.

Dakṣa: a demiurge, the son of Brahmā; Aditi is sometimes mentioned as his mother, elsewhere as his daughter.

Devī: the Goddess.

dharma: law, right, justice, religion; i.e., all that which is established or firm.

dhvajastambha: temple pillar standing in the temple compound.

Durgā: name of a goddess, "the unattainable," a form of Parvatı; a terrific aspect of the *śakti* (energy) of Śiva.

dvārapāla: "doorkeeper", a guardian figure placed on either side of a temple entrance.

Gaja Lakṣmī: a representation of the goddess Lakṣmī, in which two elephants sprinkle water to bathe or lustrate her.

gajapṛṣṭha: "elephant back"-shaped roof of an apsidal temple, i.e., curved.

gaṇas: elemental demigods represented as fat dwarfs, commonly associated with Śiva as an expression of his boundless creative energy.

Gaṇeśa: one of the most popular Hindu gods, distinguished by his elephant head, a son of

Śiva and Pārvatī, regarded as the remover of obstacles.

Garuḍa: the vehicle of the Hindu god Viṣṇu, a bird, sometimes represented as half-kite, half-man.

Gaurī: the consort of Varuna; an epithet of Pārvatī; the *śakti* (energy) of Śiva Maheśvara.

ghaṭa: a jar or a drum in the shape of a jar.

grāmadevatā: a boundary deity, especially a goddess, marking off and establishing the village locus and as guarantor of certain favors and boons such as the birth of children or an increase in family fortune.

Gupta: name of a dynasty and empire in north India and an art period flourishing from the fourth to sixth centuries A.D.

Hara: epithet of Śiva; remover, seizer, destroyer.

Hārītī: name of a mother goddess, patroness of children, reformed child-seizer.

Hoysala: name of a dynasty and art period in southwest India flourishing from the twelfth to fourteenth centuries A.D.

Ikṣvāku: name of a dynasty and an art period flourishing from the second through third centuries A.D.

Jagannātha: name of a form of Kṛṣṇa (or Viṣṇu, black in color) represented as a wooden icon worshiped in Bengal and Orissa, especially at Puri.

Jain: relating to, or worshiper of, the *jinas* (those who have achieved supreme knowledge); Jainism is a religious doctrine founded by Mahāvīra.

Jamadagni: Vedic sage (Paraśurāma's father).

Kalachuri: name of a dynasty and an art period flourishing in the fifth and sixth centuries A.D. in western India.

Kali: an epithet of several goddesses; usually, however, signifies a terrific aspect of Śiva's *śakti.*

kamala: lotus.

Kārttikeya: name of a son of Śiva and Pārvatī who was fostered by the six Kṛttikās (Pleiades) and therefore is often represented as six-headed.

kaupīna: loincloth.

kīrttimukha: lionlike mask used as a decorative motif; the lionlike face of glory, which is seen on top of the arches of doorways and niches of temples or at the top of the arch around an image of a deity.

kumbha: vase, jar, pot, or womb.

kund: temple tank.

Kuṣān: name of a north Indian dynasty and art period flourishing between the first and third centuries A.D.

Lajjā Gaurī: most widely used name for a figure of a Hindu goddess in India who is also referred to by many other names such as Aditi, Reṇuka, Nagna Kabamdha, etc.

Lakṣmī: the goddess of fortune, riches, and beauty; also a mother and fertility goddess, regarded as a personification of the earth.

Lakulīśa: "the Lord with the club"; a reformer of the Pāśupata cult who was regarded by his adherents as an *avatār* of Śiva.

liṅga: name of the phallic form symbolic of Śiva.

Mahābhārata: "the great story"; one of two great epics of India written in Sanskrit about 200 B.C.; it combines myths, folktales, legends, and history.

Mahiṣāsuramardinī: name of one of the principal forms of Durgā, under which she subdued the buffalo-demon, Mahiṣāsura.

maithuna: a pair, a loving couple, engaged in intercourse; found in temples as an auspicious symbol.

makara: a composite water creature with tapir or crocodilelike bust and foliate fishtail often seen in Indian art and throughout Asia.

makuṭa: crown, headdress.

maṇḍapa: a pillared hall in a temple before the sanctum.

mandira: temple.

Mañjuśri: in Buddhism, the god of wisdom; a very popular *dhyani bodhisattva* who is the Buddhist counterpart of the Hindu god Brahmā.

Mātājī: a goddess who may originally reflect the "Great Mother," the primeval mother of all living beings; in north India the name of the village goddess called Amma in south India.

Mātaṅgī: the mythical mother of an elephant tribe; also regarded as an epithet of Kali (or Durgā, Pārvatī).

mātṛkā: mother; divine mothers, a species of tutelary deity.

mekhalā: jeweled girdle, such as that typically worn by a woman or a goddess or as would serve as the decoration of a *pūrṇa kumbha* (brimming vase of fortune) motif around its hip.

mekhalī-ghaṭa: girdled vase.

Mitra: name of an Aditya (son of Aditi).

mūrti: manifestation, embodiment, personification, the (anthropomorphic) representation of a god; anthropomorphic images.

nāgapuṣpā: "snake flower"; an auspicious motif.

nāgara śikhara: style of temple superstructure with a square base and tapering vertical ascent; a curvilinear spire.

Naigameṣa/Naigameya: a god who is either the son or the brother of Skanda, or an aspect of Skanda himself.

nāla: temple sanctum's ablution drain.

Nanda: name of a mother goddess; a form of Pārvatī; one of the five Gaurīs.

Nandi: name of Śiva's vehicle, a bull, regarded as the theriomorphic form of Śiva, represented facing the sanctum of temples dedicated to Śiva.

Narasiṁha: name of the fourth *avatar* of Viṣṇu, as a man-lion, in which shape he rescued the world from the tyranny of the demon Hiraṇyakaśipu.

nirvāṇa: especially in Buddhism, but also in the other Indian religions, a state that is the equivalent to the end of the cycle of existence; the total extinction of all desires or passions, and therefore of all qualities that cause rebirth.

padma: lotus, symbolic of purity and the ongoing chain of existence.

Pallava: name of a dynasty and period of art that flourished in south India from the fifth to ninth centuries A.D.

Paraśurāma: name of the sixth *avatar* of Viṣṇu, in which he saved the world from the tyranny of the *kṣatriyas,* the aristocracy of warriors.

Pārvatī: name of a goddess, consort of Śiva.

Paśupata: a Śaivite sect and doctrine of faith, according to which Paśupatī, who is supplied with unsurpassed powers and active force, creates, maintains, and destroys the universe.

pītha: sanctum altar; a pedestal of an image of a *liṅga* (abstract phallic symbol of Śiva).

pralambapadāsana: a pose of some of the *mātṛkās* (mothers) and other deities who sometimes are represented seated with the legs spread.

Pratihāra: name of a dynasty and a period in art that flourished in north India from the ninth to eleventh centuries A.D.

Pṛthvī: "earth mother"; the earth personified as a goddess.

pūjā: honor, worship, adoration of the gods.

purāṇas: ancient tales or legends, chiefly concerned with gods, hence a class of sacred works, dedicated to certain gods.

pūrṇa ghaṭa: brimming vase; symbol of plenty, source of life.

pūrṇa kumbha: brimming pot or vase; brimming vase of fortune, source of life, one of a group of ancient popular symbols.

Ramāyana: one of two major epics of ancient India.

Rāṣṭrakūṭa: name of a dynasty and a period in art that flourished in the Deccan of India from the eighth to tenth centuries A.D.

Rudra: a Vedic storm god and terrific deity who, as Rudramūrti, was identified with Śiva.

Śaiva: relating to the worship of Śiva.

śakti: spear, power; all-pervading energy; the energy of a god in its personified form, comprehended as the female counterpart of a god.

śakti pitha: a mystical geometrical figure connected with *śakti* worship; a place of worship of *śakti,* the female divine energy.

śakti vahana: the vehicle of the goddess, often a lion.

śāla: oblong barrel-vaulted hall often used as decorative motif in miniature.

Saptamātṛkās: the Seven Mothers'; a group of mother deities, the number of whom is usually mentioned as seven, often a set as the female counterparts of the gods.

Sarasvatī: consort of Viṣṇu; goddess of knowledge and the arts.

satī stone: memorial stone to a dutiful wife who immolates herself on her husband's funeral pyre.

saubhagya: good fortune.

śikhara; temple superstructure; temple spire.

śirascakra: "head disk," nimbus, halo.

Śiva: name of one of the most important gods of Hinduism whose role is as the benevolent destroyer; "the auspicious one."

Śivaliṅga: name of an image of Śiva in the form of an abstract phallus.

Skanda: the war god, the leader of the army of the gods.

ślesa: pun.

śrīpada: sacred feet or footprints.

śrīvatsa: mark or sign of fortune; in art, like a whorl of hair, a triangle, or a cruciform flower; in its early form *śrīvatsa* has four upwardly curved "limbs."

stūpa: an architectural term, indicating a dome-shaped or stepped monument that contains the sacred relics of the Buddha (or other saints), which made in miniature form, is also used as a votive gift.

śukhanāsa: arched projection at base of a *śikhara* (temple spire).

Surya: name of the Hindu sun god.

swastika: a magical, auspicious mark in the form of a cross with arms in a right angle; Sanskrit *su* (well) *asti* (being).

tantra: a class of sacred texts mostly of a ritualistic character, with sacral, and chiefly magical and mystical contents; may also be interpreted as a magical formula.

tantric: relating to the *tantras.*

Tirumantiram: a tenth-century Tamil text.

toraṇa: arch, gateway; gateway to a temple.

Umā: epithet or form of the goddess Pārvatī, consort of Śiva.

Umāmaheśvara: a representation of Śiva together with Pārvatī, who sits on his left knee.

Uṣas: "the dawn"; name of one of the oldest Vedic deities, the daughter of Dyaus; sometimes mentioned as the wife of Surya.

utkuṭikāsana: seated pose, in which one sits with heels kept close to the bottom and with the back slightly curved and the forearms resting on the knees raised above the seat.

uttāna: stretched out; lying on the back, sleeping supinely or with the face upward; upright; turned so that the mouth or opening is uppermost (as a vessel), concave.

uttānapad: one whose legs are extended in parturition; name of a peculiar creative agency or productive power; vegetation, the whole creation of upward-germinating plants; in art, a pose in which the legs of figures lying on their backs make an *M*-shape; they are drawn up to the sides of the waist as if to serve as a "stand" for the torso.

vāhana: "conveyance"; vehicle or mount of a god; the vehicle of a god expresses some aspect of his nature in animal form.

Vaiṣṇava: relating to the worship of Viṣṇu.

vapi: stepwell.

Varuṇa: one of the chief Vedic gods, the lord of the waters and the guardian of the system of the world.

Veda: "knowledge"; the sacred books of Vedic religion, also regarded as the canon of later Hinduism, including the *Ṛg Veda,* the *Yajur Veda,* the *Sāma Veda,* and the *Atharva Veda.*

vedikā: fencelike uppermost plinth element on some temples with relief uprights and crossbars; railing or fence of a sacred enclosure, especially of a *stūpa.*

Venkateśvara: a form of Kṛṣṇa or Viṣṇu worshiped at Tirupati.

verul: pot.

vihāra: Buddhist monastery.

Vināya: epithet of the Hindu god Gaṇeśa, remover of obstacles.

visirikkal: "fan-stones"; anthropomorphic in shape, found in south India, datable to c. 500 B.C.

Viṣṇu: name of one of the most important gods of Hinduism, whose role is as the preserver or protector of the cosmic system.

Viṣṇukundin: name of a dynasty and a period of art in south India flourishing in the fourth century A.D.

Viśvarūpa: name of an aspect of Viṣṇu or Kṛṣṇa; "having all forms."

yakṣa: male demiurge or nature spirit (female: *yakṣi*); a wealth deity; *yakṣas* are especially associated with trees.

yoni: emblem of the goddess, womb; vessel which receives; symbol of the female principle.

Selected Bibliography

Agrawala, P. K. 1965. *Pūrna Kalaśa, the vase of plenty.* Indian Civilization Series 3, Varanasi.

———. 1974. *Śrīvatsa, the Babe of the Goddess Śrī.* Varanasi.

———. 1977. *Early Indian Bronzes.*

———. 1983a. *Goddesses in Ancient India.* Atlantic Highlands, N.J.

———. 1983b. *Mithuna.* New Delhi.

Agrawala, R. C. 1972. "Rock Cut Statues at Arnā, Jodhpur." *Journal of The Oriental Institute, M.S. University of Baroda* 21, no. 4, 351.

Agrawala, V. S. 1951. "Purna Kalasa." *Roopa Lekhā* 22, no. 1, 22–31.

Allchin, F. Raymond. 1985. "The Interpretation of a Seal from Chanhu-daro and Its Significance for the Religion of the Indus Civilization." In *South Asian Archaeology: Papers from the Seventh International Conference of the Association of South Asian Archaeologists in Western Europe, Brussels 1983,* ed. Janine Schotsman and Maurizio Taddei, Naples, 371–83.

Annigere, A. M. 1978. *Cave Temples of Badami.* Dharwar.

Archaeological Survey of India. 1906. "Excavations at Basarh." In *Annual Report 1903–4,* ed. T. Bloch, Calcutta, 81–122.

———. 1973. *Indian Archaeology 1969–70: A Review,* ed. B. B. Lal, New Delhi, pls. LXIVa, b, 75.

———. 1981. *Indian Archaeology 1978–79: A Review,* ed. B. K. Thapar, New Delhi, pl. XXXVIIIb, 53–54.

Arts Council of Great Britain. 1982. "In the Image of Man." London, 109.

Asher, Frederick, and G. S. Gai, eds. 1985. *Indian Epigraphy, Its Bearing on the History of Art.* New Delhi.

Banerjea, Jitendra Nath. 1974. *Development of Hindu Iconography.* 3d rev. ed., Delhi.

Barrett, Douglas. 1960. *Ter.* Bombay.

Bhandarkar, Ramakrishna Gopal. 1929. *Collected Works.* Vol. 4, *Vaiṣṇavism, Śaivism and Minor Religious Systems,* Bhandarkar Oriental Research Institute, Government Oriental Series, Poona.

Bhattacharya, Dipak Chandra. 1980. *Iconology of Composite Images.* New Delhi.

Bhattacharyya, N. N. 1977. *The Indian Mother Goddess.* 2d ed., Delhi.

Bolon, Carol Radcliffe. 1985. "The Kudavelli Saṅgameśvara Temple and the Aihole Durgā Temple: A Sculptural Review." *Ars Orientalis* 15, 46–64.

———. 1986. "A Late 8th Century Mātṛkā Set from Aihole." In *Dimensions of Indian Art Pupul Jayakar Seventy,* ed. Lokesh Chandra, Delhi, 51–55.

Bosch, F. D. K. 1960. *The Golden Germ; an Introduction to Indian Symbolism.* The Hague, Mouton.

Boston Museum of Fine Arts. 1977. *From River Banks and Sacred Places: Ancient Indian Terracottas.* Boston.

Brereton, Joel. 1981. *The Ṛgvedic Ādityas* (American Oriental Series, vol. 63). New Haven, chap. 4: "Aditi," 192–251.

Brubaker, Richard Lee. 1978. "The Ambivalent Goddess." Ph.D. diss., University of Chicago.

Burgess, James. 1981. *The Rock Temples of Elura or Verul.* repr. ed., New Delhi.

Chandra, Moti. 1973. "Studies in the Cult of the Mother Goddess in Ancient India." *Prince of Wales Museum Bulletin* 12, 1–47.

Chandra, Pramod. 1971. "The Cult of Śri Lakshmi and Four Carved Discs." *Chhavi,* ed. Anand Krishna. Banares, 139–48.

Chapekar, B. N. 1969. *Report on the Excavation at Ter, 1958.* Poona.

Chhabra, B. C. 1961. "Antiquities from Jhusi and Other Sites." *Lalit Kala* 9, 11–15.

Codrington, Kenneth de Burgh. 1926. *Ancient India.* London.

———. 1935 (May). "Iconography: Classical and Indian." *Man* 35, no. 70, 65–66.

Coomaraswamy, A. K. 1927. "The Origin of the Buddha Image." *Art Bulletin,* 9, no. 4, 287–329.

———. 1927–28. "Notes on Indian Coins and Symbols," *Ostasiatische Zeitschrift*, n.s. IV, 183–84.

———. 1929. "Early Indian Iconography II: Śrī Lakṣmī." *Eastern Art* I, 33–41.

———. 1935a. "The Conqueror's Life in Jaina Painting." *Journal of the Indian Society of Oriental Art* 3, 127–44.

———. 1935b. *Elements of Buddhist Iconography.* Cambridge, Mass.

———. 1953. "Archaic Indian Terracottas." *Marg* 6, no. 2, 22–35.

———. 1971. *Yakṣas.* 2 vols. Repr. of 1928–31 ed., New Delhi.

———. 1972. *The Origin of the Buddha Image,* New Delhi (reprint of 1927 article).

Cousens, Henry. 1902. "Ter-Tagara." *Archaeological Survey of India Annual Report 1902–03.* 195–204.

———. 1926. *The Chalukyan Architecture of the Kanarese Districts.* Archaeological Survey of India Reports, 42, Calcutta.

Dagens, Bruno. 1984. *Entre Alampur et Śrīśailam.* Institut Français d'Indologie, no. 67.1–2, Pondichéry.

Das, Sudhender Kumar. 1934. *Śakti or Divine Power.* Calcutta.

Dasgupta, C. C. 1961. *Origin and Evolution of Indian Clay Sculpture.* Calcutta.

Dasgupta, P. C. 1959. "Early Terracottas from Chandraketugarh." *Lalit Kalā* 6, 45–52.

de Lippe, Aschwin. 1978. *Indian Mediaeval Sculpture.* Amsterdam.

Deo, S. B. 1973. *Mahurjhari Excavation 1970–72.* Nagpur.

———. 1974. *Excavations at Bhokardan.* Nagpur.

———, and M. K. Dhavalikar. 1968. *Paunar Excavation (1967).* Nagpur.

Deo, S. B., and J. P. Joshi. 1972. *Pauni Excavation 1969–70.* Nagpur.

Desai, Devangana. 1975. *Erotic Sculpture of India.* Delhi.

———. 1984. "Shades of Eroticism in Temple Art." In *Symbols and Manifestations of Indian Art,* ed. Saryu Doshi. Bombay. 42–64.

Dhavalikar, M. K. 1977. *Masterpieces of Indian Terracotta.* Bombay.

———. 1979–80. "Lajjāgaurī," *Bulletin Deccan College Research Institute* 40, 30–35.

———. 1986. "The Goddess of Mahakut." In *Government of Karnataka, Directorate of Archaeology and Museums, Centenary Celebration 1885–1985,* National Seminar on Karnataka Archaeology, Mysore. Ms. 1–22.

Dhere, R. C. 1978. *Lajjā Gaurī* (in Marathi). Pune.

Dikshit, S. K. 1957. *A Guide to the State Museum, Dhubela, Nowgong (BKD) Vindhya Pradesh 1955–57.* Nowgong.

———. n.d. *The Mother Goddess.* Poona.

Divakaran, O. 1981. "The Beginnings of Early Western Chalukya Art." *Chhavi II,* ed. Anand Krishna. Banares. 59–66.

Donaldson, Thomas. 1975. "Propitious-Apotropaic Eroticism in the Art of Orissa." *Artibus Asiae* 37, nos. 1–2, 75–100.

———. 1976. "Doorframes on the Earliest Orissan Temples." *Artibus Asiae* 38, nos. 2–3, 189–218.

———. 1985. *Hindu Temple Art of Orissa.* Leiden. *Studies in South Asian Culture,* vol. XII, ed. Janice Stargardt.

Egnor, Margaret Trawick. 1978. "The Sacred Spell and Other Conceptions of Life in Tamil Culture." Ph.D. diss., University of Chicago.

Eliade, Mircea. 1973. *Yoga: Immortality and Freedom.* Princeton.

Elmore, W. T. 1925. *Dravidian Gods in Modern Hinduism.* Madras.

Eschmann, Anncharlott, Hermann Kulke, and Gaya Charan Tripathi, eds. 1978. *The Cult of Jagannātha and the Regional Tradition of Orissa.* South Asia Institute, New Delhi Branch, Heidelberg University, Manohar Publications, New Delhi.

Fleet, John Faithful. 1881. "Sanskrit and Old Canarese Inscriptions." *Indian Antiquary* 10, 103.

Foucher, Alfred. 1905–51. *L'art Greco-Bouddhique du Gandhara.* Paris.

Gaur, R. C. 1983. *Excavations at Atranjīkherā.* New Delhi.

Gerow, Edwin. 1971. *A Glossary of Indian Figures of Speech.* The Hague and Paris.

Ghosh, Niranjan. 1979. *Concept and Iconography of the Goddess of Abundance and Fortune in Three Religions of India.* Burdwan.

Gimbutas, Marija. 1982. *The Goddesses and Gods of Old Europe.* Berkeley and Los Angeles.

Gonda, Jan. 1954. *Aspects of Early Viṣṇuism.* Utrecht.

———. 1970. *Viṣṇuism and Śivaism: A Comparison.* London.

Gopinatha Rao, T. A. 1968. *Elements of Hindu Iconography.* Repr. of 1914 ed., Delhi.

Gorakshekar, Sadasiv. 1982. "The Parel Mahādeva Reassessed and Two Newly Discovered Images from Parel." *Lalit Kalā* 20, 2–3.

Gulder, Alois. 1960–62. *Die urnenfelderzeitliche "Frauenkröte" von Maissau und ihr geistesgeschichtlicher Hintergrund.* Mitteilungen der Prähistorischen Kommission der Österreichischen Akademie der Wissenschaften, vol. x, Vienna.

Gupta, Chandrashekar. 1981. "Māndhal Sculptures" (in Hindi). *Purnā,* 143–46.

———. 1987. "Some Interesting Images of the Goddess Lajjā." In *Giridharaśrī, G. S. Dikshit Felicitation Volume,* ed. A. V. Narasimha Murthy and K. V. Ramesh, Delhi, 45–50.

Gupta, P. L., ed. 1965. *Patna Museum Catalogue of Antiquities.* Patna.

Gupta, Swarajya Prakash. 1980. "The Problem of the Origin of Śrīvatsa." In *The Roots of Indian Art.* New Delhi, 325–28.

Hall, Fritz-Edward. 1859. "The Śrī-Sūkta, or Litany to Fortune." *Journal of the Asiatic Society of Bengal* 28, 121–35.

Harle, James. 1969. "Le temple de Nāganātha à Nagaral." *Arts Asiatiques* 19, 53–83.

———. 1986. *The Art and Architecture of the Indian Subcontinent.* Harmondsworth, Middlesex: Penguin.

Hopkins, E. W. 1968. *Epic Mythology.* Repr. of 1915 ed., Varanasi.

Hunter, G. A. P. 1933. "Antiquities from Mahurjhari." In *Shardashrama Varshika,* ed. Y. K. Deshpande. Yavatmal, 30–35.

Huntington, Susan L., and John C. Huntington. 1985. *The Art of Ancient India.* New York and Tokyo.

Illustrated London News. 1971 (August). "Central India 3000 Years Ago," 41–43.

Inglis, Stephen. 1984. "Creators and Consecrators: A Potter Community of South India." Ph.D. diss., University of British Columbia.

James, E. O. 1959. *The Cult of the Mother Goddess.* London.

Jamindar, Ramesh. forthcoming. "An Unpublished Sculpture of Pārvatī from Gujarat."

Jamkhedkar, A. P. 1985. "Buddhist Bronzes from Ramtek." *Lalit Kalā* 22, 13–19.

Janssen, Frans. 1989. "Over de oorsprong en de ontwikkeling van Lajjā Gaurī." Ph.D. diss. Rijksuniversiteit Utrecht.

Jayakar, Pupul. 1981. *The Earthen Drum.* New Delhi.

Joshi, J. R. 1977. *Some Minor Divinities in Vedic Mythology and Ritual,* chap. 9, "Śrī and Lakṣmī." Deccan College Post Graduate and Research Institute, Pune.

Joshi, N. P. 1968 (March). "Two Mātṛkā Plaques." *Bulletin of Museums and Archaeology in U.P. Sangrahalya Puratattva Patrika, U.P.* 18–19.

Kala, S. C. 1946. *Sculptures in the Allahabad Municipal Museum.* Allahabad.

———. 1950. *Terracotta Figurines from Kauśāmbī.* Allahabad.

———. 1957. *Terracotta Figurines in the Allahabad Museum.* Allahabad.

———. 1958–60. "Antiquities from Jhusi." *Journal of Indian Museums* 14–16, ed. Moti Chandra, Bombay, pl. 7a, 7.

———. 1980. *Terracottas in the Allahabad Museum.* Delhi.

Kinsley, David. 1986. *Hindu Goddesses: Visions of the Divine Feminine in the Hindu Religious Tradition.* Berkeley and Los Angeles.

Kosambi, D. D. 1962. *Myth and Reality.* Bombay.

Kramrisch, Stella. 1928. *Vishnudharmottara Part III.* 2d ed., Calcutta.

———. 1956. "An Image of Aditi-Uttānapad." *Artibus Asiae* 19, nos. 3–4, 259–70; repr. 1982 in *Exploring India's Sacred Art,* ed. Barbara Stoler Miller, Philadelphia, 148–58.

———. 1975. "The Indian Great Goddess." *Journal of the History of Religion* 14, no. 4 (May), 235–65.

———. 1976. *The Hindu Temple.* 2 vols. 2d ed., Delhi.

———. 1978. "The Mahāvīra Vessel and the Plant Pūtika." *Journal of the American Oriental Society* 95, no. 2, 222–35.

———. 1981. *The Presence of Śiva.* Princeton.

Krisnamurthy, K. 1967. "Pūrṇa Ghaṭa in Early Indian Literature and Art." *Orissa Historical Research Journal* 16, nos. 1–2, 9–14.

Kumar, Pushpendra. 1974. *Śakti Cult in Ancient India.* Varanasi.

Lal, Shyam Kishore. 1980. *Female Divinities in Hindu Mythology and Ritual.* Poona.

Larson, Gerald James, Pratapaditya Pal, and Rebecca P. Gowen. 1980. *In Her Image.* UCSB Art Museum, University of California, Santa Barbara.

L'Hernault, Françoise. 1987. *Darasuram.* Ecole française d'Extrême-Orient, Mémoires archéologiques, vol. 16, Paris.

Liebert, Gösta. 1976. *Iconographic Dictionary of the Indian Religions*. Studies in South Asian Culture, v, ed. J. E. Van Lohuizen-de Leeuw, Leiden.

Margabandhu, C. 1975–76. "An Unique Frog-Amulet from Atranjikhera." *Journal of the Indian Society of Oriental Art* 7, 86–90.

———. 1976. "Some Mother Goddess Plaques from Western India and their Cultural Significance." In *Homage to a Historian, Professor N. Subrahmanian Felicitation Volume,* ed. N. Jagadesan. Madurai, 205–16.

———. 1981. "Early Historic Terracottas from Gujarat—A Study." In *Madhu: Recent Researches in Indian Archaeology and Art History,* ed. M. S. Nagaraja Rao, Delhi, 99–112.

Marglin, Frederique A. 1980. "The Wives of the God King." Ph.D. diss., Brandeis University.

———. 1985. *The Wives of the God King*. Oxford.

Marshall, John. 1912. "Excavations at Bhīṭa." *Archaeological Survey of India Annual Report 1911–12,* 25–94.

Maury, Curt. 1969. *Folk Origins of Indian Art*. New York.

Meister, Michael. 1986. "Regional Variations in *Mātṛkā Conventions.*" *Artibus Asiae* 47, nos. 3–4, 233–60.

———, and M. A. Dhaky, eds. 1983, 1986, 1987. *Encyclopedia of Indian Temple Architecture*. Vol. 1, pts. 1–2, Oxford; vol. 2, pts. 1–2, Philadelphia.

Miller, Barbara Stoler, ed. 1983. *Exploring India's Sacred Art: Selected Writings of Stella Kramrisch*. Philadelphia.

Misra, Om Prakash. 1985. *Mother Goddess in Central India*. Delhi, pl. 48, 140.

Misra, Ram Nath. 1981. *Yaksha Cult and Iconography*. Delhi.

Mookerjee, Agit. 1967. *Tantra Art*. New York.

———. 1971. *Tantra Asana*. Basel.

———, and Madhu Khanna. 1977. *The Tantric Way*. Boston.

Monier-Williams, Monier. 1976. *Sanskrit-English Dictionary*. reprint of 1899 ed., Oxford.

Mukhopadhyay, Samir K. 1972. "Terracottas from Bhīṭā." *Artibus Asiae* 34, no. 1, 71–94.

Muley, P. M. 1979. "Lajjāgaurī Shilpe." In *Vidarbha Samsodhana Mandal Varshika,* Nagpur, 187–89.

Murray, M. A. 1934. "Female Fertility Figures." *Journal of the Royal Anthropological Institute of Great Britain and Ireland* 64, 93–100.

Najaraja Rao. M. S. 1978. *Progress of Archaeology in Karnataka 1956–1972*. Mysore.

Nagaswamy, R. 1978. "A Tantric Image at Darasuram and Takkayagapparani." *South Indian Studies* 1, 134–45.

———. 1981 (1 November). "A Sculptural Representation of Kamakala." Paper read at Birth Centenary of Mahamahopadhyaya Professor Kuppuswami Sastri, Kuppuswami Sastri Research Institute, Madras.

———. 1986. "From Aditi to Kundalini (From Prehistoric Visirikkal to Historic Sri Cakra)." In *Dimensions of Indian Art Pupul Jayakar Seventy,* ed. Lokesh Chandra, Delhi, 323–31, and 130–34 in vol. 2.

Nandi, R. N. 1973. *Religious Institutions and Cults in the Deccan 600–1000*. Delhi.

Narasimhaswami, H. K. 1952. "Nagarjunikonda Image Inscription," *Epigraphia Indica* 29, pt. 5, 137–39.

Neumann, Erich. 1955. *The Great Mother*. New York.

Oppert, Gustav. 1893. *On the Original Inhabitants of Bharatavarṣa or India*. Westminster.

Padmanabhan, Seetha, ed. 1969. *Śrīpraśnasamhitā*. Kendriya Sanskrit Vidyapeetha Series, 12.

Panofsky, Erwin. 1955. *Meaning in the Visual Arts*. Garden City, N.Y.

Poster, Amy. 1986. *From Indian Earth: 4,000 Years of Terracotta Art*. Brooklyn Museum, New York.

Prasad, B. Rajendra. 1980. *Art of South India, Andhra Pradesh*. Delhi.

Radcliffe, C. 1981. "Early Chalukya Sculpture." Ph.D. diss., New York University, Institute of Fine Arts.

Rahman, Muklesur. 1965. "The Early History of the Cult of the Mother Goddess in Northern Indian Hinduism . . ." Ph.D. diss., University of London.

Rao, S. R. 1966. "Excavations at Amreli—A Kshatrapa Gupta Town." *Bulletin Museum and Picture Gallery Baroda* 18, 1–114.

Ramesan, N. 1969. *Temples and Legends of Andhra Pradesh*. Bombay.

Rawson, Philip. 1968. *Erotic Art of the East*. New York.

———. 1978. *The Art of Tantra*. New York.

———. n.d. *Tantra*. New York.

Ray, Amita. 1983. *Life and Art of Early Andhradesa*, Delhi.

Roşu, Arion. 1966. "Pūrṇaghata et le symbolisme du lotus dans l'Inde." *Arts Asiatiques* 8, no. 3, 163–94.

Sankalia, H. D. 1960. "The Nude Goddess or 'Shameless Woman' in Western Asia, India, and South Eastern Asia." *Artibus Asiae* 23, no. 2, 111–23.

———. 1978. "The Nude Goddess in Indian Art." *Marg* 31, 4–10.

———, and M. G. Dikshit. 1952. *Excavations at Brahmapuri (Kolhapur) 1945–46*. Poona.

Sankalia, H. D., and M. K. Dhavalikar. 1969. "The Terracotta Art of India." *Marg* 23, no. 1, 33–54.

Saraswati, Bhandana. 1971. "History of the Worship of Śrī in North India to cir. A.D. 550." Ph.D. diss., University of London.

Sarkar, H., and B. N. Misra. 1972. *Nāgārjunakoṇḍa*. New Delhi.

Sarma, I. K. 1972 (September). "The Names 'Satavāhana' and 'Sātakarni' and the Significance of the Śrīvatsa Symbol on the Sātavāhana Coinage." *Indica* 9, no. 2, 87.

———. 1979. "Early Historical Vestiges at Vijayawada and Some Trimurti Cult Plaques." *Itihas Journal of the Andra Pradesh State Archives (India)* 7, no. 2, 23–32.

———. 1982. *The Development of Early Śaiva Art and Architecture with special reference to Andhradesa*. Delhi.

———. 1987. "The Brahmanical Brick Temples and Cult Objects from Keesaragutta." In *Kusumāñjali, C. Sivaramamurti Memorial Volume*, ed. M. S. Nagaraja Rao, Delhi, 233–40.

Sastri, T. V. G. 1967–68. "A Stone Relief from Konidani, Guntur District." *Journal of the Indian Society of Oriental Art* n.s. 2, 16–22.

———. 1986. "Lajja Gauri from Alampur and Its Symbolism." Government of Karnataka, Directorate of Archaeology and Museums Centenary Celebration 1885–1985, National Seminar of Karnataka Archaeology, Mysore.

Sastry, Anathakrishna R. 1951. *Lalitā-sahasranāman*. Madras.

Schastok, Sara. 1980. "Sixth Century Indian Sculptures from Śāmalājī: Style and Iconography." Ph.D. diss., University of Michigan.

———. 1985. *The Śāmalājī Sculptures and Sixth Century Art in Western India*. XI. *Studies in South Asian Culture*, ed. J. E. van Lohuizen-de Leeuw. Leiden.

Seshadri, M. 1972. "Buddhist Monuments in Mysore." *Artibus Asiae* 34, nos. 2–3, 160–70.

Settar, D. S. 1979. "Roots, Relations and Relevance, the Chalukya Backdrop." *In Praise of Aihole, Badami, Mahakuta, Pattadakal. Marg*, ed. Sarayu Doshi, Bombay, 9–32.

Shah, U. P. 1955–56. "Some Early Sculptures from Ābū and Bhinmāl." *Bulletin: Museum and Picture Gallery Baroda* 12, 43–56.

———. 1960. "Sculptures from Śāmalājī and Roḍā (North Gujarat) in the Baroda Museum." *Bulletin Museum and Picture Gallery Baroda* 13, special number.

Sharma, G. R. 1969. "Excavations at Kauśāmbī 1949–50." *Memoires of the Archaeological Survey of India* 74, Delhi.

Sharma, Y. D. 1955–56. "Past Patterns in Living as Unfolded by Excavations at Rupar." *Lalit Kalā* 1–2, 121–29.

Shere, S. A. 1961. *Terracotta Figurines in Patna Museum*. Patna.

Shetti, B. V. 1971. "A Note on South Indian Metal Sculptures in the Prince of Wales Museum." *Prince of Wales Museum Bulletin* 11, 46–53.

Sircar, D. C. 1948. "The Śākta Pīṭhas." *Journal of the Royal Asiatic Society of Bengal* 14, pt. 1, 1–108.

———. 1980. "Aspects of the Cult of the Indian Mother Goddess." *Journal of Indian Museums* 36, 9–20.

Sisodia, Vishnu. 1969 (September–December). "A Jain Goddess from Rajasthan." *East and West* n.s. 19, nos. 3–4, 410–12.

Sivaramamurti, Calumbar. 1941. "Goddess Lakshmī and her Symbols." *U.P. [Uttar Pradesh] Historical Society Journal* 14, no. 1, 21–24.

———. 1942. "Amaravati Sculptures in the Madras Government Museum." *Bulletin of the Madras Government Museum* n.s. 4.

———. 1950. "Geographical and Chronological Factors in Indian Iconography." *Ancient India* 6, 21–63.

———. 1954. "Early Eastern Chalukya Sculpture." *Bulletin of the Madras Government Museum* 7, no. 2.

———. 1957. "Early Eastern Chaḷukya Sculpture."

Bulletin of the Madras Government Museum n.s. 7, no. 2, pl. Ia, p. 12.

———. 1963. *South Indian Bronzes.*

———. 1979. "Early Andhra Art and Iconography." Government of Andhra Pradesh Archaeological Series 52. Hyderabad.

———. 1982. *Śrī Lakshmī in Indian Art and Thought.* New Delhi.

Snellgrove, David Llewellyn. 1978. *The Image of the Buddha.* New York.

Sonawane, V. H. 1986. "Some Remarkable Sculptures of Lajjā Gaurī from Gujarat." *Lalit Kalā* 23, 27–35.

Spink, Walter. 1967. "Ellora's Earliest Phase." *Bulletin American Academy Benares* I, 11–22.

———. 1983. "Elephanta: A Study of Its Sources." In *Essays on Gupta Culture,* ed. Bardwell Smith, Delhi, 235–84.

Srinivasan, P. R. 1981. "Four Pieces of Sculpture." *Chhavi II,* ed. Anand Krishna. Banares, 36–37.

Srivastava, A. L. 1979. "The Śrīvatsa Symbol in Indian Art." *East and West* 29, 37–60.

Srivastava, Balram. 1978. *Iconography of Śakti A Study Based on Śrītattvanidhi.* Chaukhambha Oriental Research Studies no. 9, Varanasi, figs. 7–8, p. 10.

Srivastava, M. C. P. 1979. *Mother Goddess in Indian Art and Archaeology.* Delhi.

Stutley, James, and Margaret Stutley. 1977. *Harper's Dictionary of Hinduism.* New York.

Sundara, A. 1977. "An Inscribed Gaja Lakshmi from Kuppagadde." *Archaeological Studies* 2, Karnatak University, Dharwar, 87–89.

———. 1979. "A Unique Lajjā Gaurī Plaque from Majati." *Archaeological Studies* 4, Karnatak University, Dharwar, 56–58.

Sundara Rajan, K. V. 1981. *Glimpses of Indian Art and Culture.* Delhi.

———. 1983. *Indian Religious Art: Ideas and Ideals.* Delhi.

Tartakov, Gary. 1980. "The Beginnings of Dravidian Architecture in Stone." *Artibus Asiae* 42, no. 1, 39–99.

Tartakov, Gary, and Vidya Dehejia. 1984. "Sharing, Intrusion, and Influence: The Mahiṣāsuramardinī Imagery of the Calukyas and the Pallavas." *Artibus Asiae* 45, 4, 287–345.

Tiwari, Jagdish Narain. 1971. "Studies in the Goddess Cult in Northern India with Special Reference to the 1st to 7th century A.D." Ph.D. diss., Australian National University.

———. 1985. *Goddess Cults in Ancient India.* Delhi.

von Schroeder, Ulrich. 1981. *Indo-Tibetan Bronzes.* Hong Kong.

Vora, Manibhai, and Narottam Palan. 1971. "Tasabir na Dhank," (Gujarati) *Swadhyaya* 8, no. 3, 357–59.

Wadley, Susan S., ed. 1980. *The Powers of Tamil Women.* South Asian Series 6, Syracuse University.

Waheed Khan, Mohammed Abdul. 1963. *A Monograph on Yēlēśwaram Excavations, Devanakonda Taluk, Nalgonda District, Andhra Pradesh.* Hyderabad.

———. 1969a. *Kesanapalli Excavation Report.* Andhra Pradesh Government Archaeological Series, 27, Hyderabad.

———. 1969b. *A Monograph of the Early Buddhist Stupa at Kesanapalli.* Hyderabad.

———. 1973. *Stone Sculptures in the Alampur Museum.* Hyderabad.

West, E. W. 1881. "The Divine Mothers or Local Goddesses of India." *Indian Antiquary* 10, 245–46.

Whitehead, Henry. 1921. *The Village Gods of South India.* Calcutta.

Williams, Joanna Gottfried. 1984. "Śiva and the Cult of Jagannātha: Iconography and Ambiguity." In *Discourses on Śiva,* ed. M. Meister, Philadelphia, 298–311.

Index

Illustrations

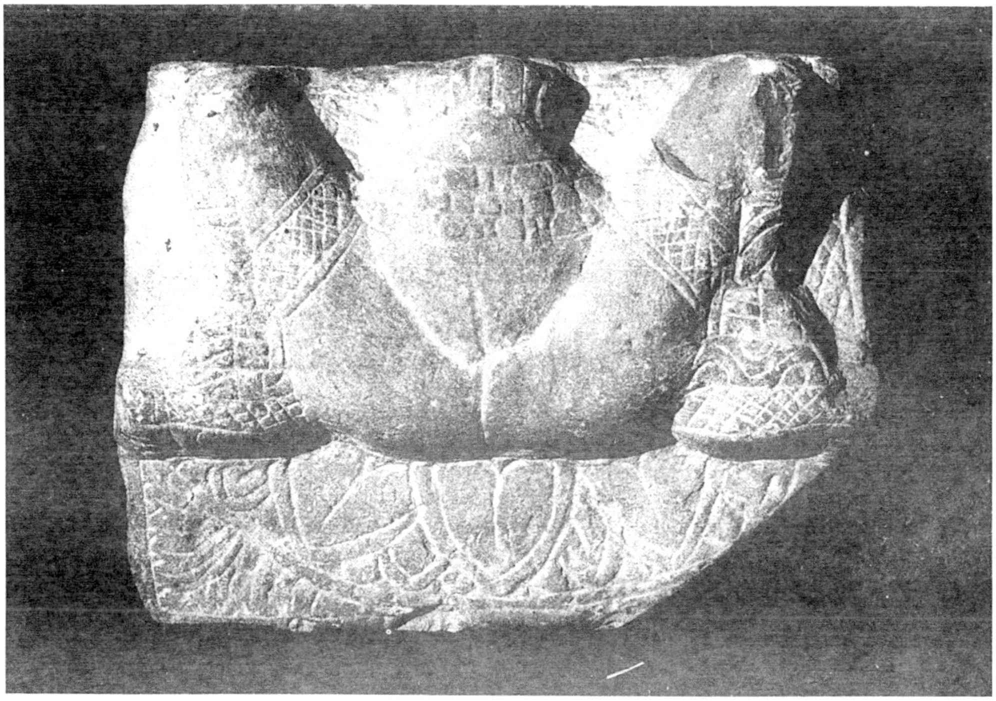

Fig. 1. Ter, Osmanabad District, Maharashtra, Ter Museum, 3¾ × 5 inches, stone, third–fourth century

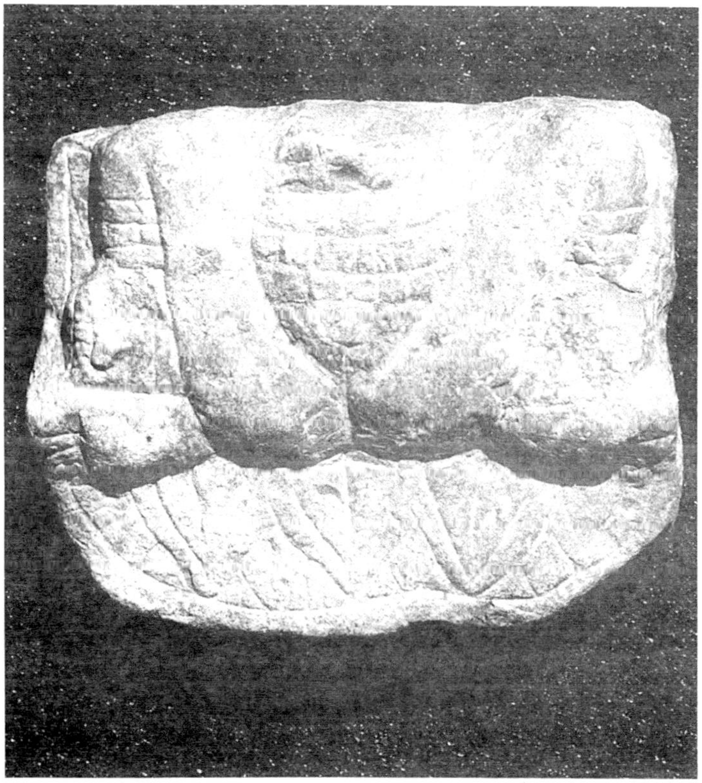

Fig. 2. Ter, Osmanabad District, Maharashtra, Ter Museum 9.144, 2 × 2¼ inches, stone, third– fourth century

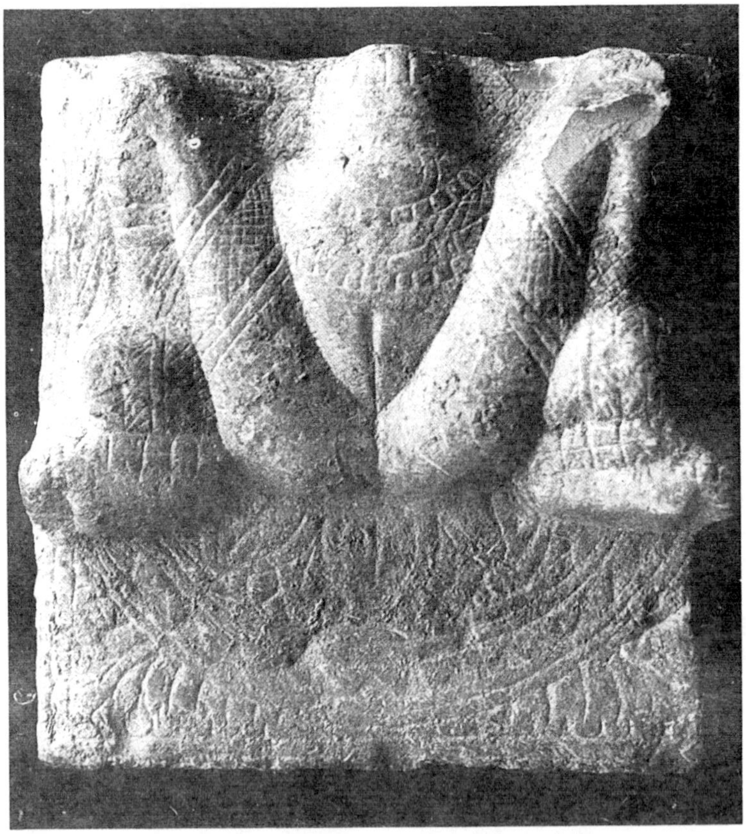

Fig. 3. Ter, Osmanabad District, Maharashtra, Ter Museum RC 9.120, 4⅝ × 5 inches, stone, third–fourth century

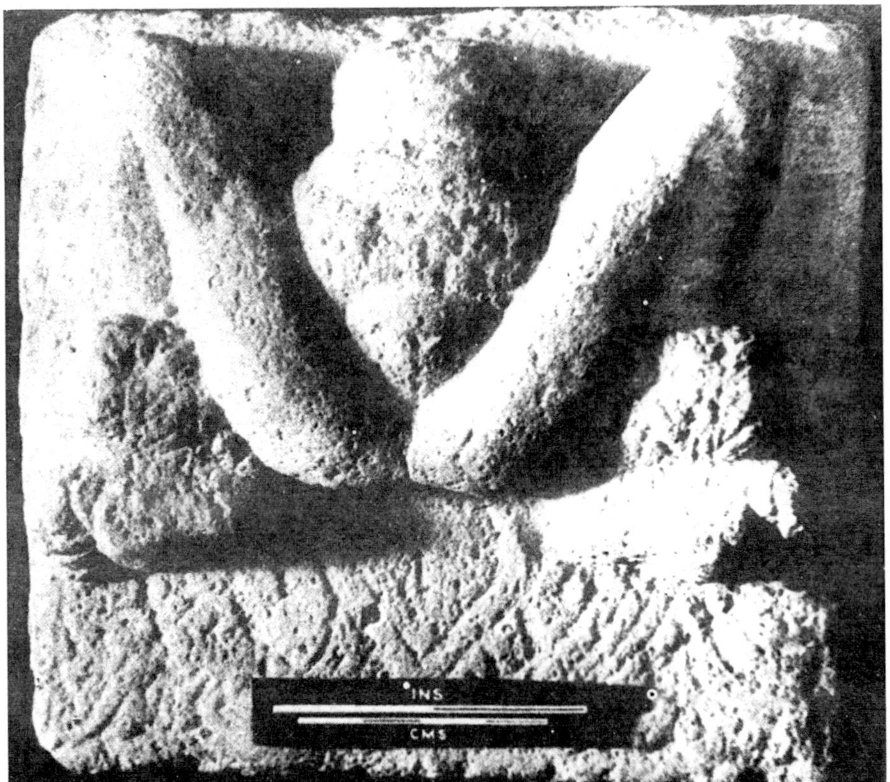

Fig. 4. Nevase, Ahmadnagar District, Maharashtra, Deccan College Museum, Poona, 2½ × 2½ inches, stone, third–fourth century

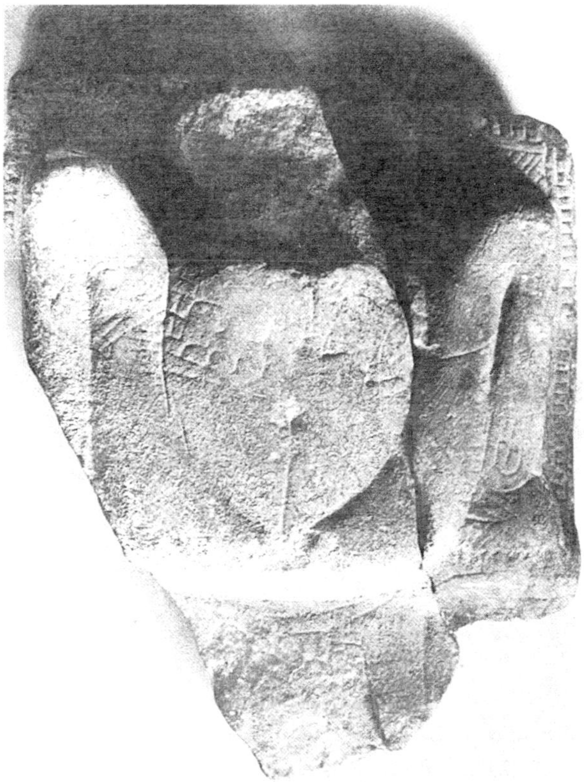

Fig. 5. Yellesvaram, Nalgonda District, Andhra Pradesh, Andhra Directorate of Archaeology and Museums 1718, 7 × 6½ inches, stone, third–fourth century

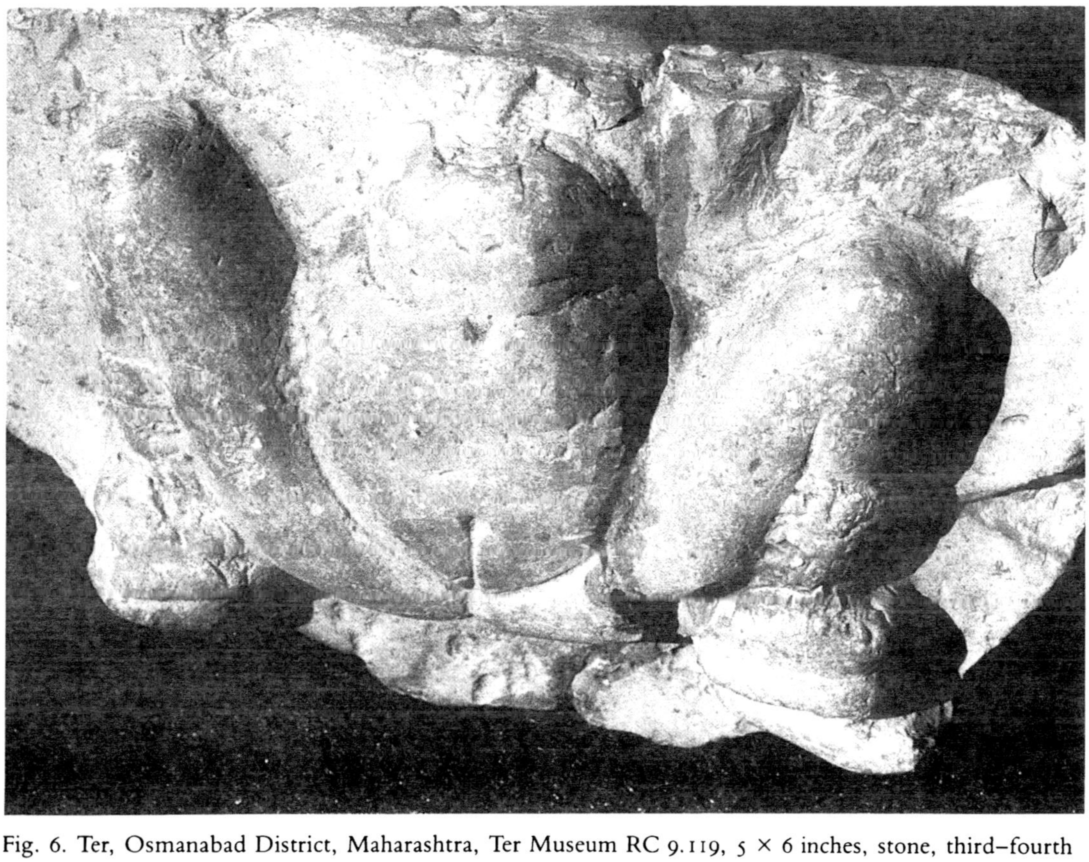

Fig. 6. Ter, Osmanabad District, Maharashtra, Ter Museum RC 9.119, 5 × 6 inches, stone, third–fourth century

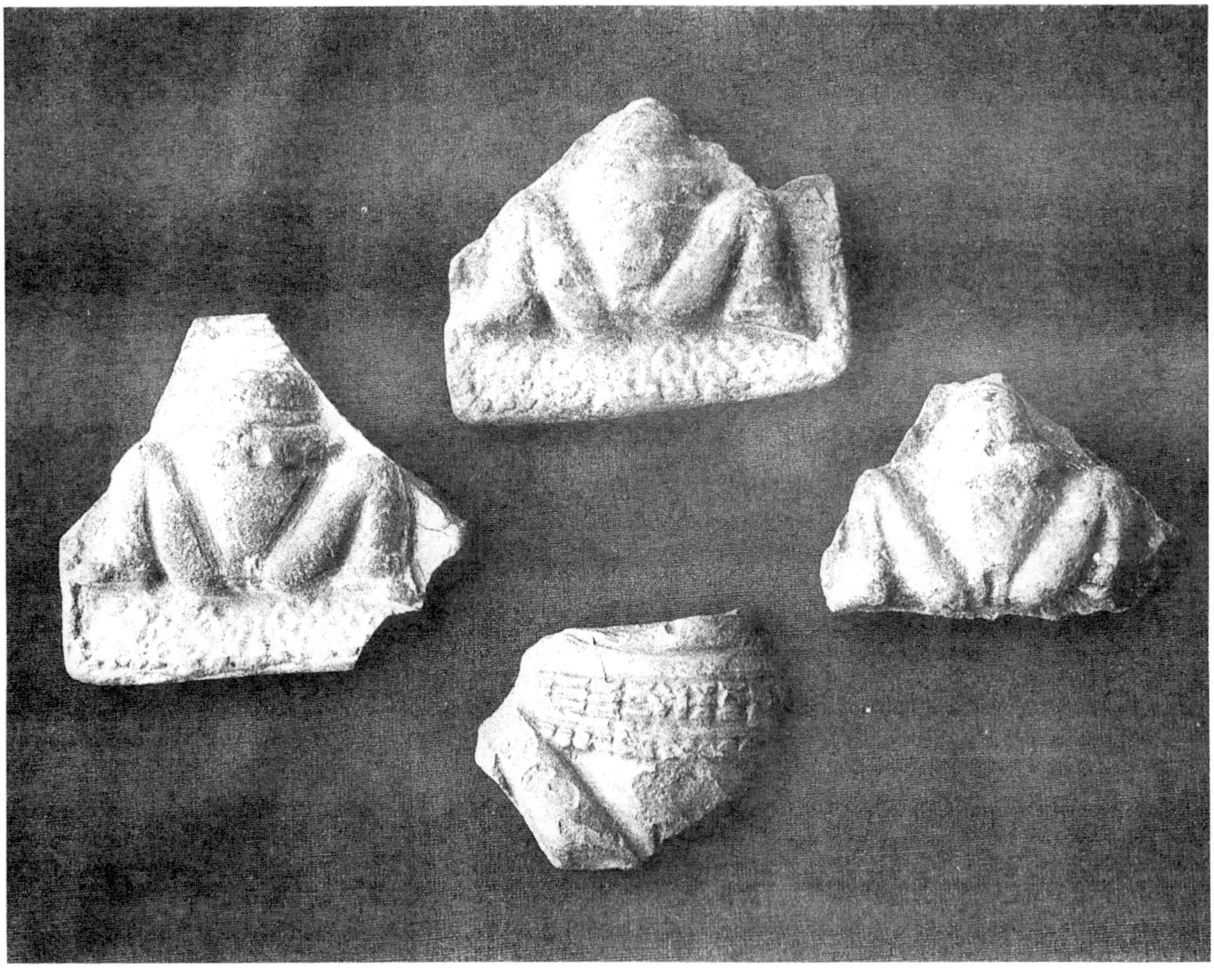

Fig. 7. Sannati, Gulbarga District, Karnataka, Karnataka Directorate of Archaeology and Museums, 2 × 2 inches, terra-cotta, third–fourth century

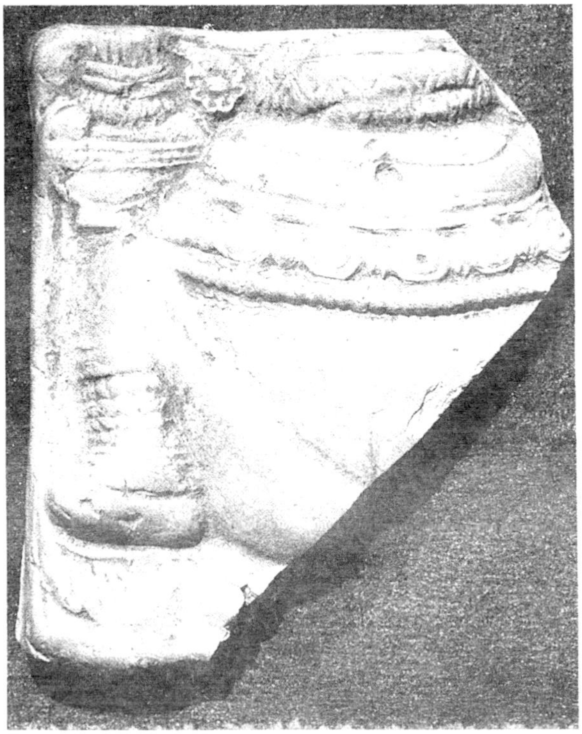

Fig. 8. Kondapur, Khammam District, Andhra, Andhra Directorate of Archaeology and Museums 119, 3½ × 3 inches, terra-cotta, third–fourth century

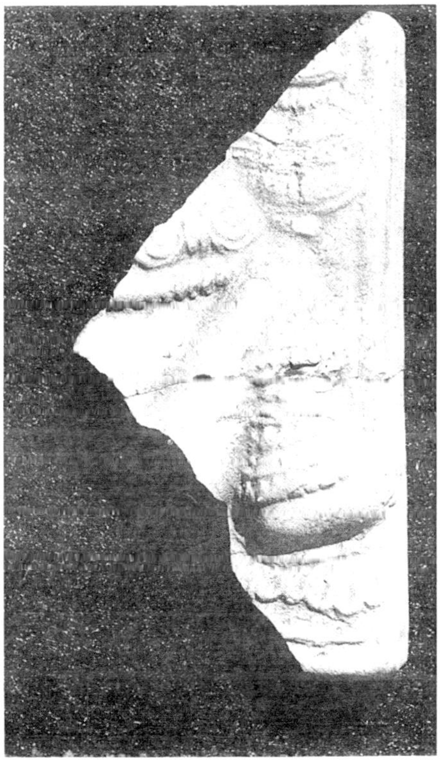

Fig. 9. Ter, Osmanabad District, Maharashtra, Ter Museum RC 1.258, 3½ × 2 inches, terra-cotta, third century

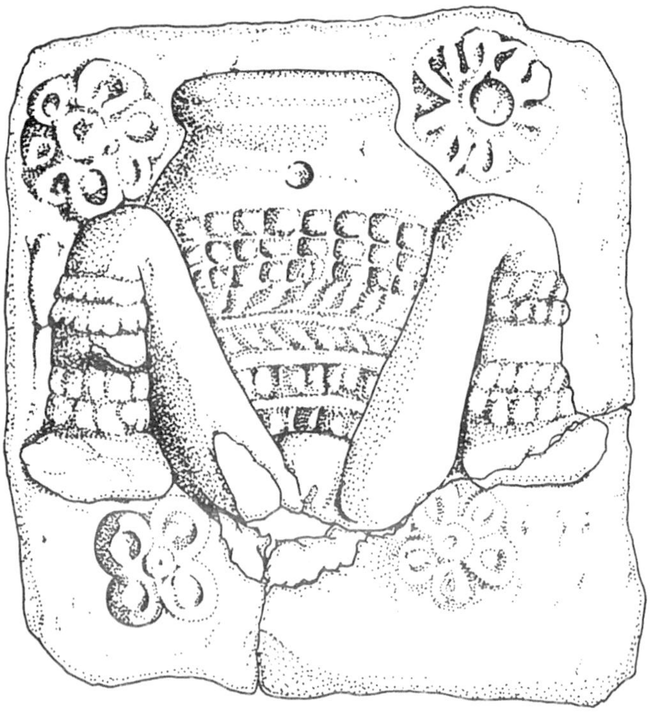

Fig. 10. Ter, Osmanabad District, Maharashtra, Ter Museum 785, size?, terra-cotta, third–fourth century

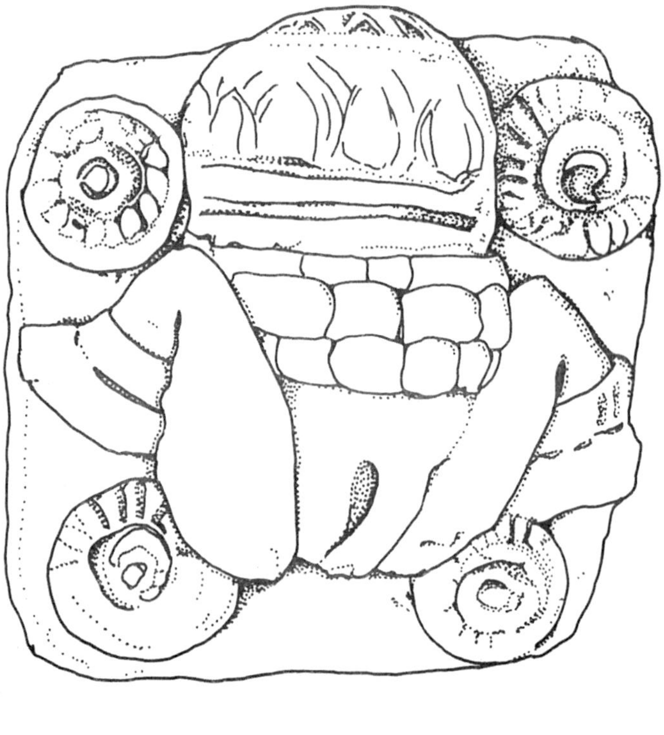

Fig. 11. Nagarjunakonda (a), Guntur District, Andhra, Archaeological Museum, Nagarjunakonda, 2 × 2 inches, terra-cotta, third–fourth century

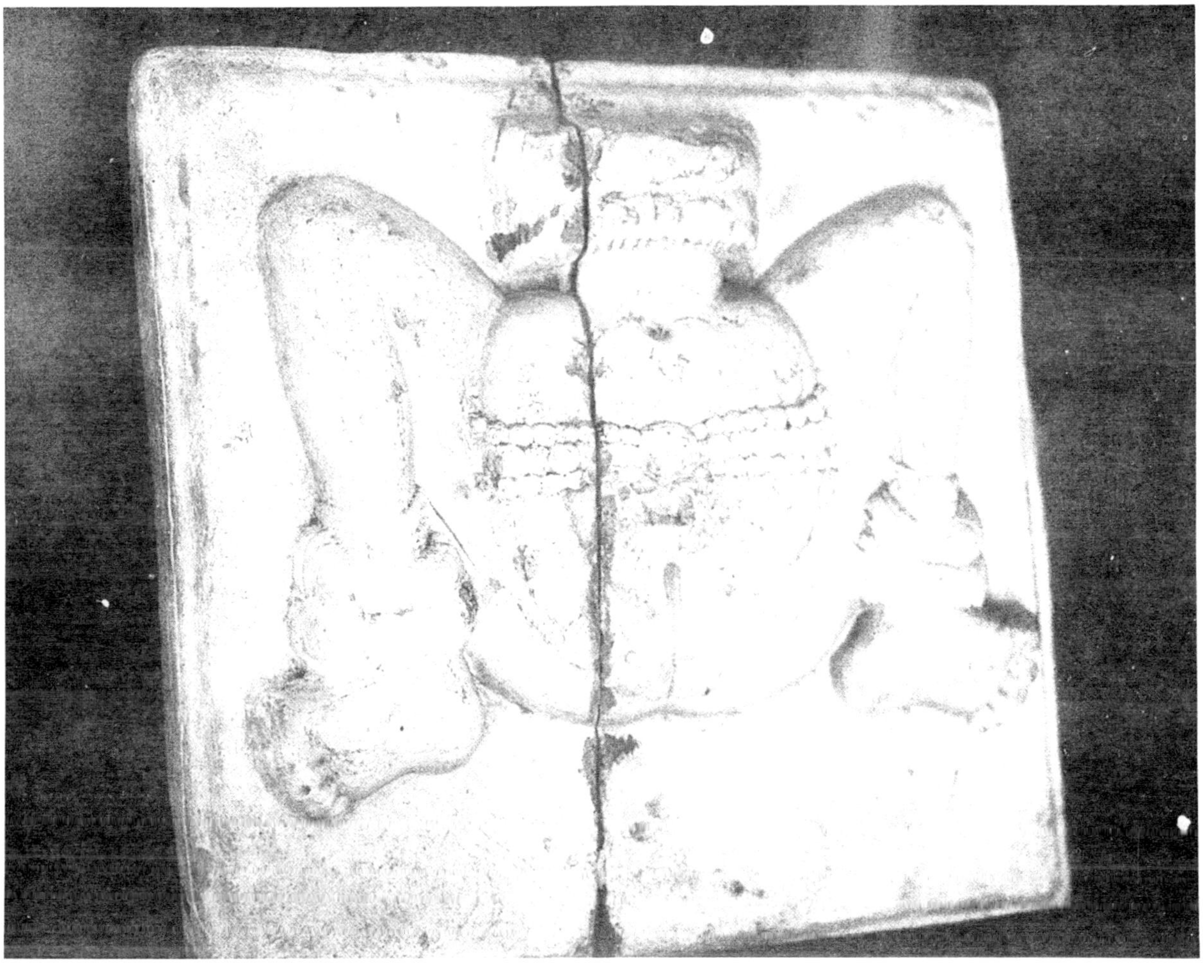

Fig. 12. Karlapalem, Guntur District, Andhra, Victoria Jubilee Museum, Vijayawada, 10 × 10 inches, stone, third–fourth century

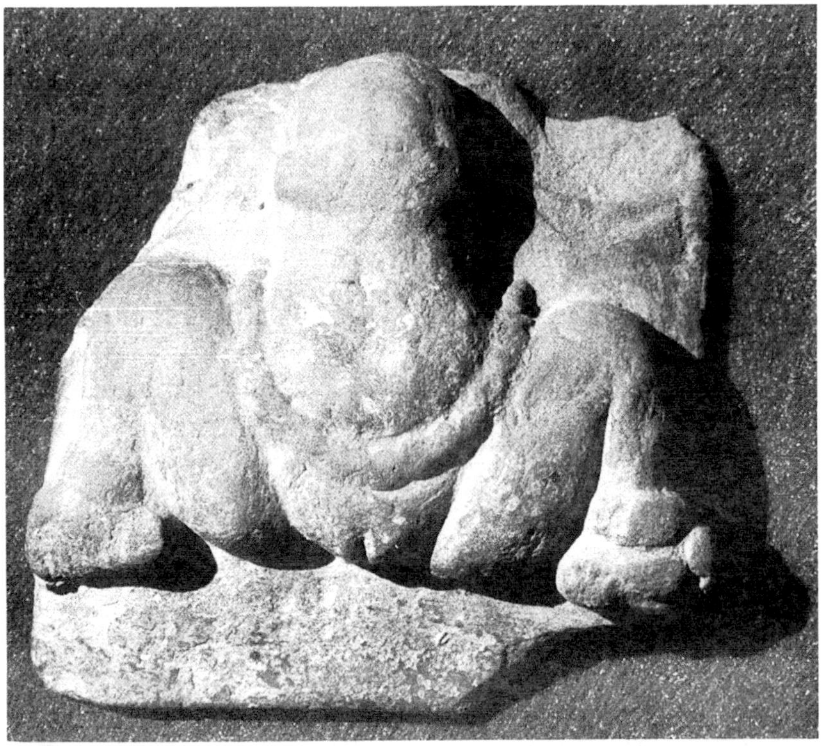

Fig. 13. Ter, Osmanabad District, Maharashtra, Ter Museum 7.219, 2¼ × 2¼ inches, terracotta, third–fourth century

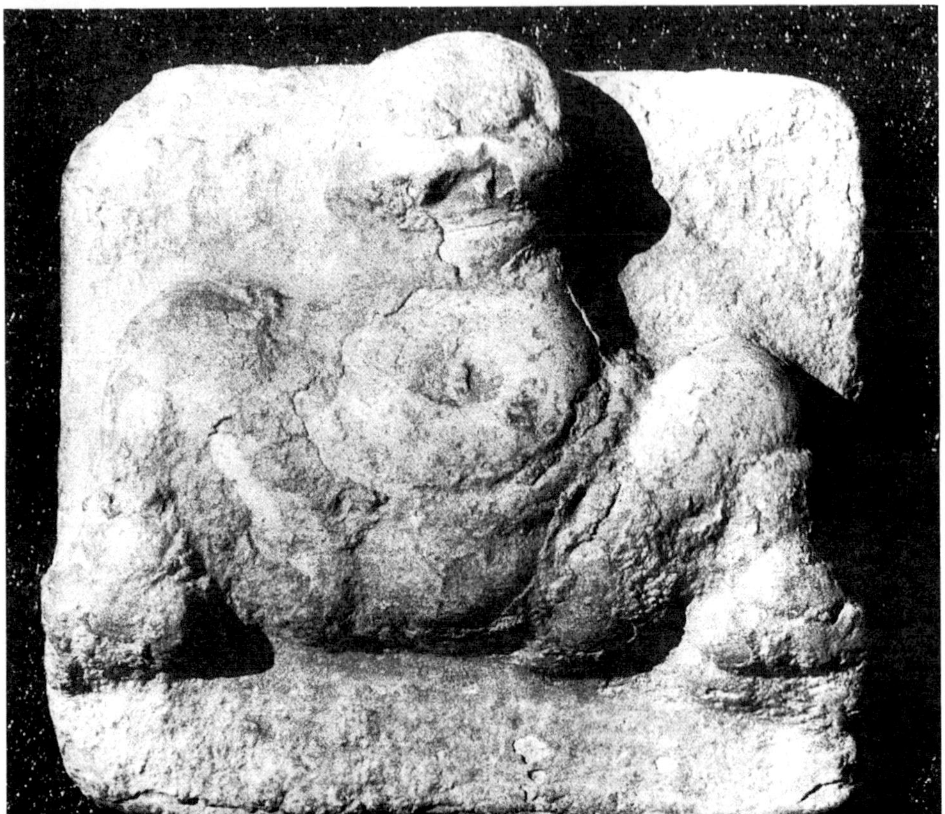

Fig. 14. Ter, Osmanabad District, Maharashtra, Ter Museum RC 7.220, 2½ × 2½ inches, terra-cotta, third–fourth century

Fig. 15. Bhita, Allahabad District, Uttar Pradesh, Allahabad Municipal Museum 299, 5 7/10 × 5 1/2 inches, stone, third–fourth century

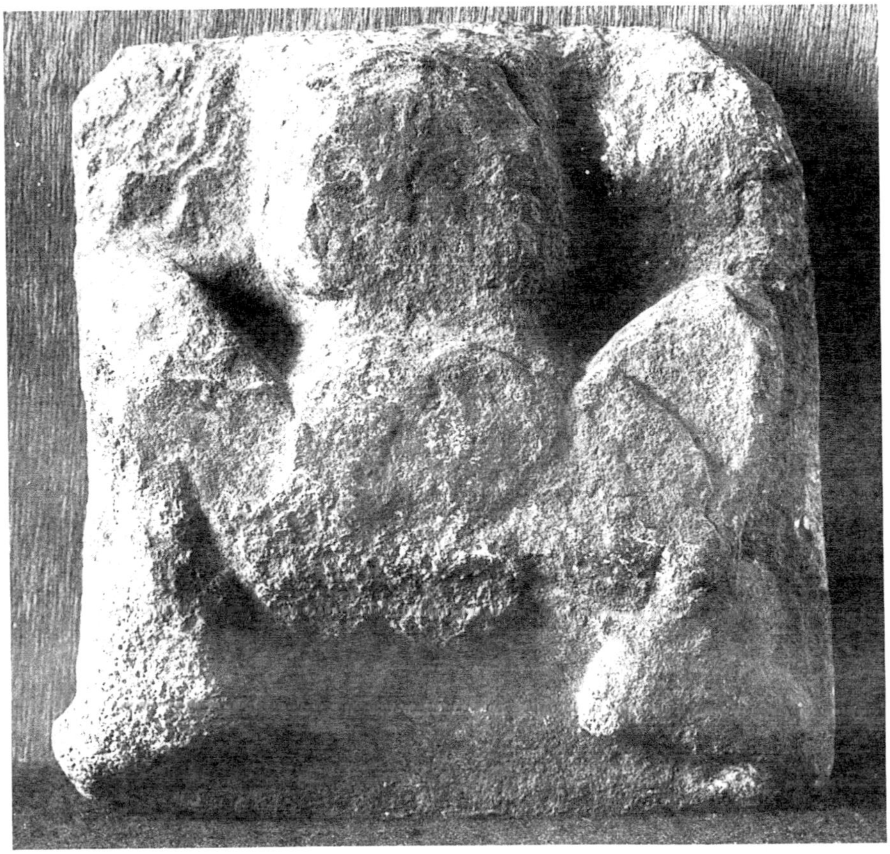

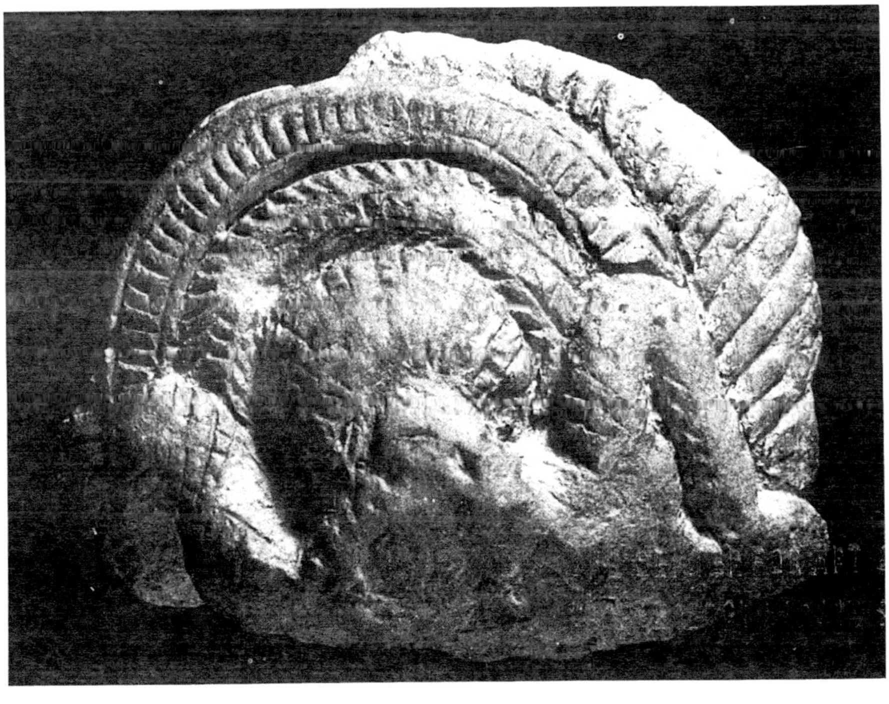

Fig. 16. Kausambi, Allahabad District, Uttar Pradesh, Allahabad Municipal Museum K5053, 1 1/4 × 2 inches, terracotta, third century

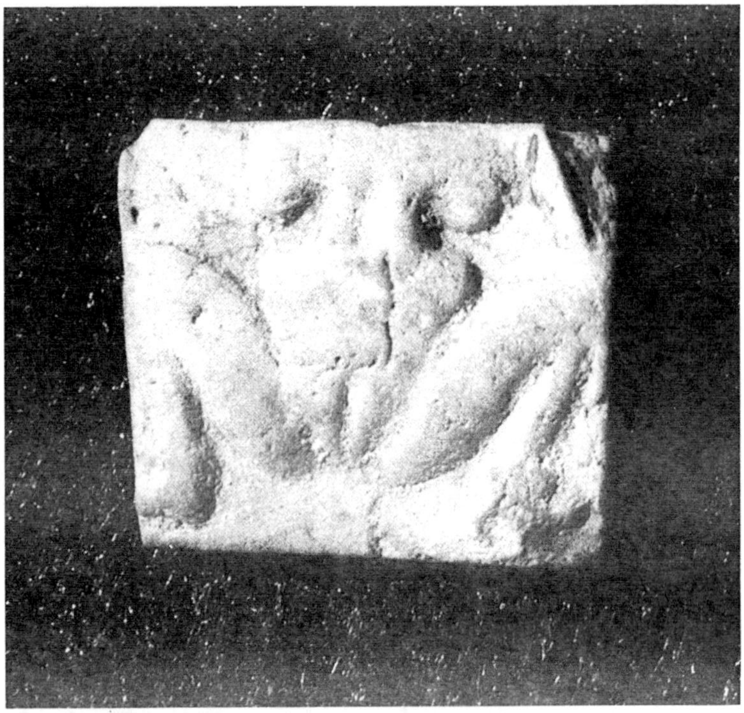

Fig. 17. Ter, Osmanabad District, Maharashtra, Ter Museum 3.80, 7/8 × 7/8 inches, faience, third century

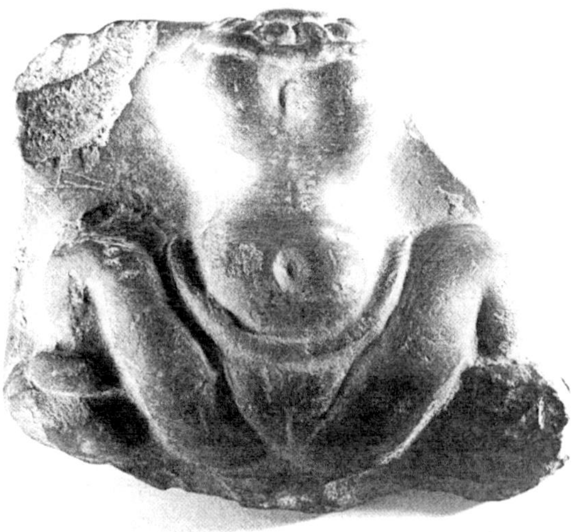

Fig. 18. Ter, Osmanabad District, Maharashtra, British Museum 1958.10–17.2, 2½ × 2½ inches, terra-cotta, second–third century

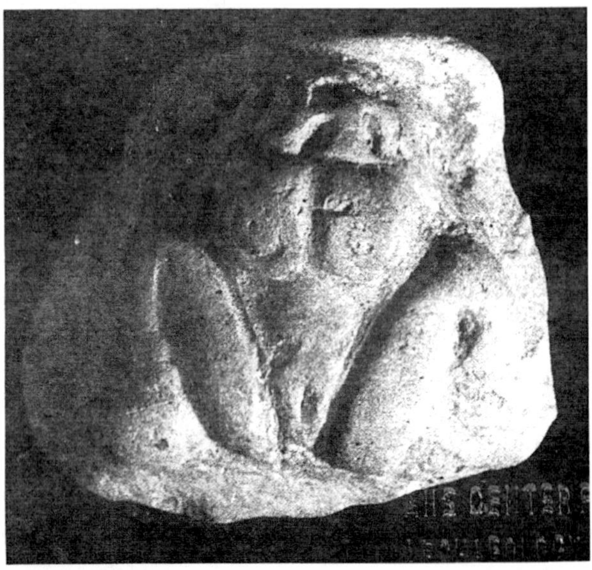

Fig. 19. Kausambi, Allahabad District, Uttar Pradesh, Allahabad Museum K3904, 1¼ × 1¼ inches, terra-cotta, fourth–fifth century

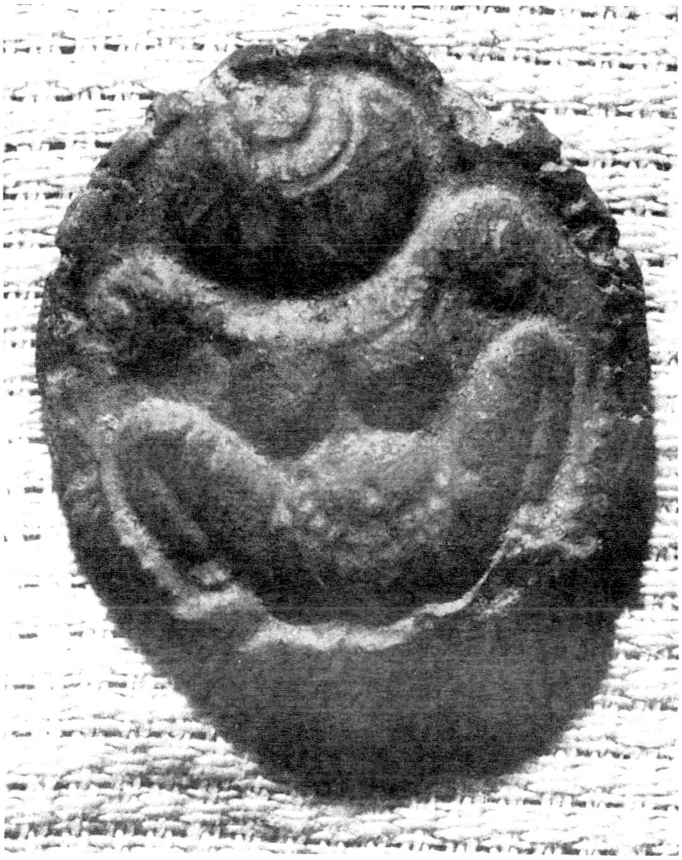

Fig. 20. Site unknown, Uttar Pradesh, Kanoria Collection, Patna, Bihar, 4-inch diameter, terra-cotta, fourth–fifth century

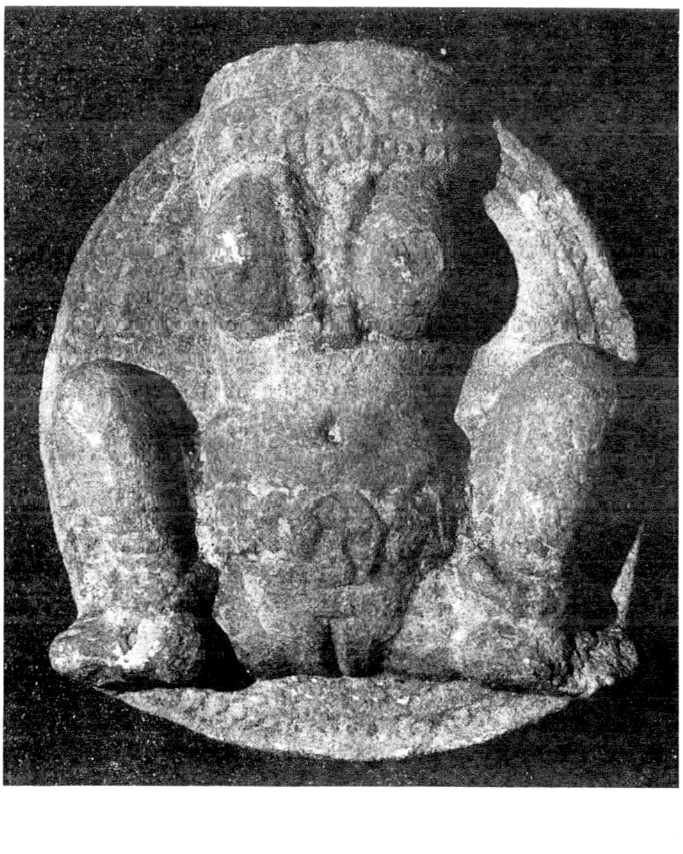

Fig. 21. Kausambi, Allahabad District, Uttar Pradesh, Indian Museum, Calcutta AI2688, 5 × 4½ inches, stone, fourth–fifth century

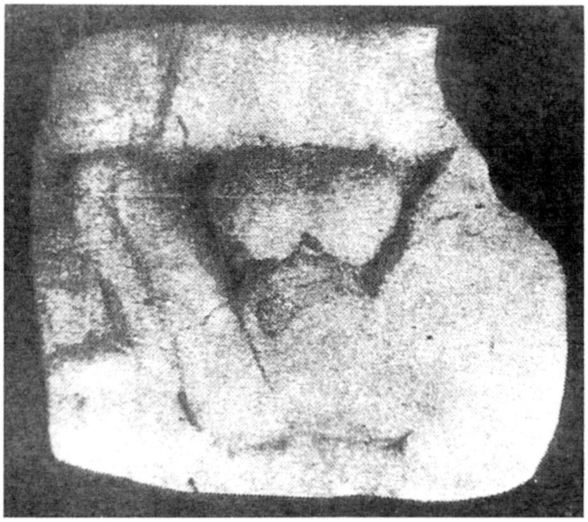

Fig. 22. Alapur (a), Aurangabad District, Maharashtra, Marathwada University Museum, 4 × 4 inches, stone, fourth–sixth century

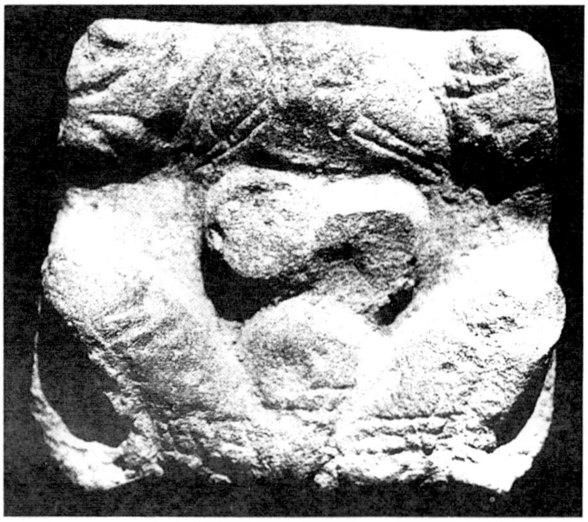

Fig. 23. Alapur (b), Aurangabad District, Maharashtra, Nagpur University Museum, 2¼ × 2½ inches, stone, fourth–sixth century

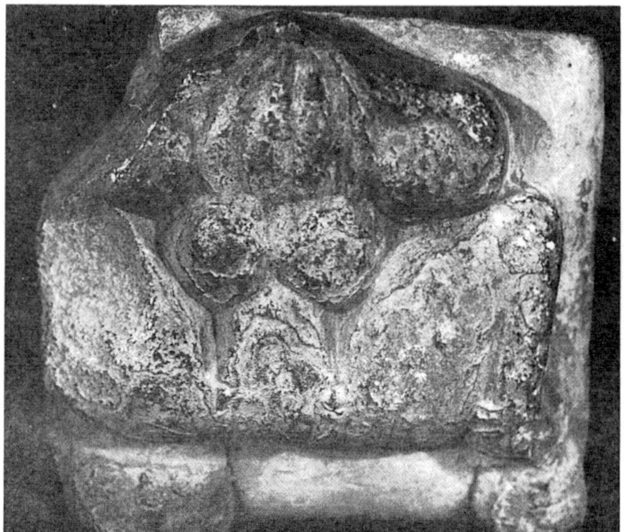

Fig. 24. Paunar (a), Wardha District, Maharashtra, private collection, 4½ × 4½ inches, stone, fourth century

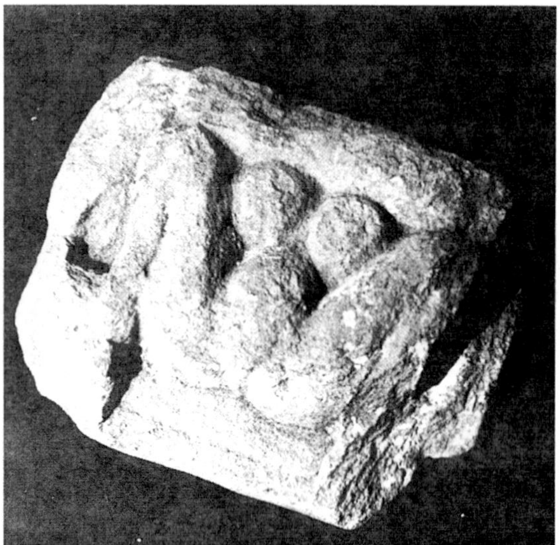

Fig. 25. Paunar (b), Wardha District, Maharashtra, private collection, 4¼ × 3 inches, stone, fourth century

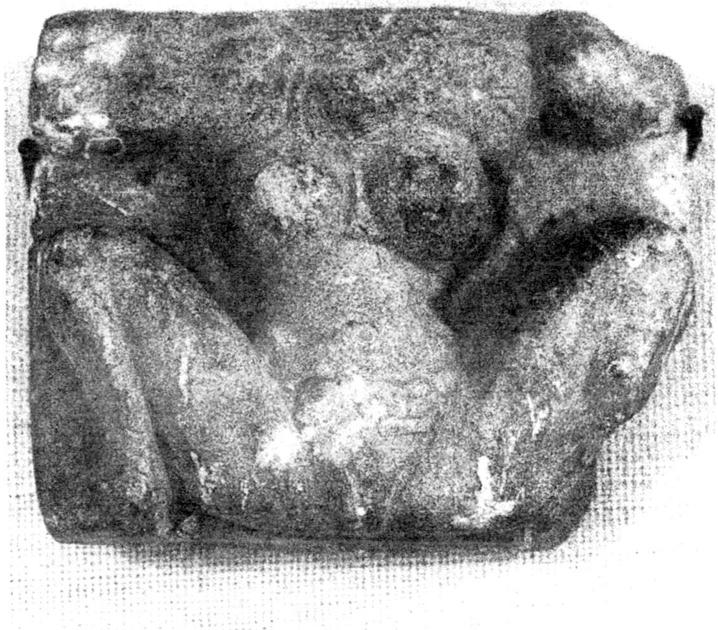

Fig. 26. Sanchi, Raisen District, Madhya Pradesh, Archaeological Museum, 2 × 2 inches, stone, fourth century

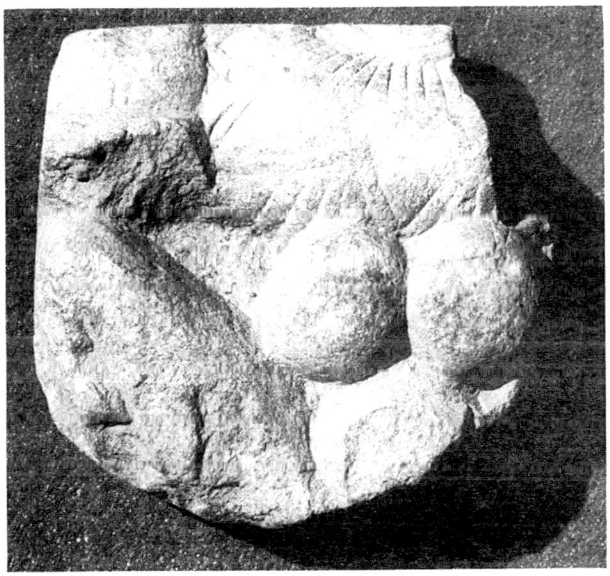

Fig. 27. Ter, Osmanabad District, Maharashtra, Ter Museum 9.148, 2¼ × 2¼ inches, stone, fourth century

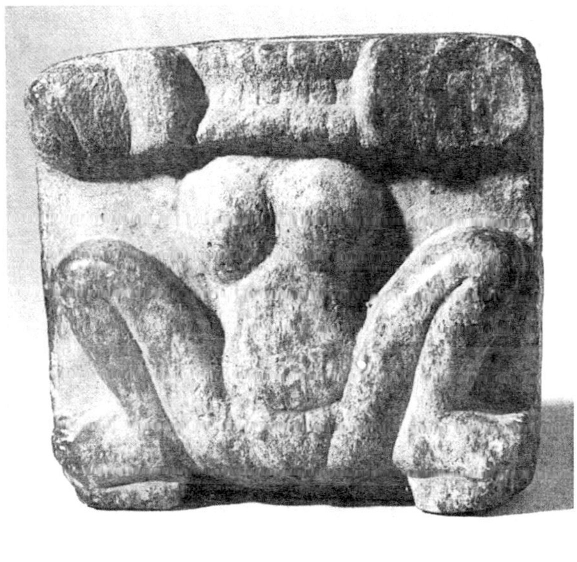

Fig. 28. Pauni, Nagpur District, Maharashtra, British Museum 1976.4–5.2, 2⅝ × 3 inches, stone, fourth–fifth century

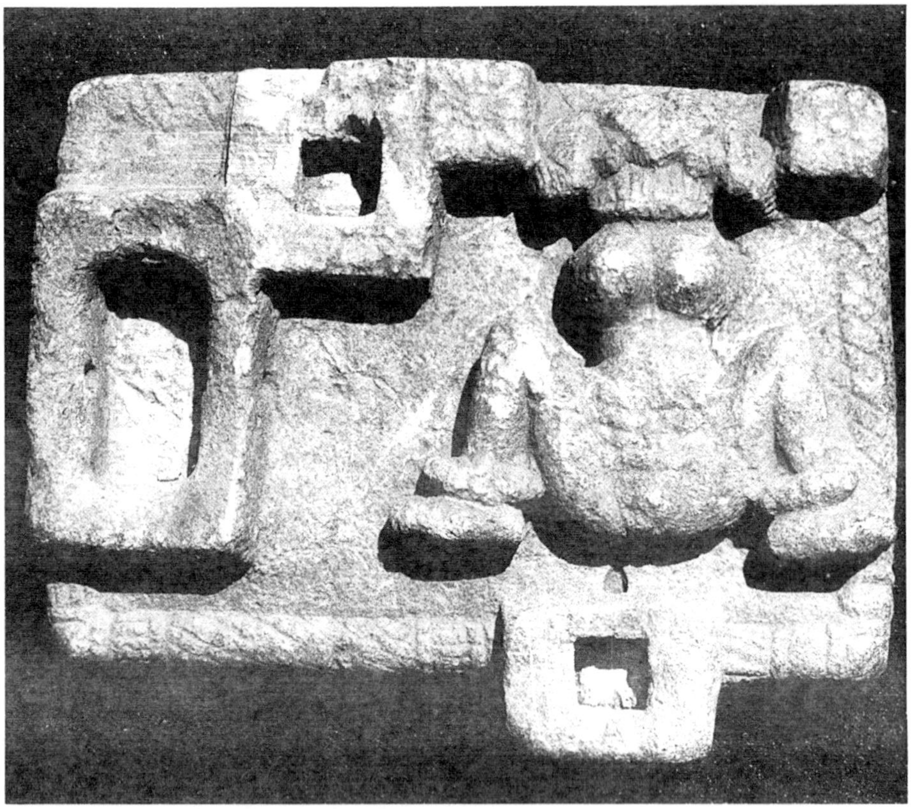

Fig. 29. Ramatola (a), Bhandara District, Maharashtra, Central Museum, Nagpur, 6 × 8¾ inches, stone, fourth–sixth century

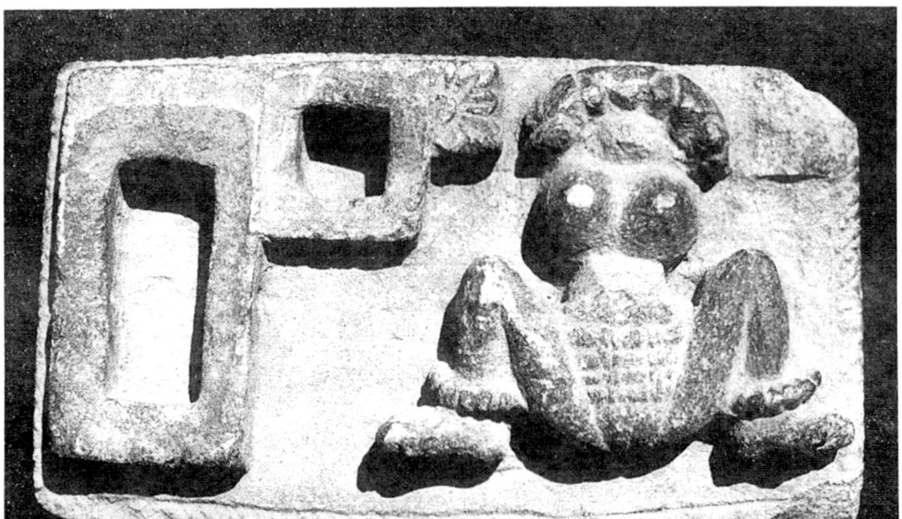

Fig. 30. Ramatola (b), Bhandara District, Maharashtra, Central Museum, Nagpur, 5 × 7¾ inches, stone, fourth–sixth century

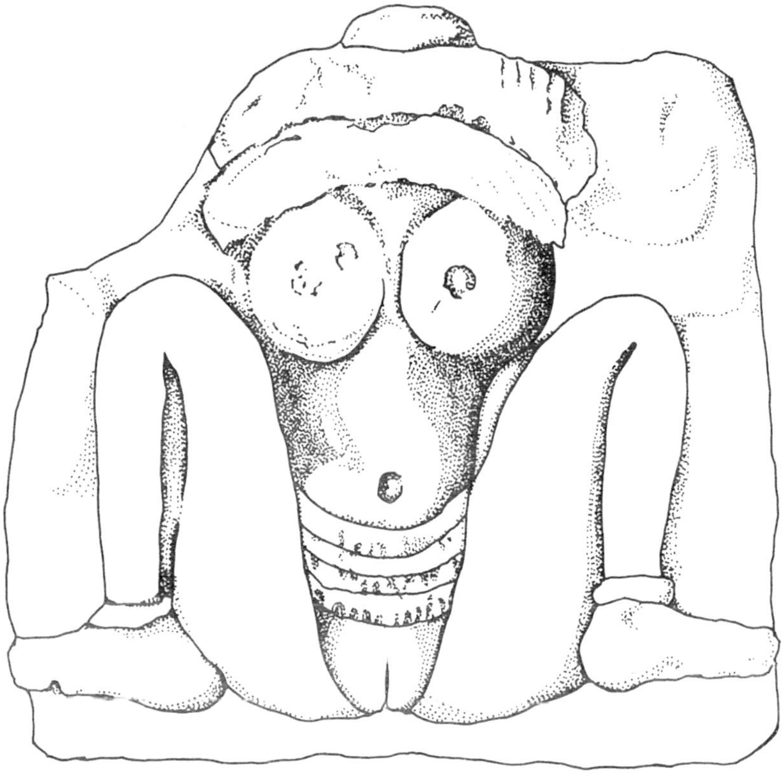

Fig. 31. Mahurjhari (a), Nagpur District, Maharashtra, Sharadasrama, Yeotmal, size?, stone, seventh century

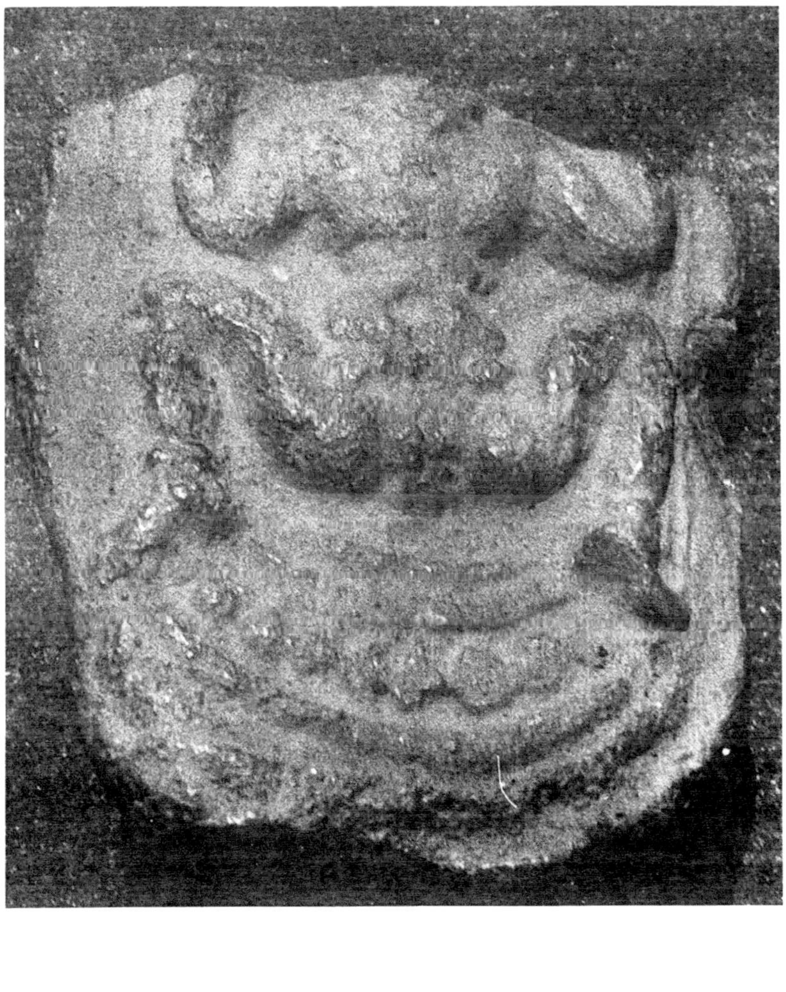

Fig. 32. Yellesvaram, Nalgonda District, Andhra Pradesh, Andhra Directorate of Archaeology and Museums 31, 2 × 1¾ inches, terracotta, third century

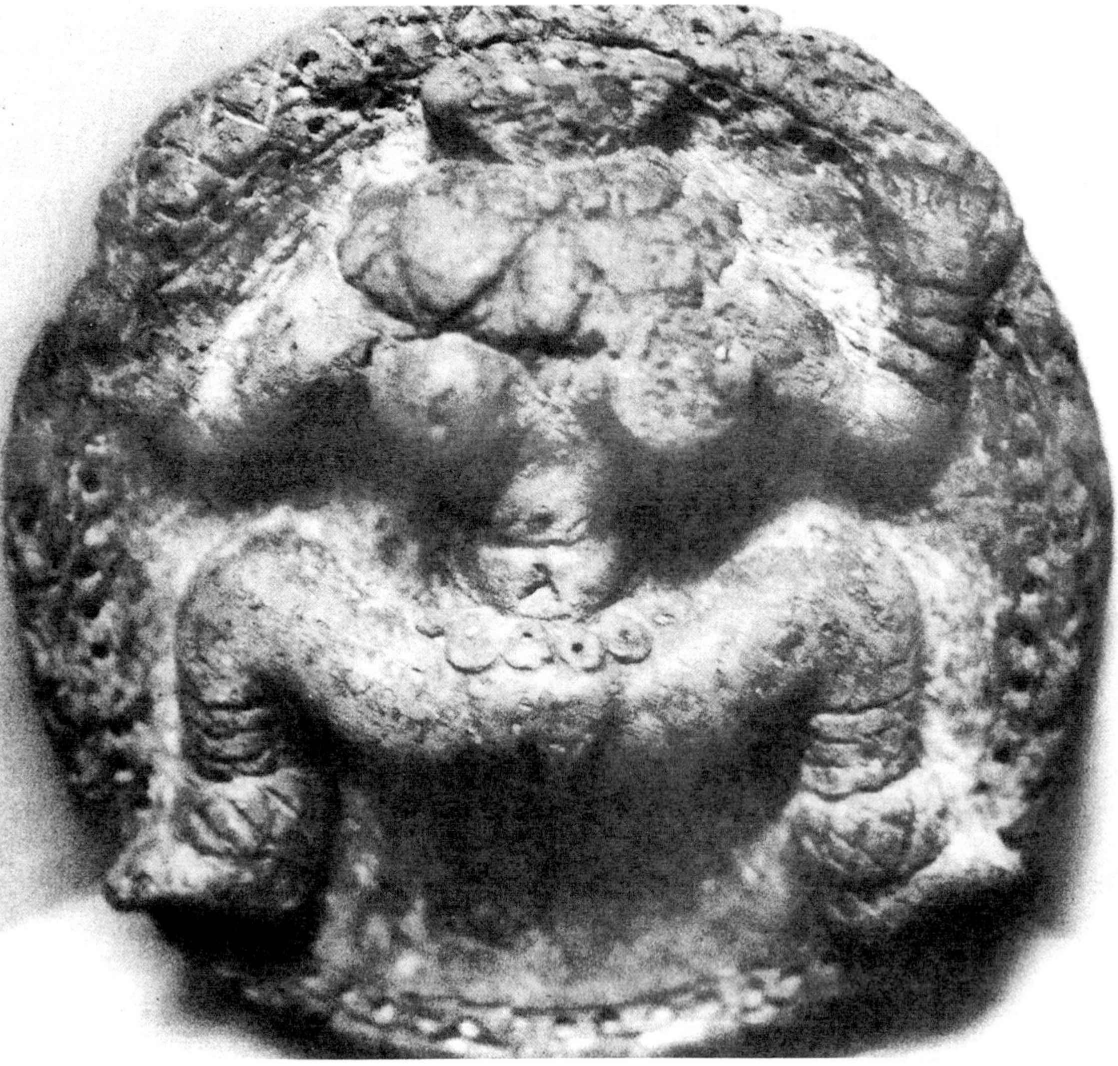

Fig. 33. Bhita, Allahabad District, Uttar Pradesh, Indian Museum, Calcutta AI0431, 4⅝ inches diameter, terra-cotta, fourth–sixth century

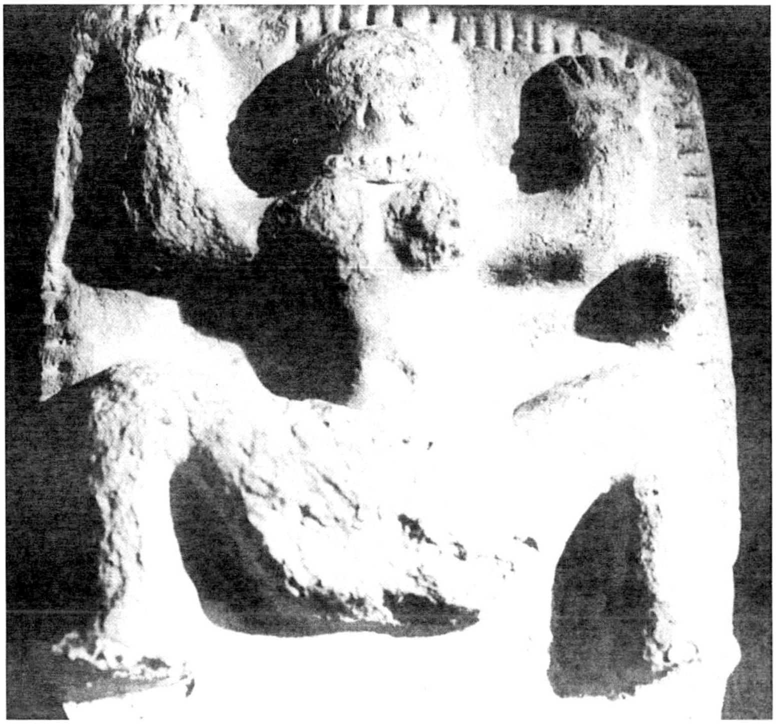

Fig. 34. Kausambi, Allahabad District, Uttar Pradesh, Patna Museum Arch 7716, 7½ × 6⅞ inches, terra-cotta, third–fourth century

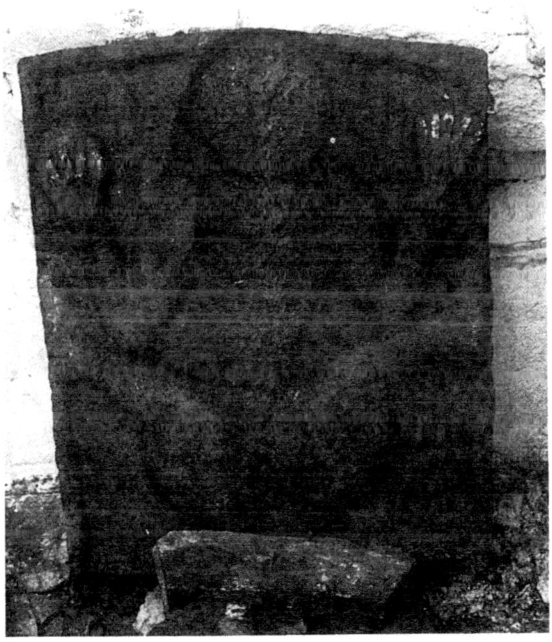

Fig. 35. Bilagi, Siddheśvara temple, Bijapur District, Karnataka, c. 4 feet, stone, twentieth century

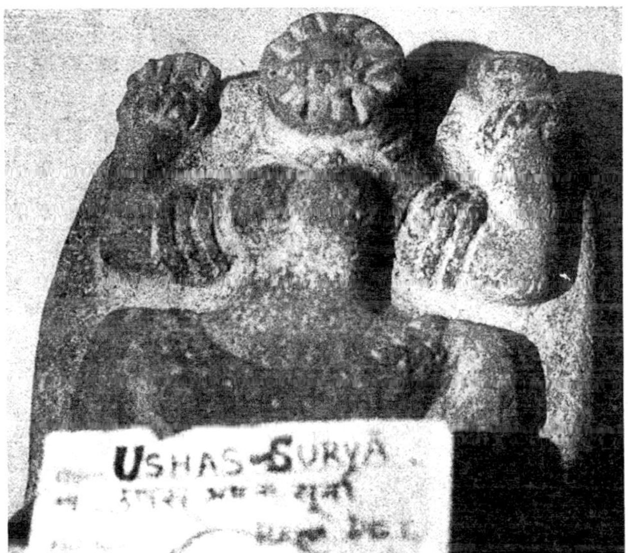

Fig. 36. Bundelkhand, Rewa District, Madhya Pradesh, State Museum, Dhubela, M.P., 5 × 5 inches, stone, third–fourth century

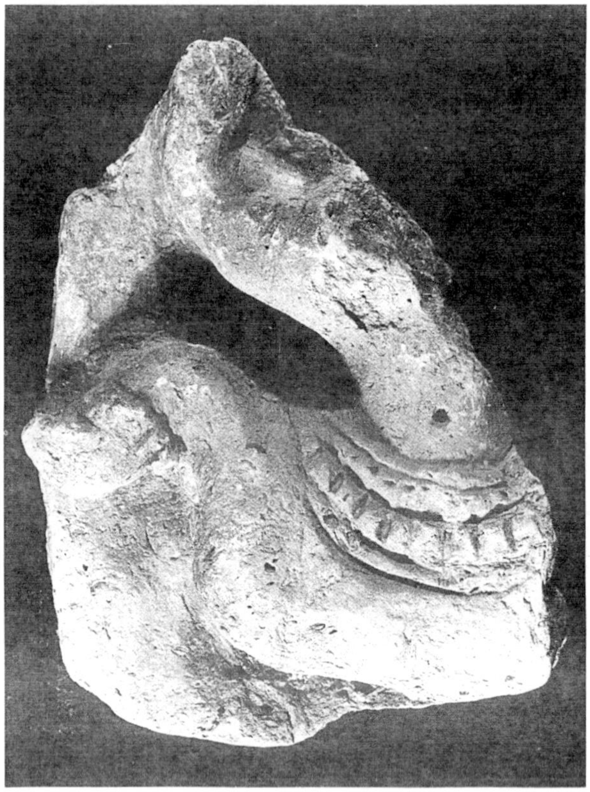

Fig. 37. Kausambi, Allahabad District, Uttar Pradesh, Allahabad Municipal Museum 5034, 6¼ × 4¼ inches, terra-cotta, third–fourth century

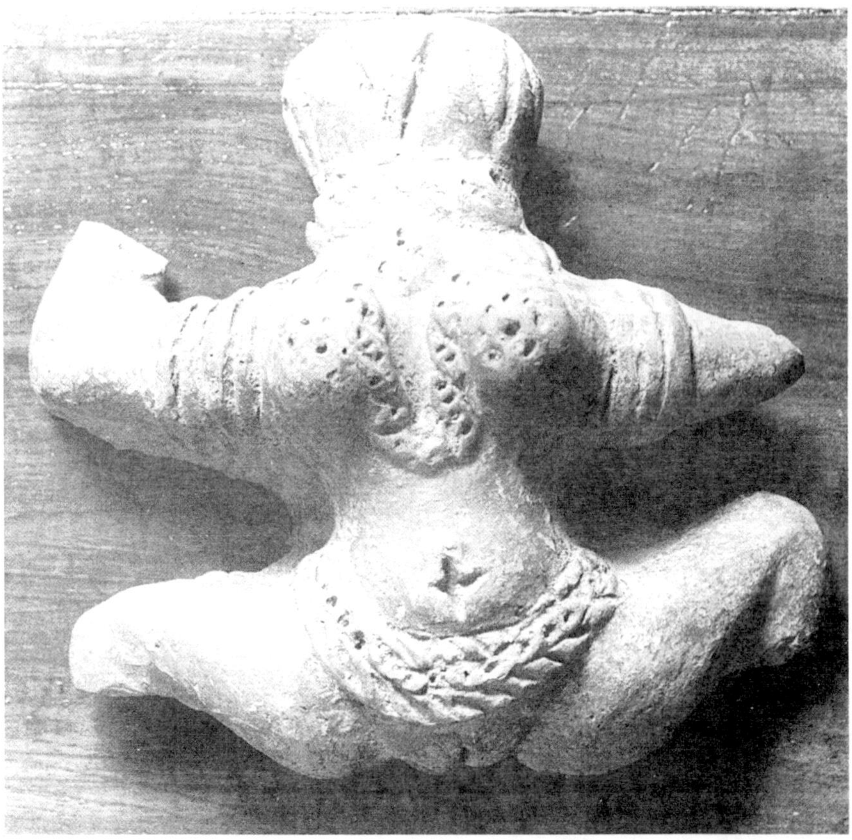

Fig. 38. Jhusi, Allahabad District, Uttar Pradesh, Allahabad Municipal Museum 4617, 5 × 5½ inches, terra-cotta, fourth century

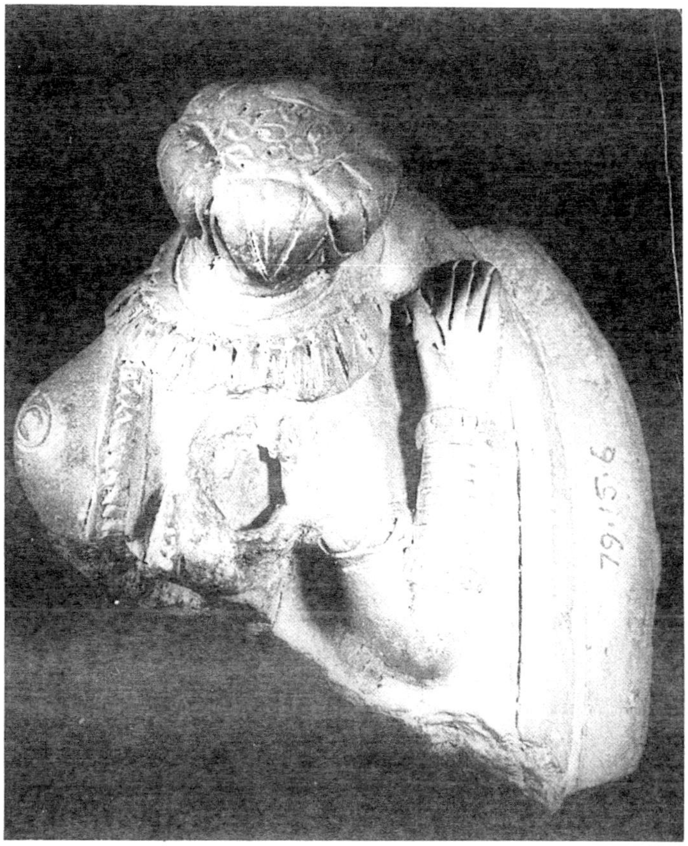

Fig. 39. Kausambi, Allahabad District, Uttar Pradesh, State Museum, Lucknow 79.15.6, height 8 inches (fragment), terra-cotta, fourth century

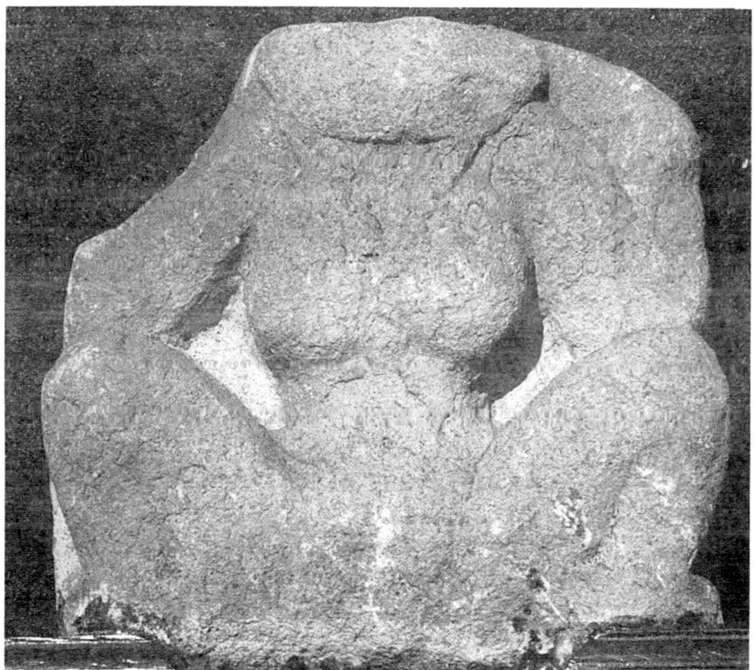

Fig. 40. Kausambi, Allahabad District, Uttar Pradesh, Patna Museum 7606, 5 × 5½ inches, stone, date?

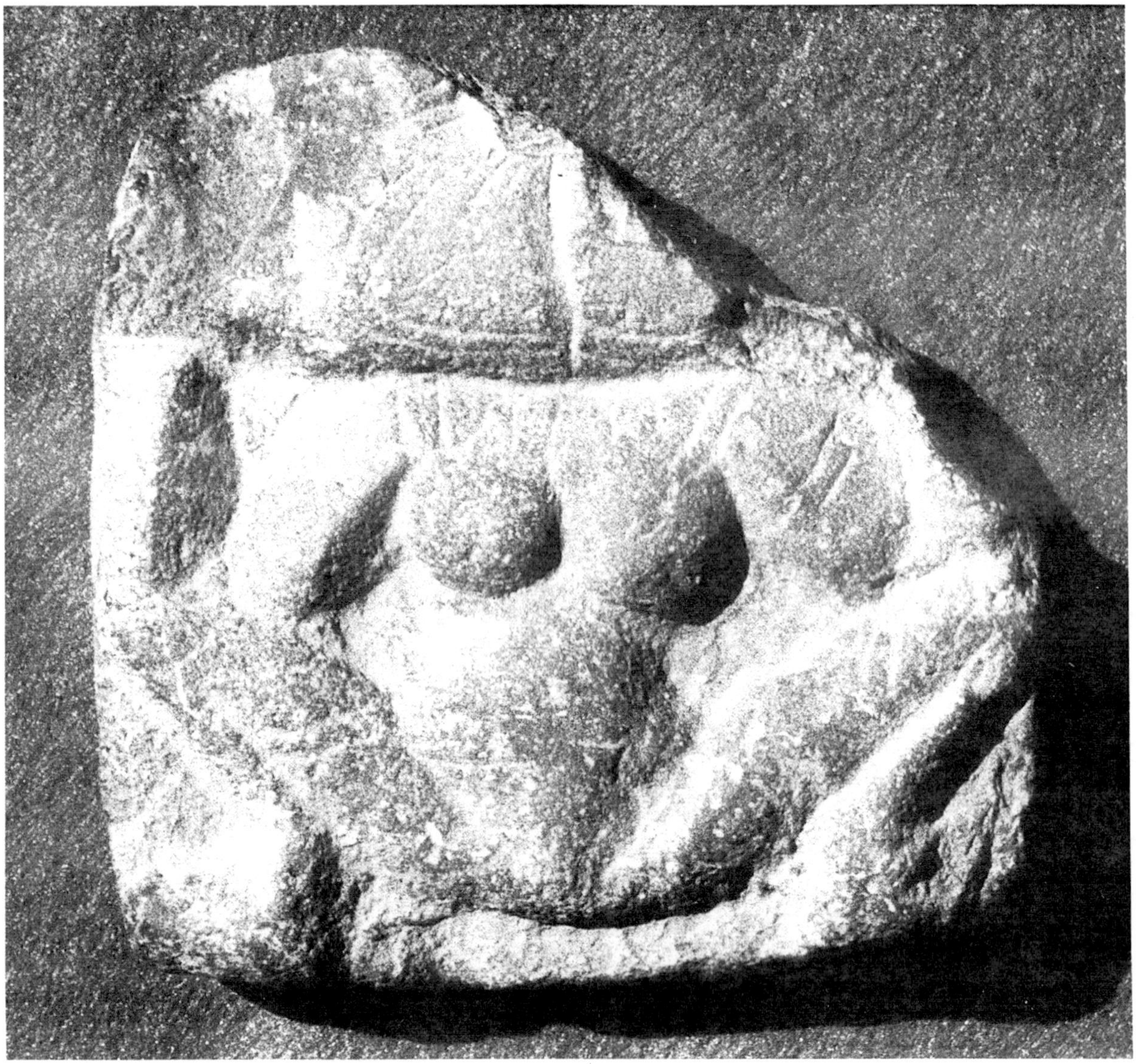

Fig. 41. Ter, Osmanabad District, Maharashtra, Ter Museum 9.147, 2¾ × 2¾ inches, stone, fourth century

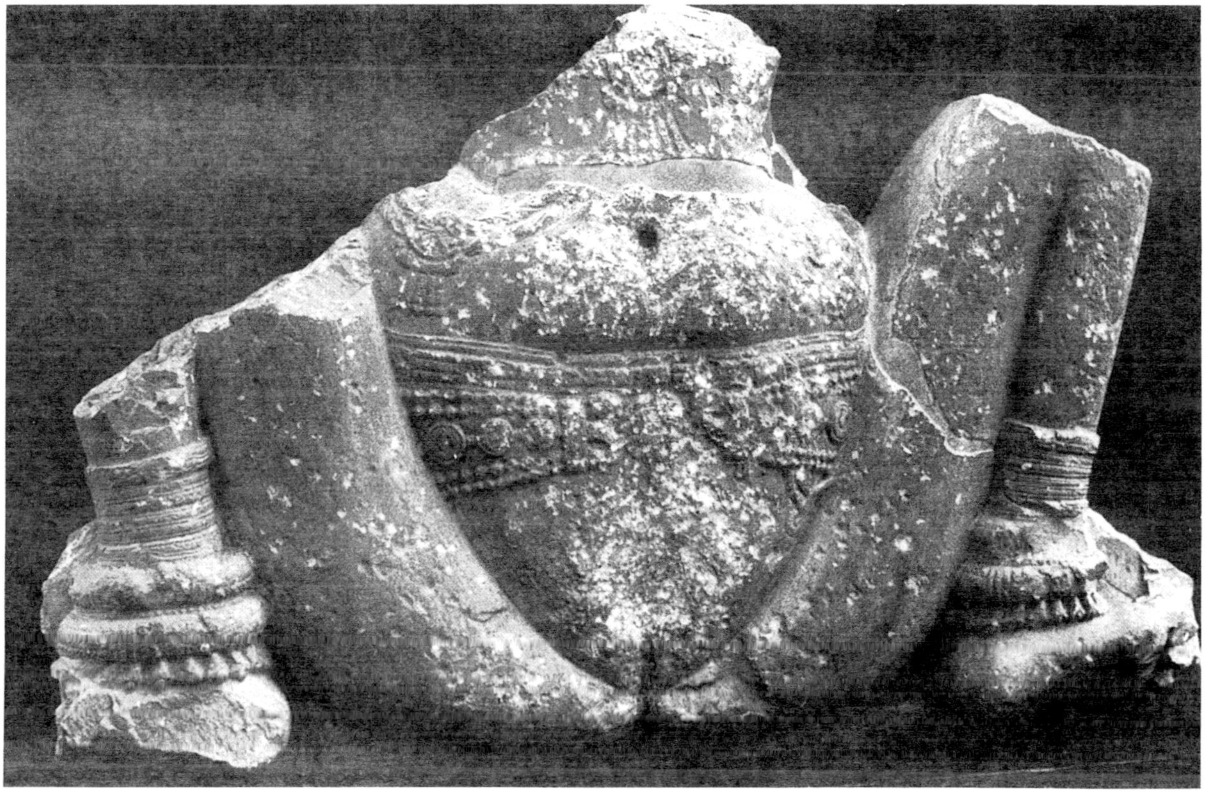

Fig. 42. Nagarjunakonda (b), Guntur District, Andhra Pradesh, Archaeological Museum, Nagarjunakonda, 3–4 feet square, stone, late third–early fourth century

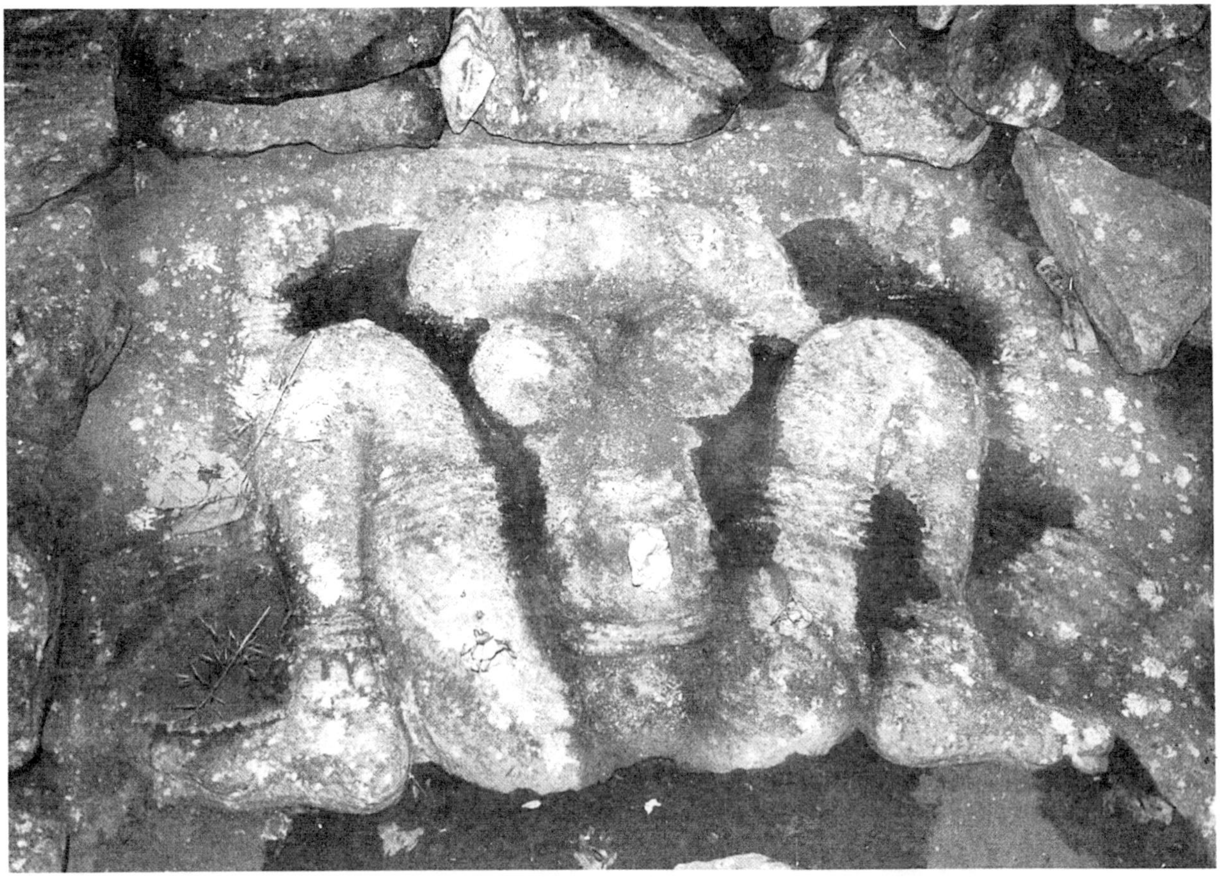

Fig. 43. Siddhanakolla, Lakulīśa temple, Bijapur District, Karnataka, 32 × 39 inches, stone, late seventh century

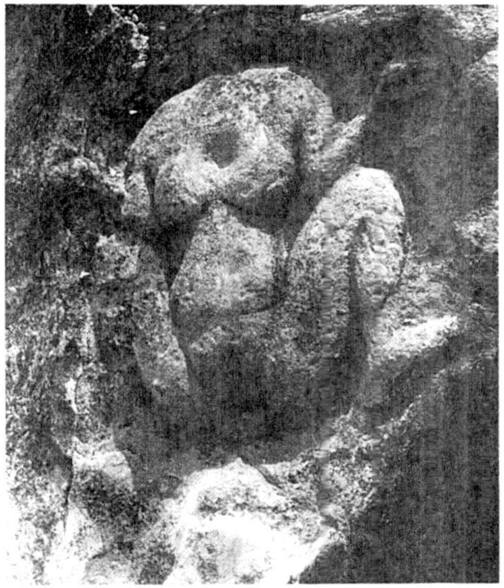

Fig. 44. Siddhanakolla, path marker

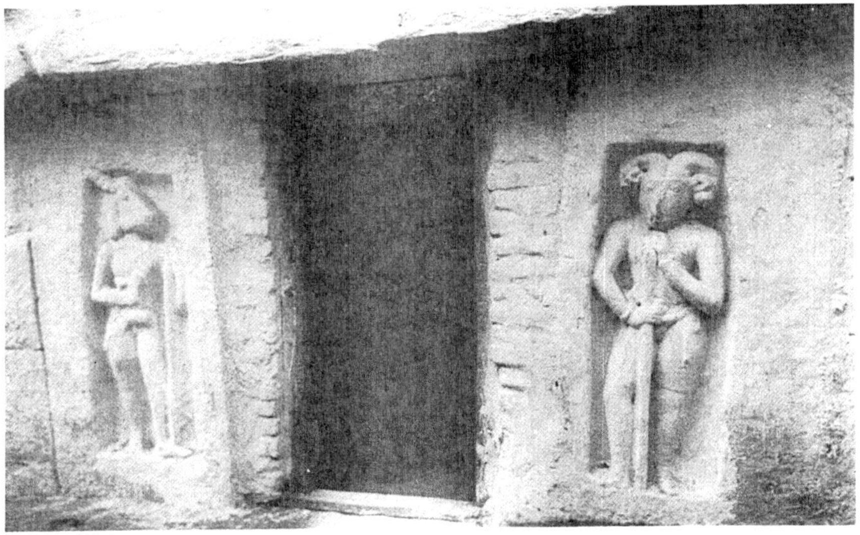

Fig. 45. Siddhanakolla, Lakulīśa temple subshrine, Bijapur District, Karnataka, goat-headed guards, late seventh century

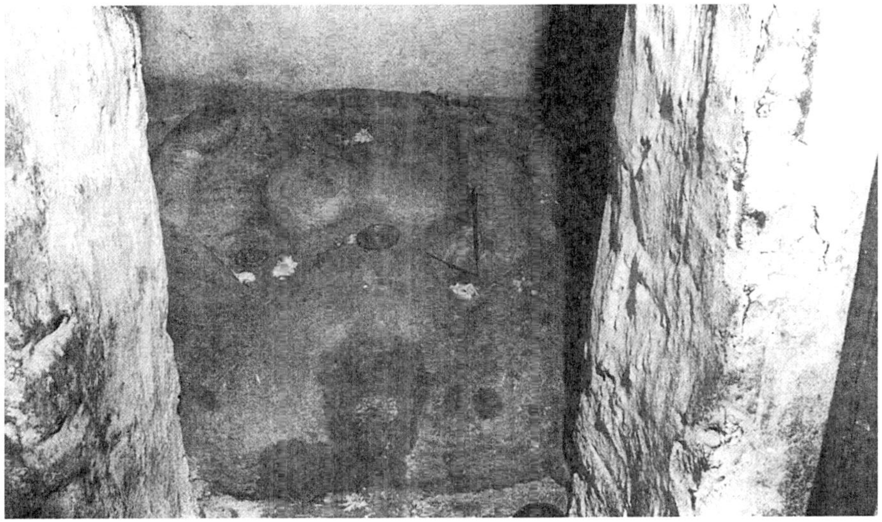

Fig. 46. Alampur, Bala Brahmā temple, Kurnool District, Andhra Pradesh, 3–4 feet square, stone, late seventh century

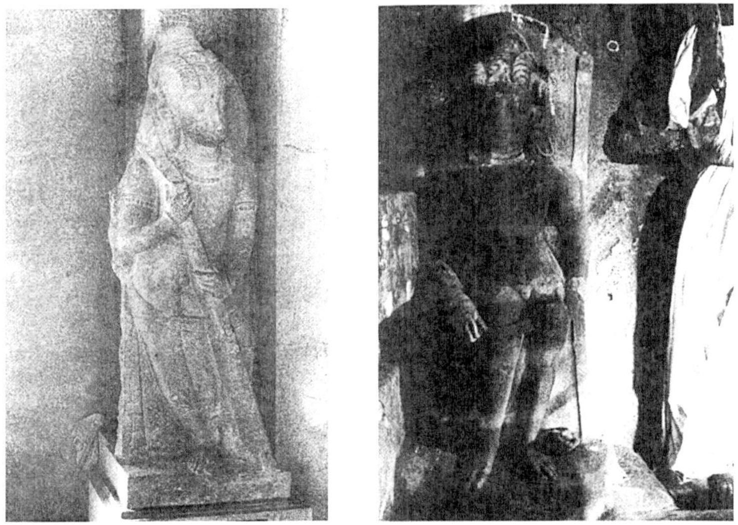

Fig. 47. a, b. Alampur, Kurnool District, Andhra Pradesh, goat-headed guards, Alampur Museum and Bala Brahmā temple, late seventh century

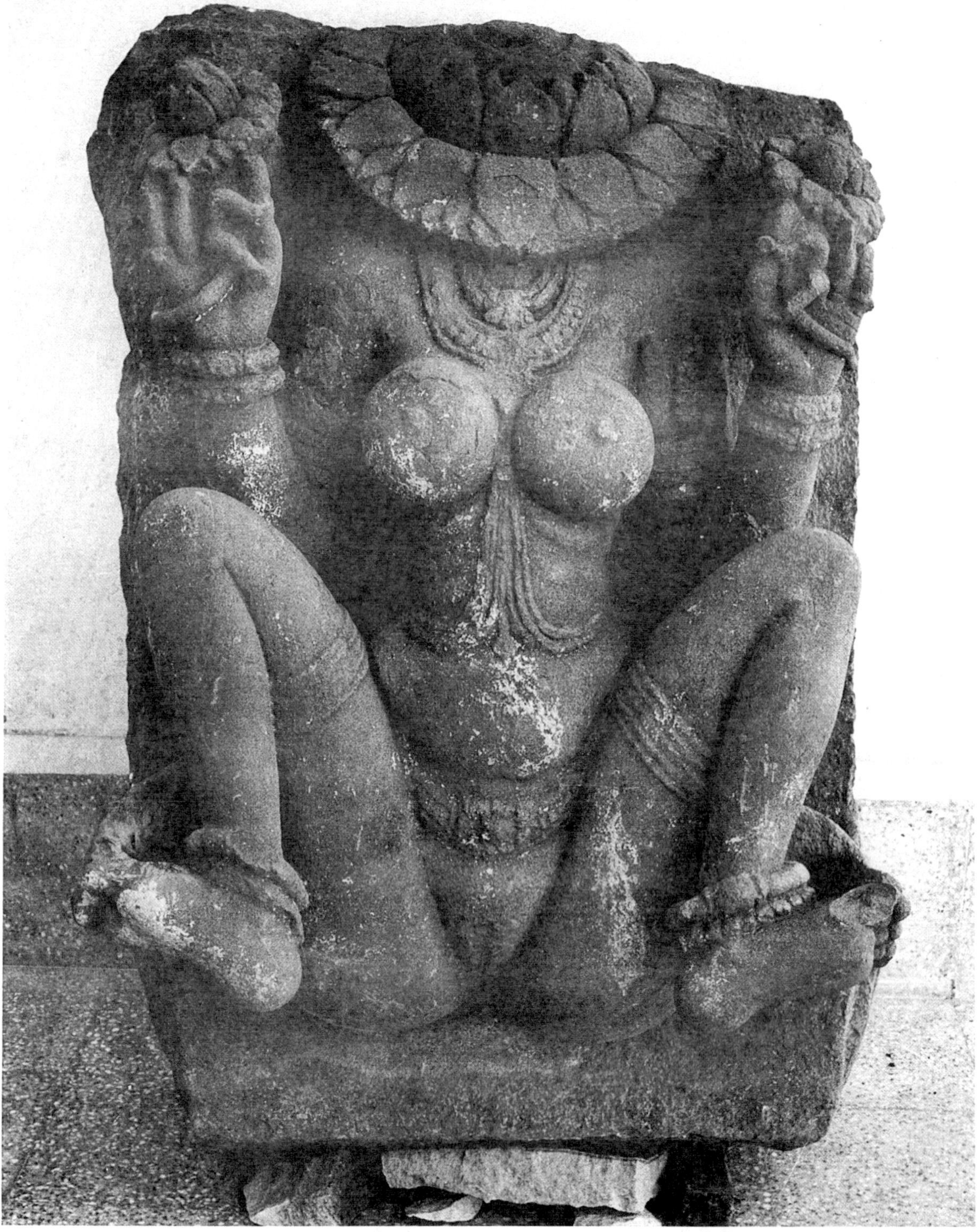

Fig. 48. Naganathakolla, Nāganātha temple, Bijapur District, Karnataka, Badami Museum B36, 38 × 28 inches, stone, late seventh century

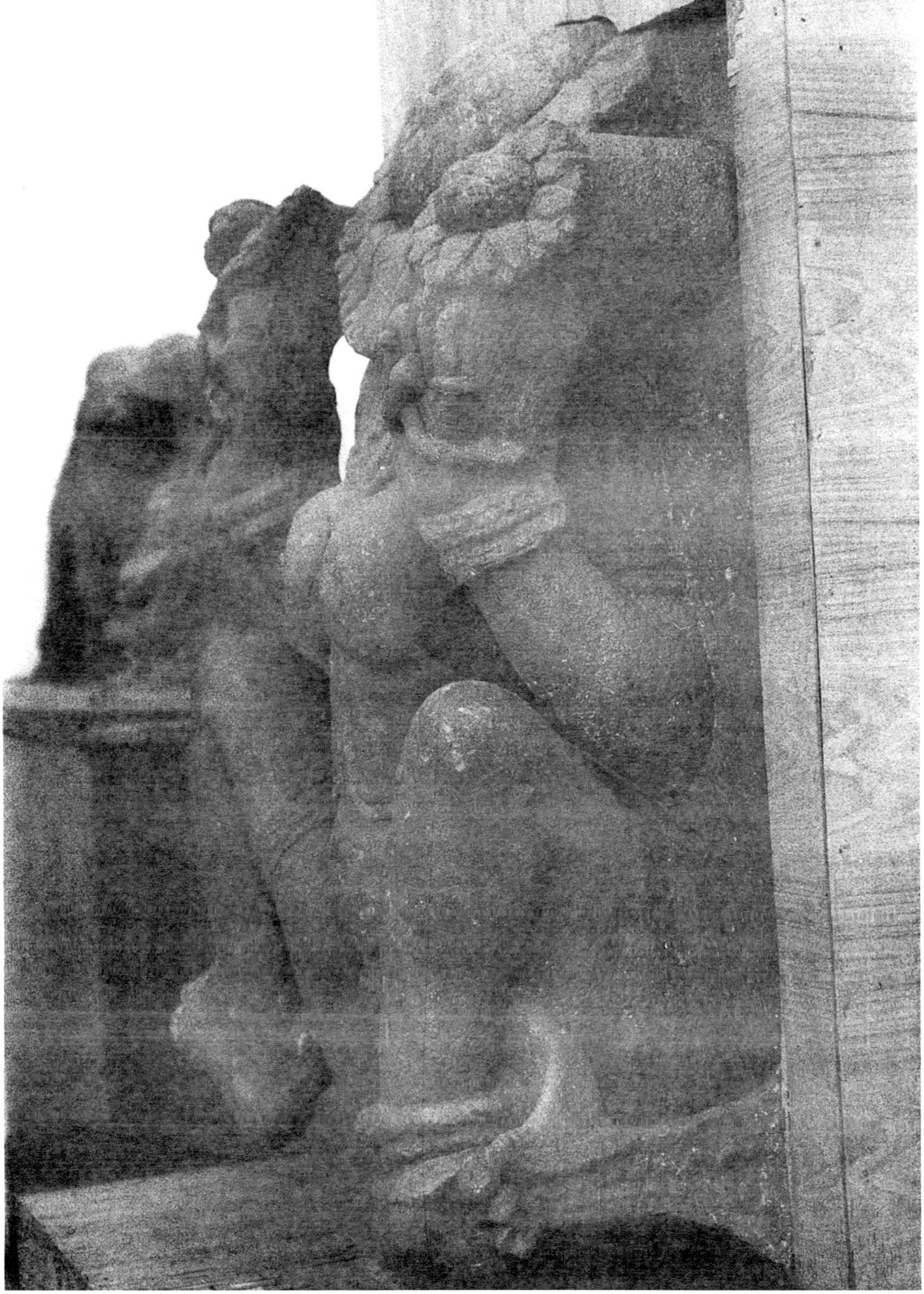

Fig. 49. Naganathakolla, Nāganātha temple, Bijapur District, Karnataka, Badami Museum B36, 38 × 28 inches, stone, late seventh century, side view

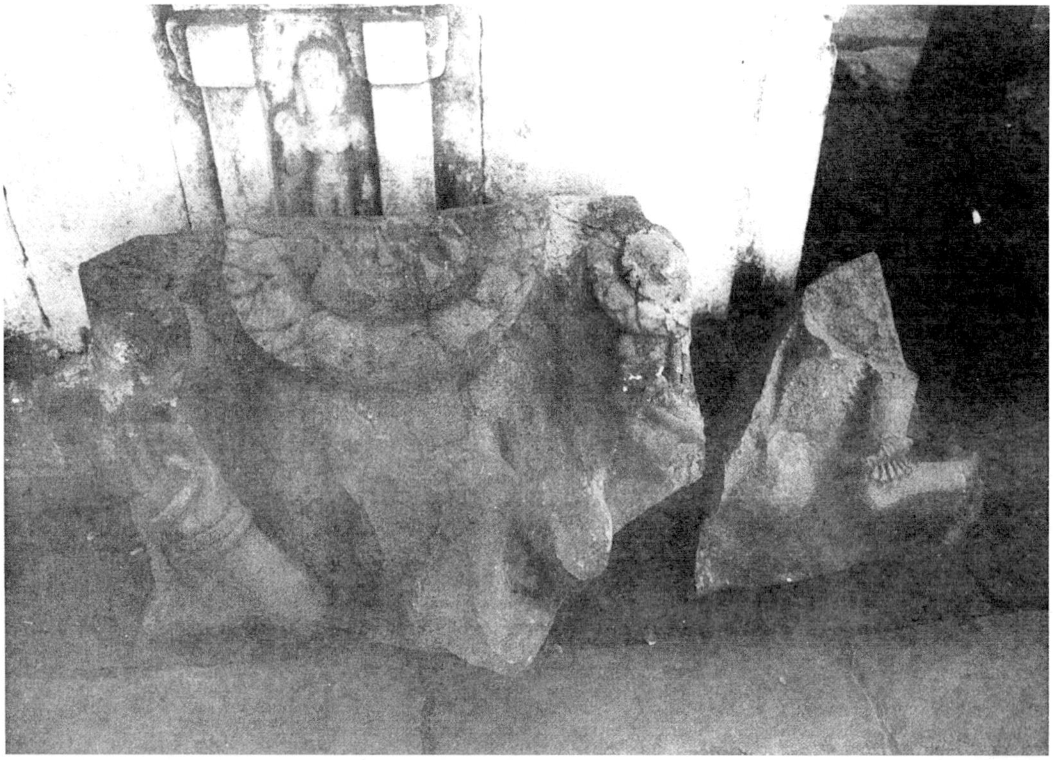

Fig. 50. Mahakuta, Mahakuteśvara temple, Bijapur District, Karnataka, 39 × 38 inches, stone, late seventh century

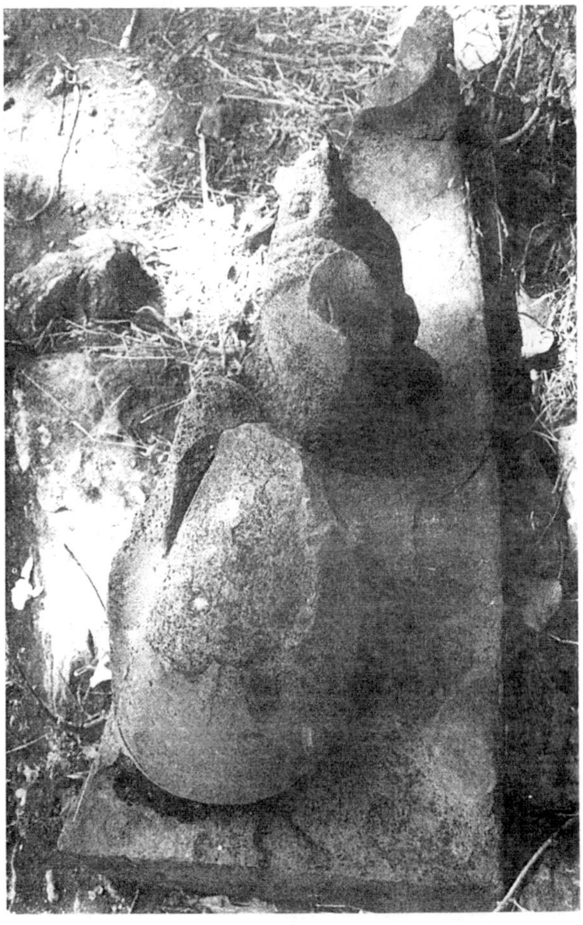

Fig. 51. Chikkamahakuta, Bijapur District, Karnataka, 39½ × 16½ inches (fragment), stone, late seventh century

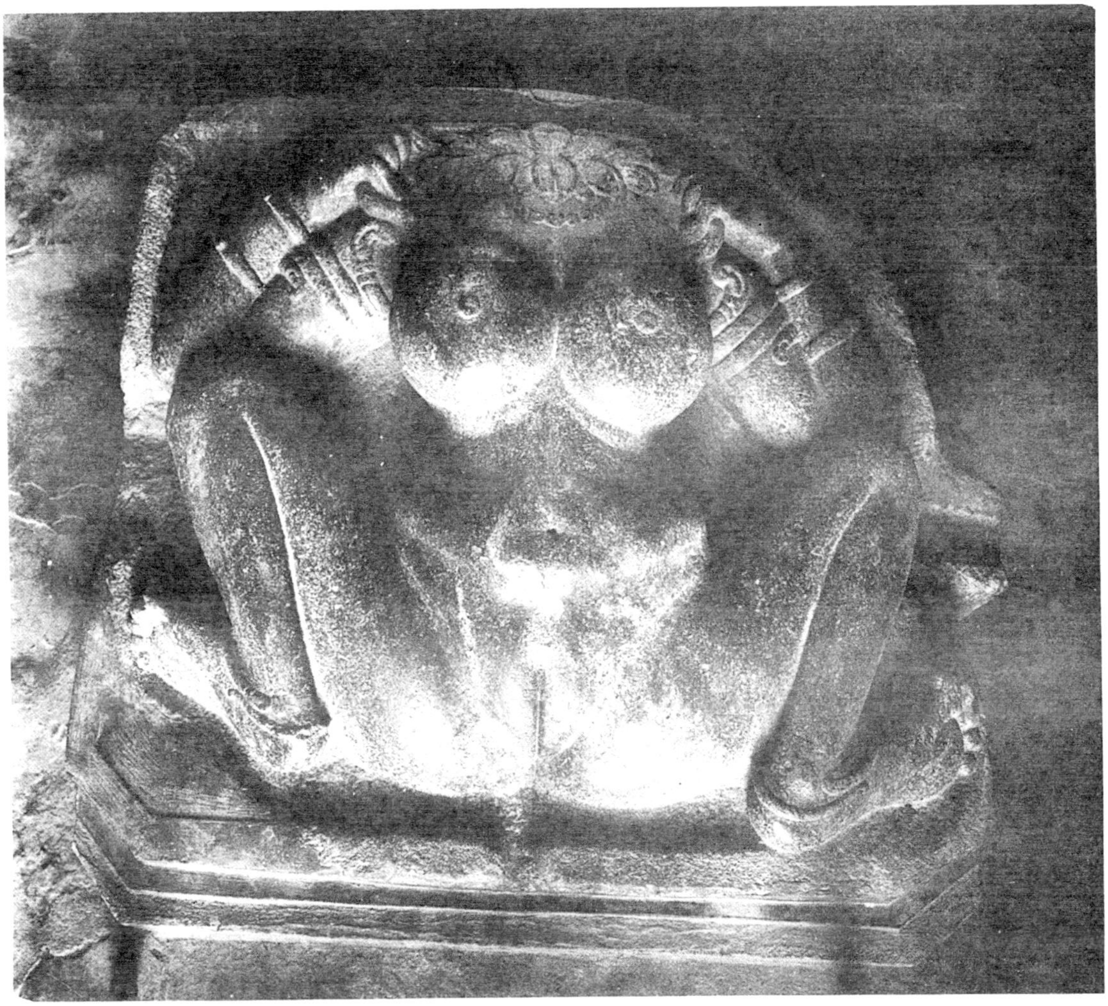

Fig. 52. Kudavelli (a), Saṅgameśvara temple, Kurnool District, Andhra Pradesh, Alampur Museum, 35 × 41 inches, stone, late seventh century

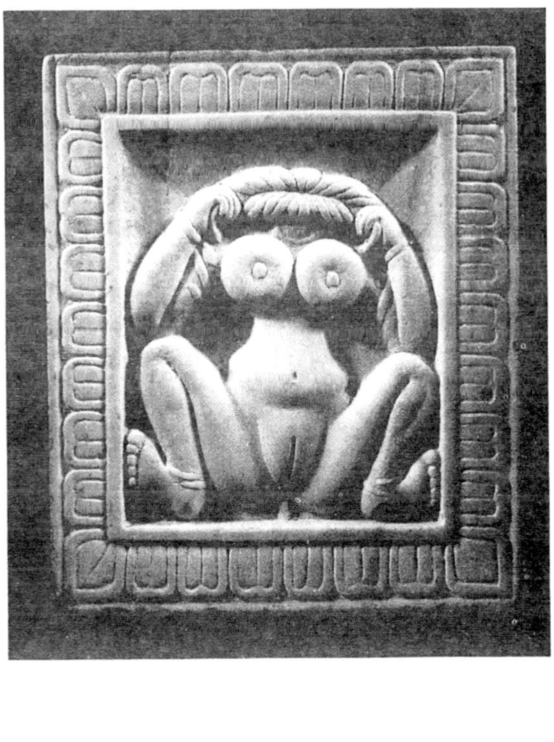

Fig. 53. Copy after Kudavelli (a) late seventh century, made in Rajasthan, private collection, United Kingdom, 12½ × 14½ inches, marble, nineteenth–twentieth century

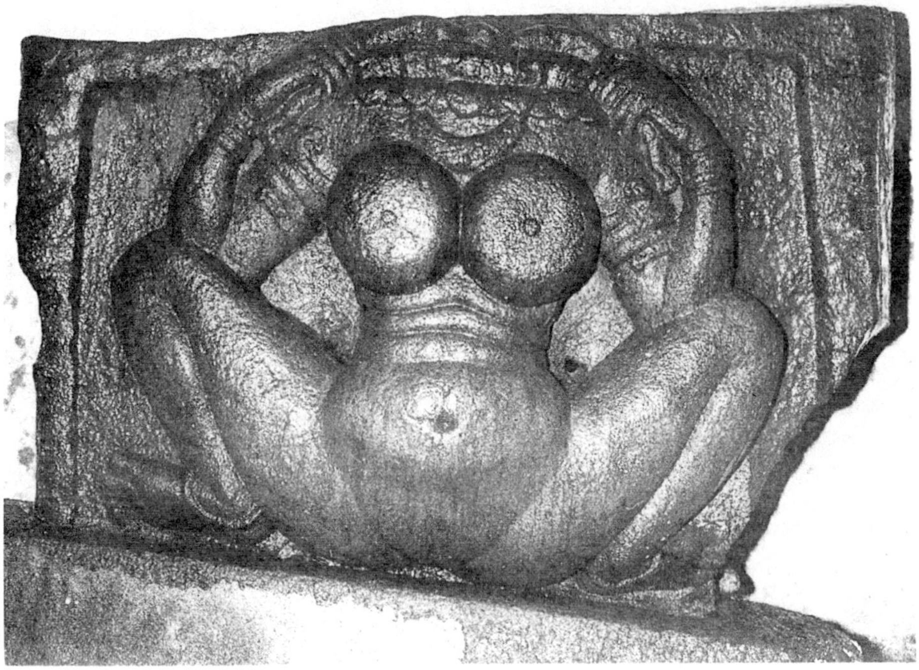

Fig. 54. Darasuram, Chakrāyi temple, Tanjore District, Tamil Nadu, 45 × 33 inches, stone, late seventh century

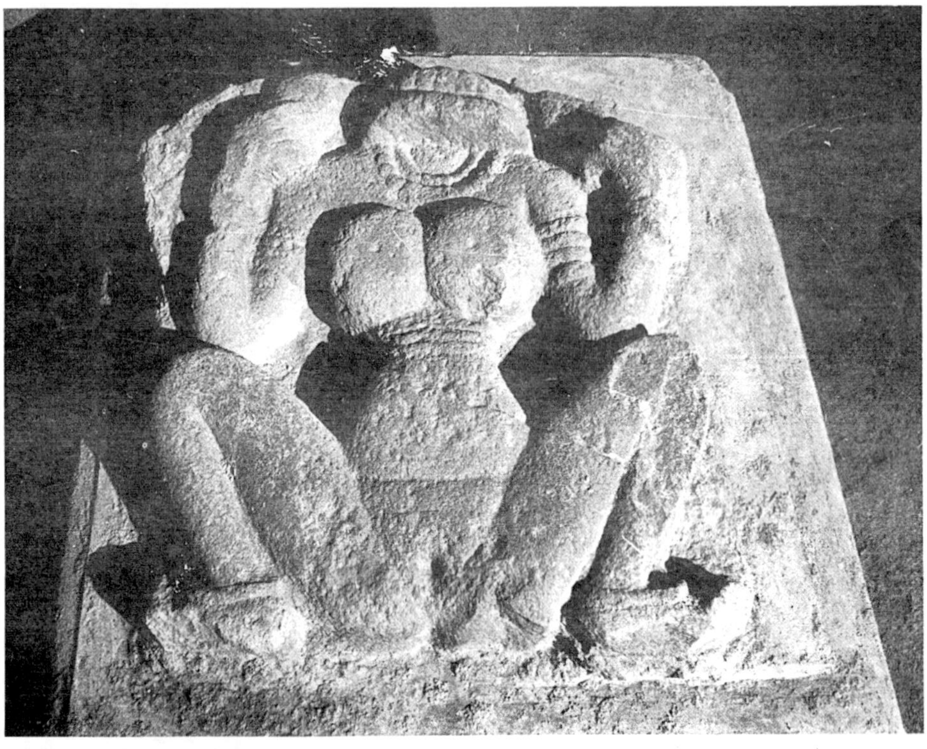

Fig. 55. Kudavelli (b), Saṅgameśvara temple, Kurnool District, Andhra Pradesh, Alampur Museum, 2½ × 2¼ inches, stone, late seventh century

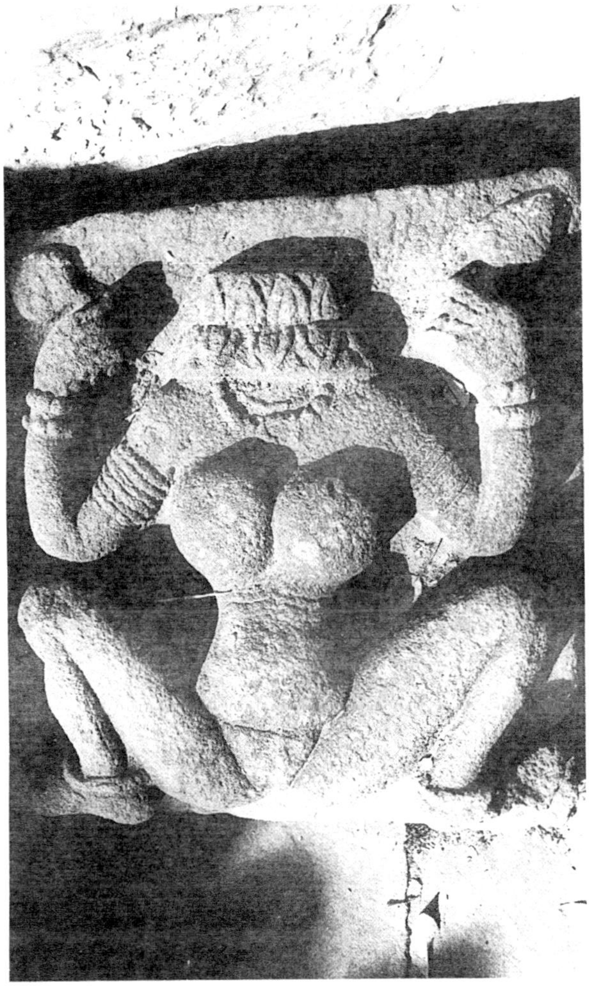

Fig. 56. Panchalingala, Pañchaliṅgeśvara temple, Kurnool District, Andhra Pradesh, c. 3 feet square, stone, late seventh century

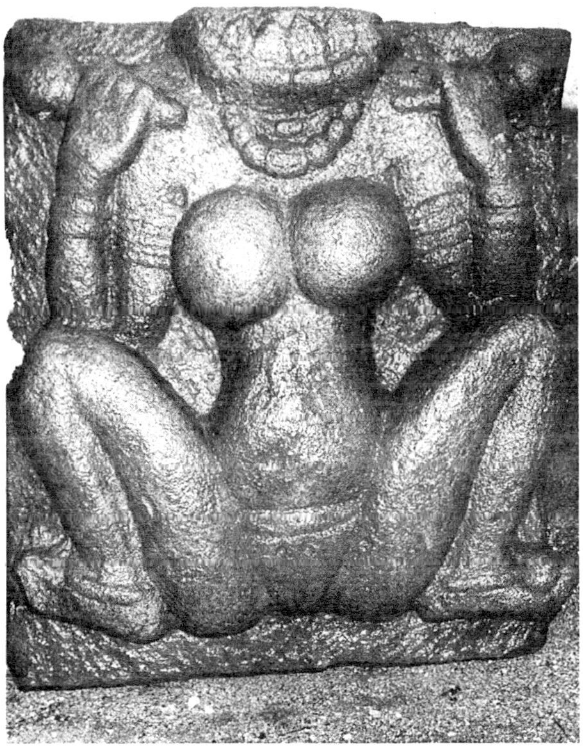

Fig. 57. Yellala, Kurnool District, Andhra Pradesh, Andhra Directorate of Archaeology and Museums, 36 × 36 inches, stone, late seventh century

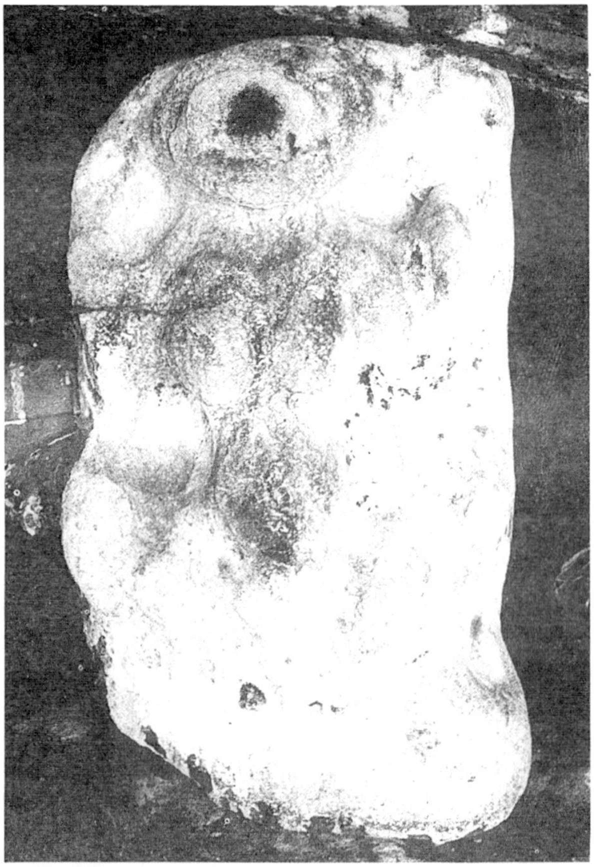

Fig. 58. Bhadranayika Jalihal (a), Hulligamakolla, Bijapur District, Karnataka, 34 × 24 inches, stone, late seventh century

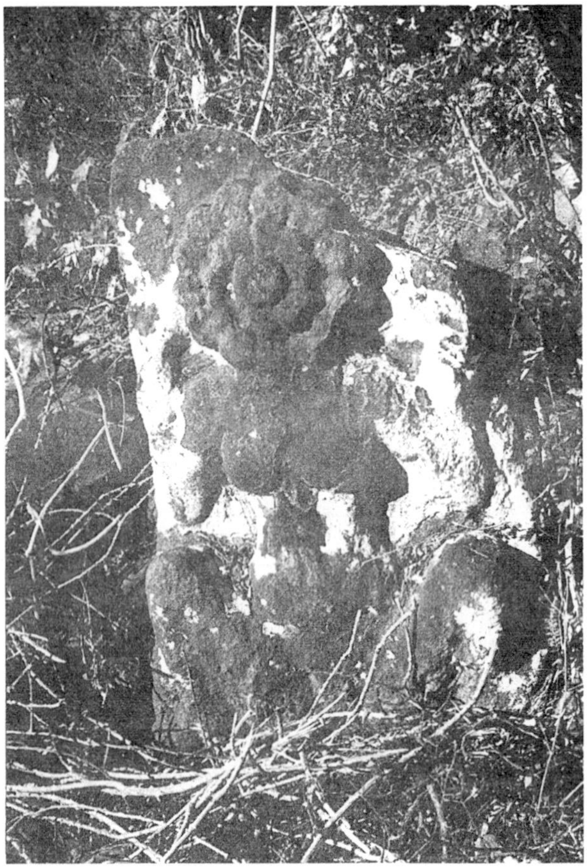

Fig. 59. Bhadranayika Jalihal (b), Hulligamakolla, Bijapur District, Karnataka, 23 × 13 inches, stone, late seventh century

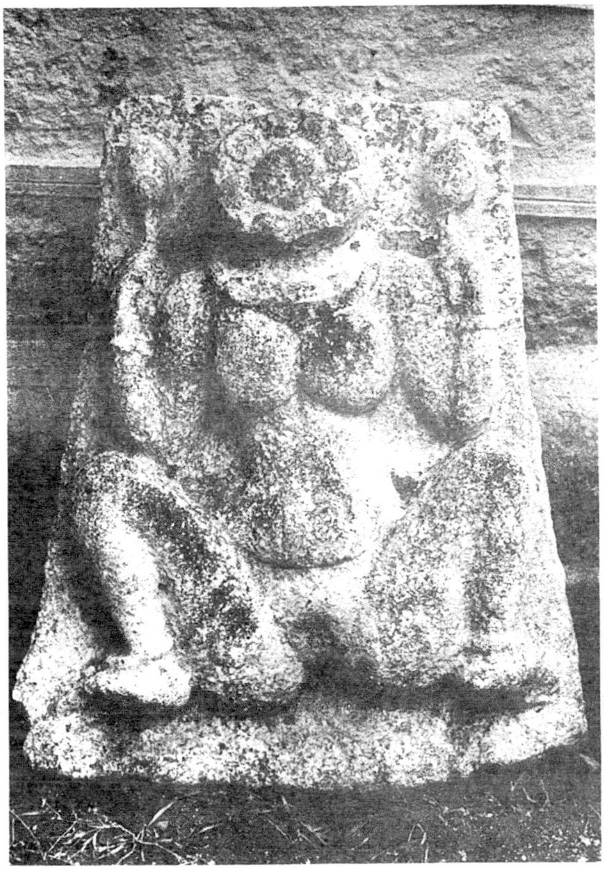

Fig. 60. Bhavanasi, Nivrittisaṅgameśvara temple, Kurnool District, Andhra Pradesh, height 41 inches, stone, seventh–eighth century

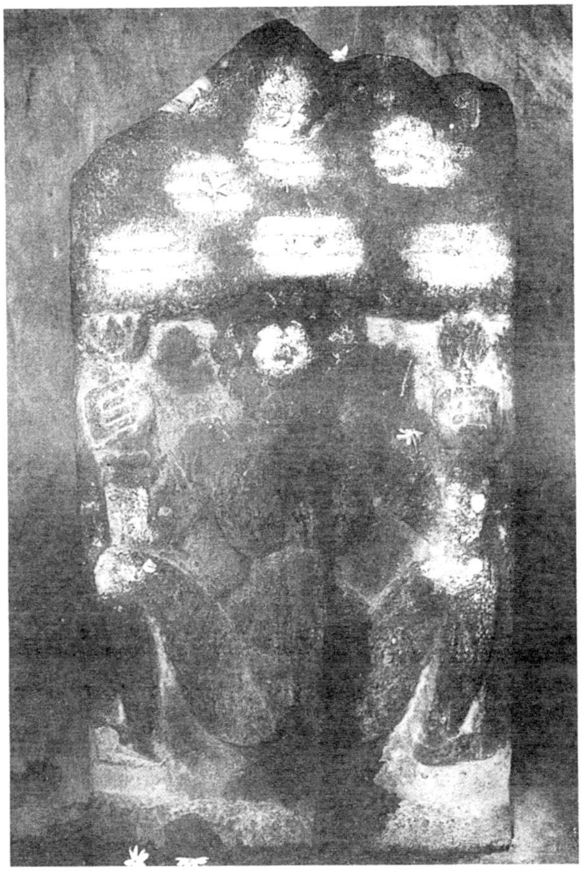

Fig. 61. Belligamve, Kedareśvara temple, Shimoga District, Karnataka, 28 × 15 inches, stone, eighth century

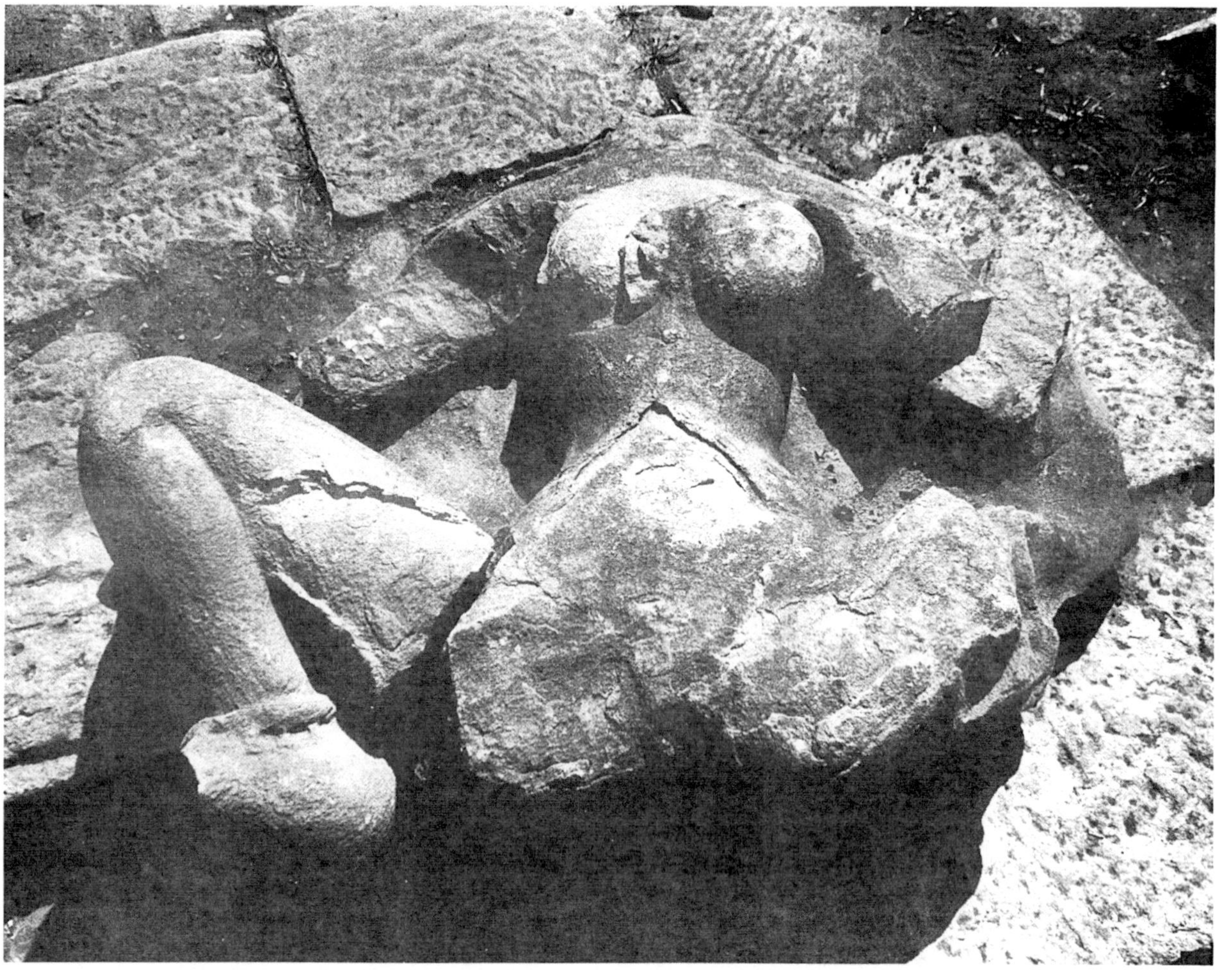

Fig. 62. Aihole, Galagnātha temple area, Bijapur District, Karnataka, 41 × 41 inches, stone, eighth century

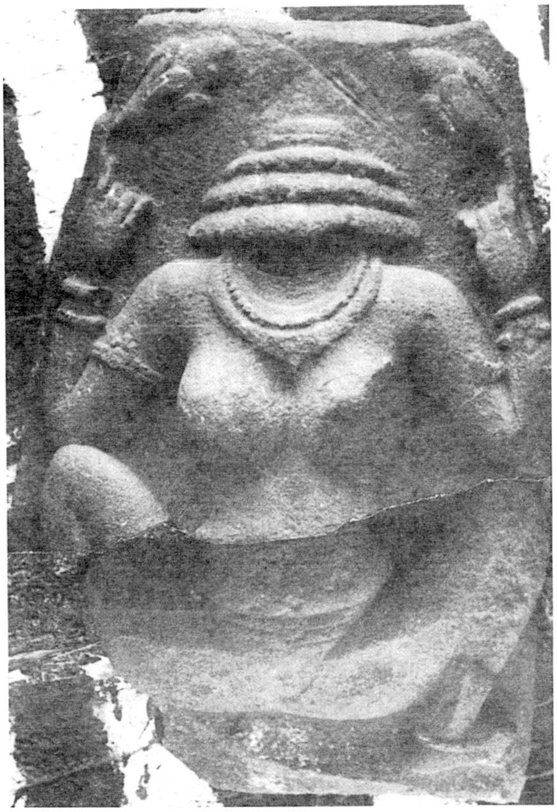

Fig. 63. Pratakota, Nageśvaraswami temple, Kurnool District, Andhra Pradesh, height c. 3–4 feet, stone, eighth–ninth century

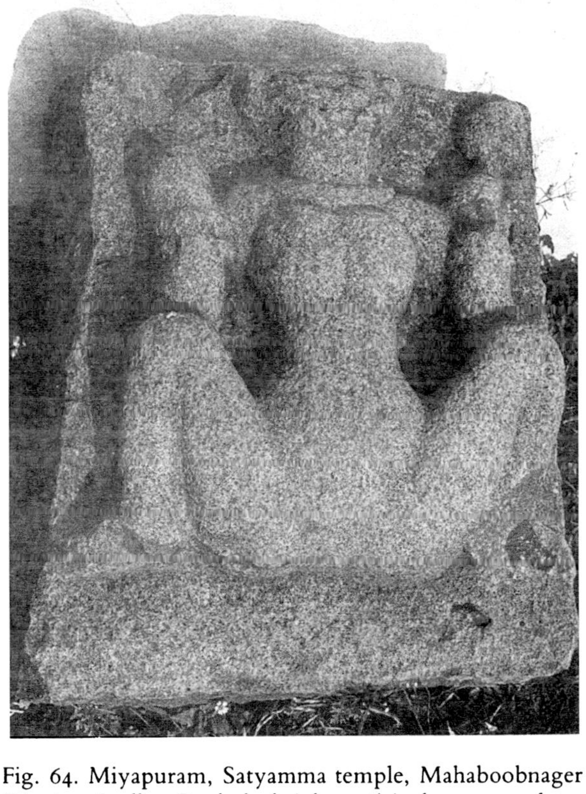

Fig. 64. Miyapuram, Satyamma temple, Mahaboobnager District, Andhra Pradesh, height 23½ inches, stone, late seventh century

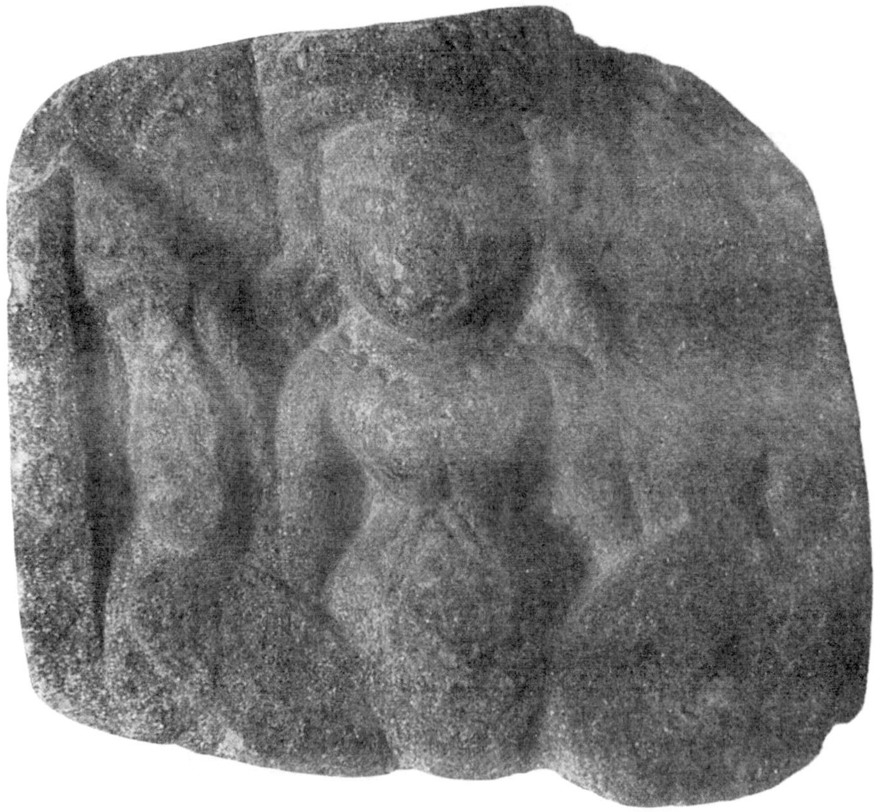

Fig. 65. Amreli, Amreli District, Gujarat, Collection of U.P. Shah, Baroda, 2 × 2 inches, stone, sixth century

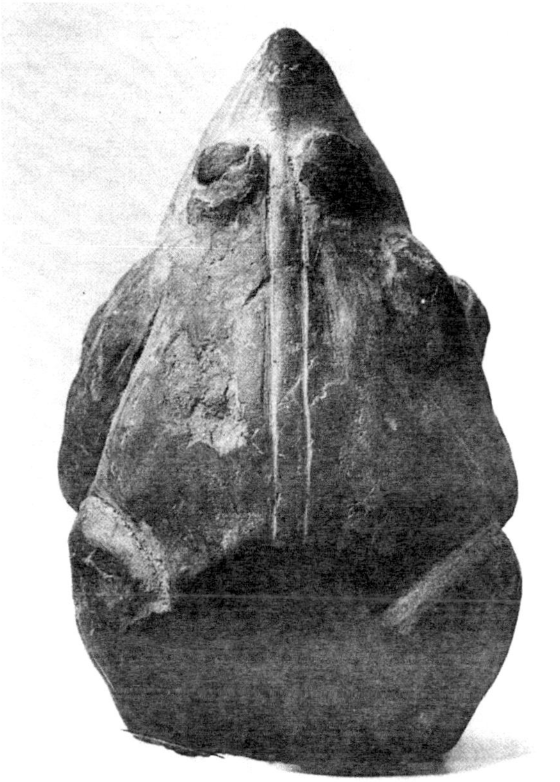

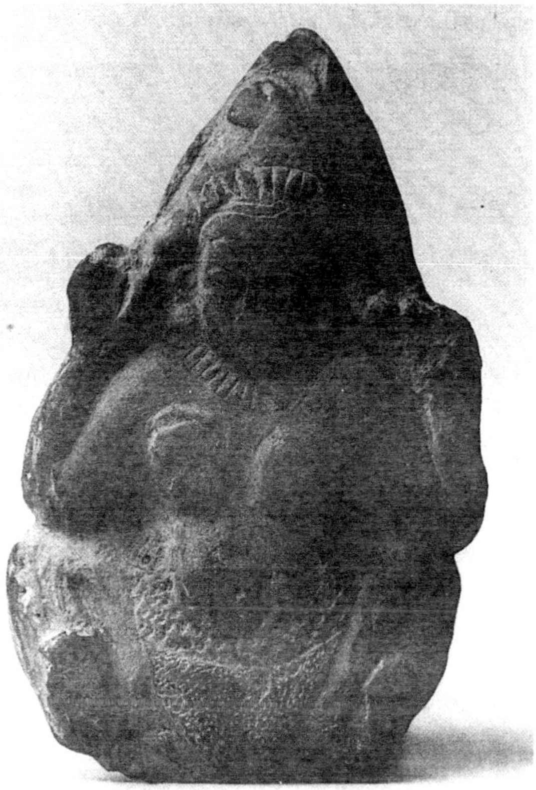

Fig. 66. Mathura, Mathura District, Uttar Pradesh, Victoria and Albert Museum 177, height 3⅘ inches, terra-cotta, second century?

Figs. 67–68. Mathura, Mathura District, Uttar Pradesh, Victoria and Albert Museum 177, height 3⅘ inches, terra-cotta, second century?, back and side views

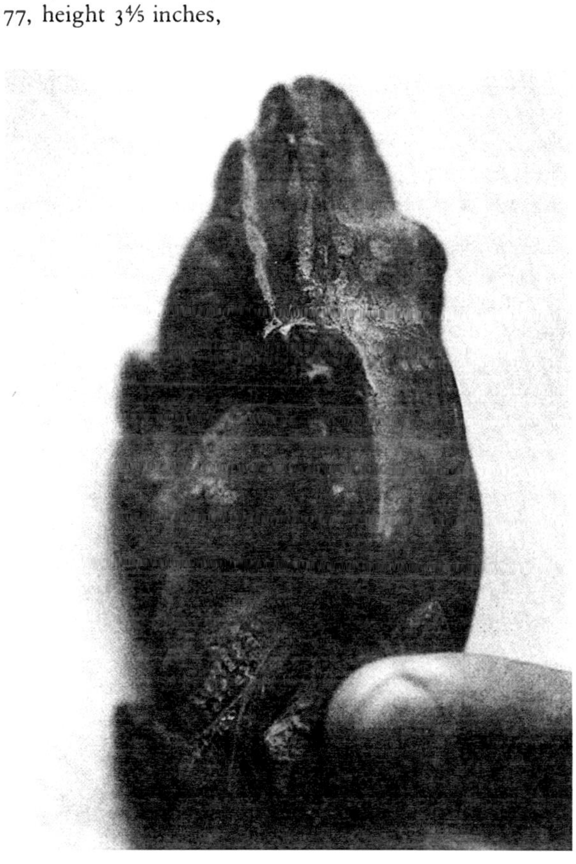

68.

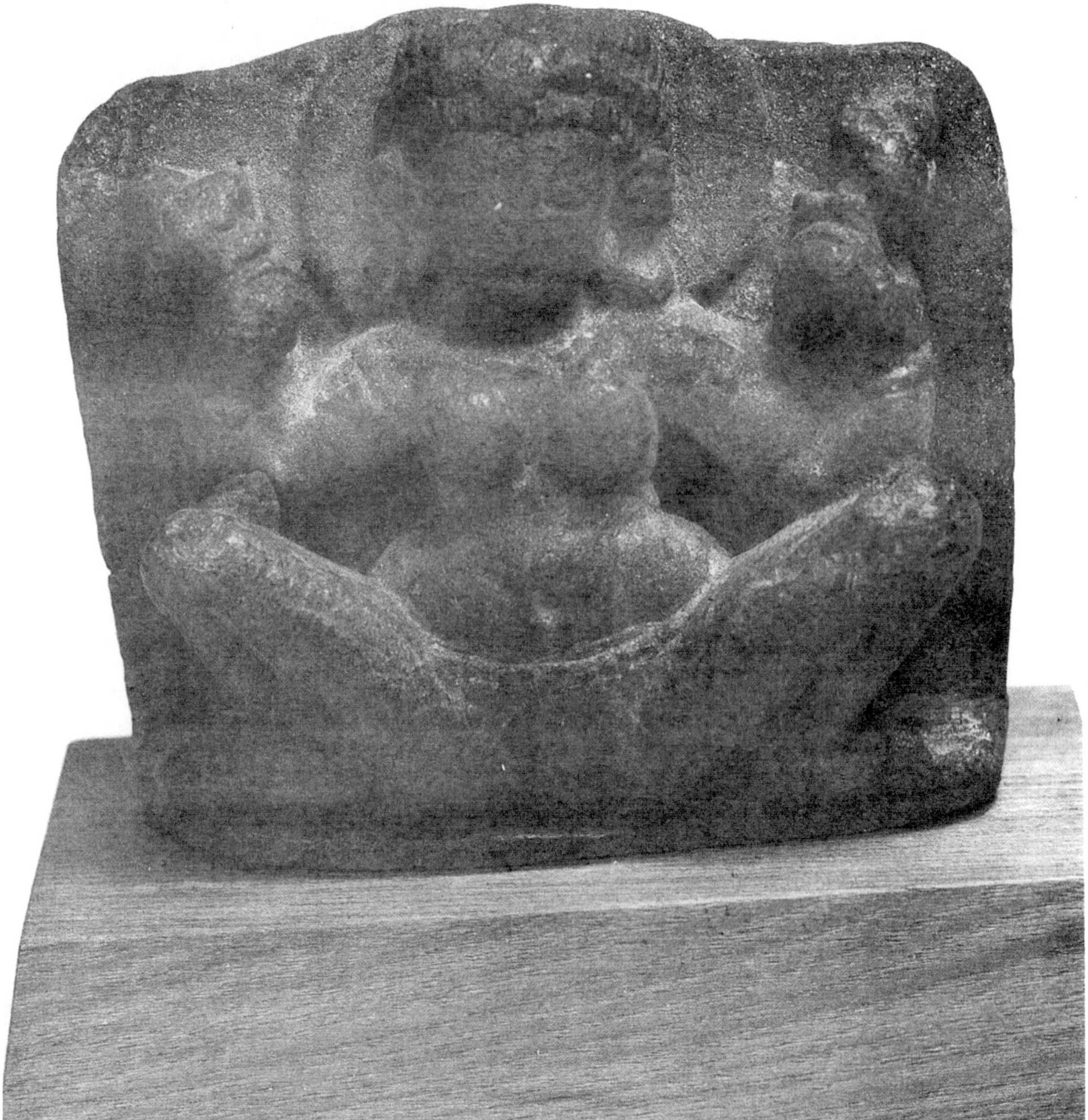

Fig. 69. Site unknown, North India, National Museum, New Delhi 82.363, Collection of Ajit Mookerjee, 4 inches, stone, sixth century

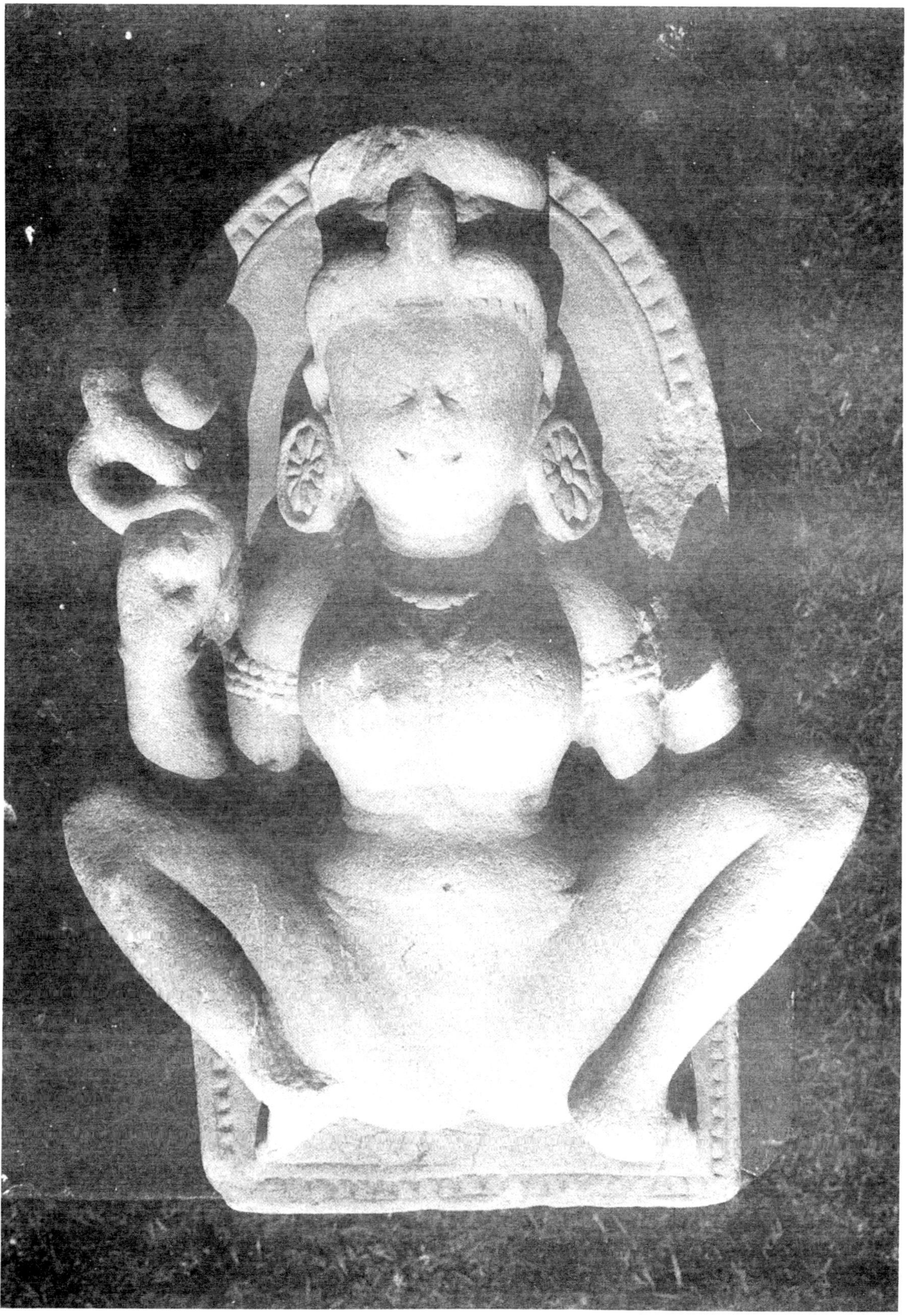

Fig. 70. Site unknown, Central India, Archaeological Museum, Mathura 15.597, 11 × 5½ inches, stone, eighth century

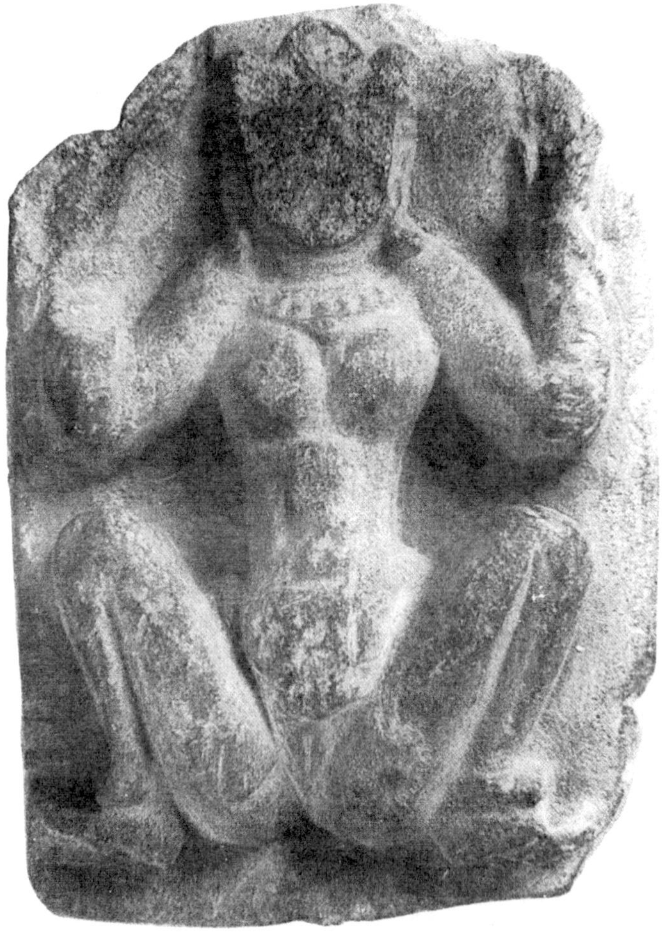

Fig. 71. Pavi-Jetpur, Baroda District, Gujarat, Department of Archaeology and Ancient History, M.S. University, Baroda, 5 × 3½ inches, stone, seventh century

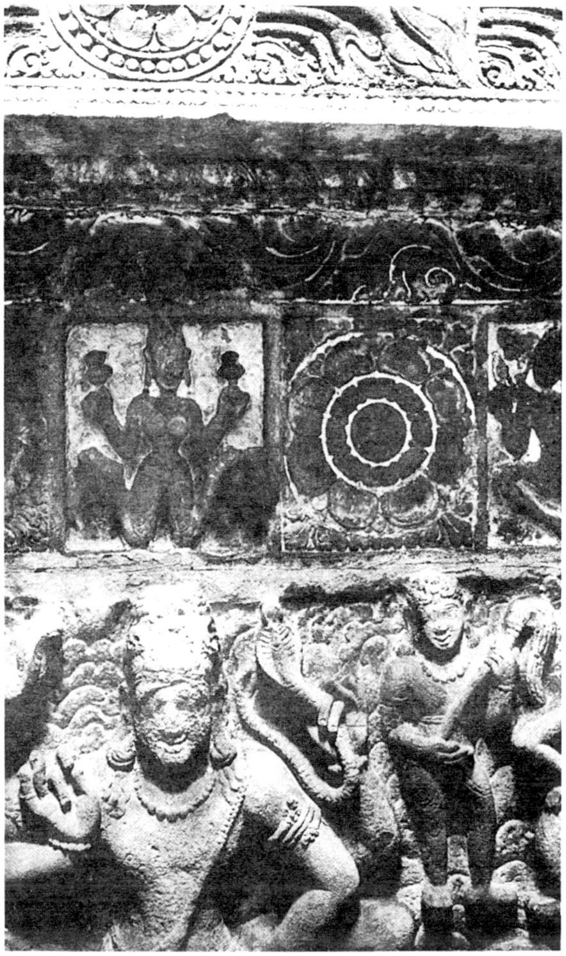

Fig. 72. Aihole, Huchchapayya temple ceiling border, Bijapur District, Karnataka, stone, c. 700

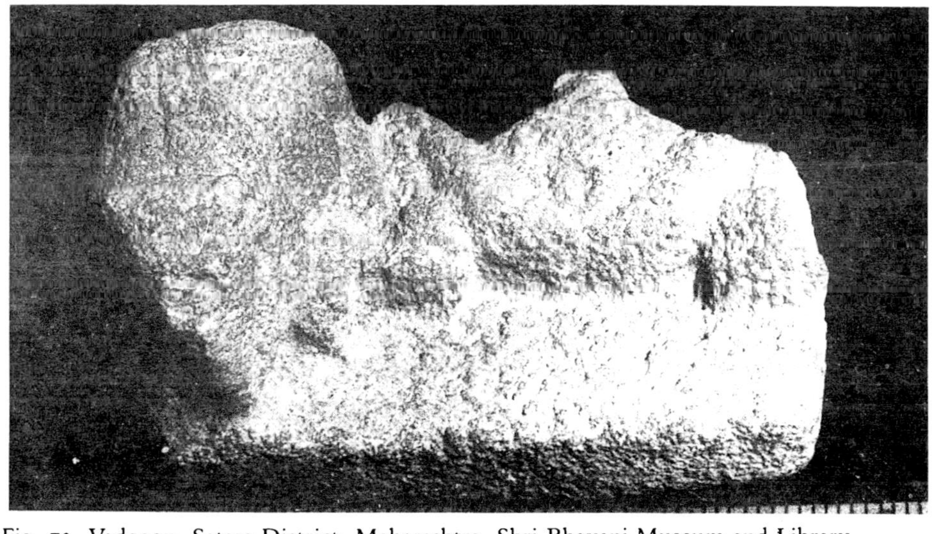

Fig. 73. Vadgaon, Satara District, Maharashtra, Shri Bhavani Museum and Library, Aundh, 3 × 4 inches, stone, fourth century

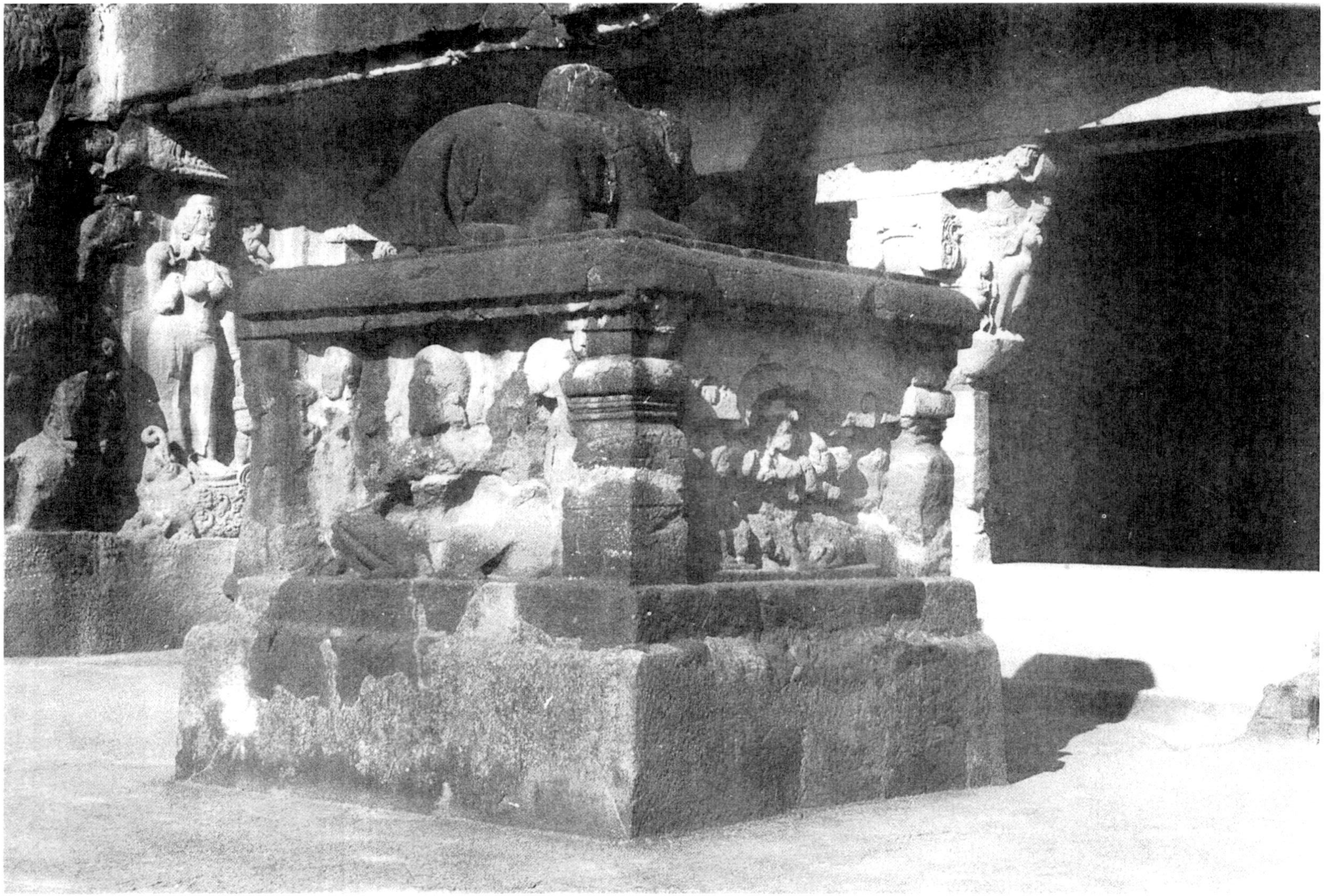

Fig. 74. Ellora, Rāmeśvara temple (21), Aurangabad District, Maharashtra, Nandi *maṇḍapa*, stone, sixth century

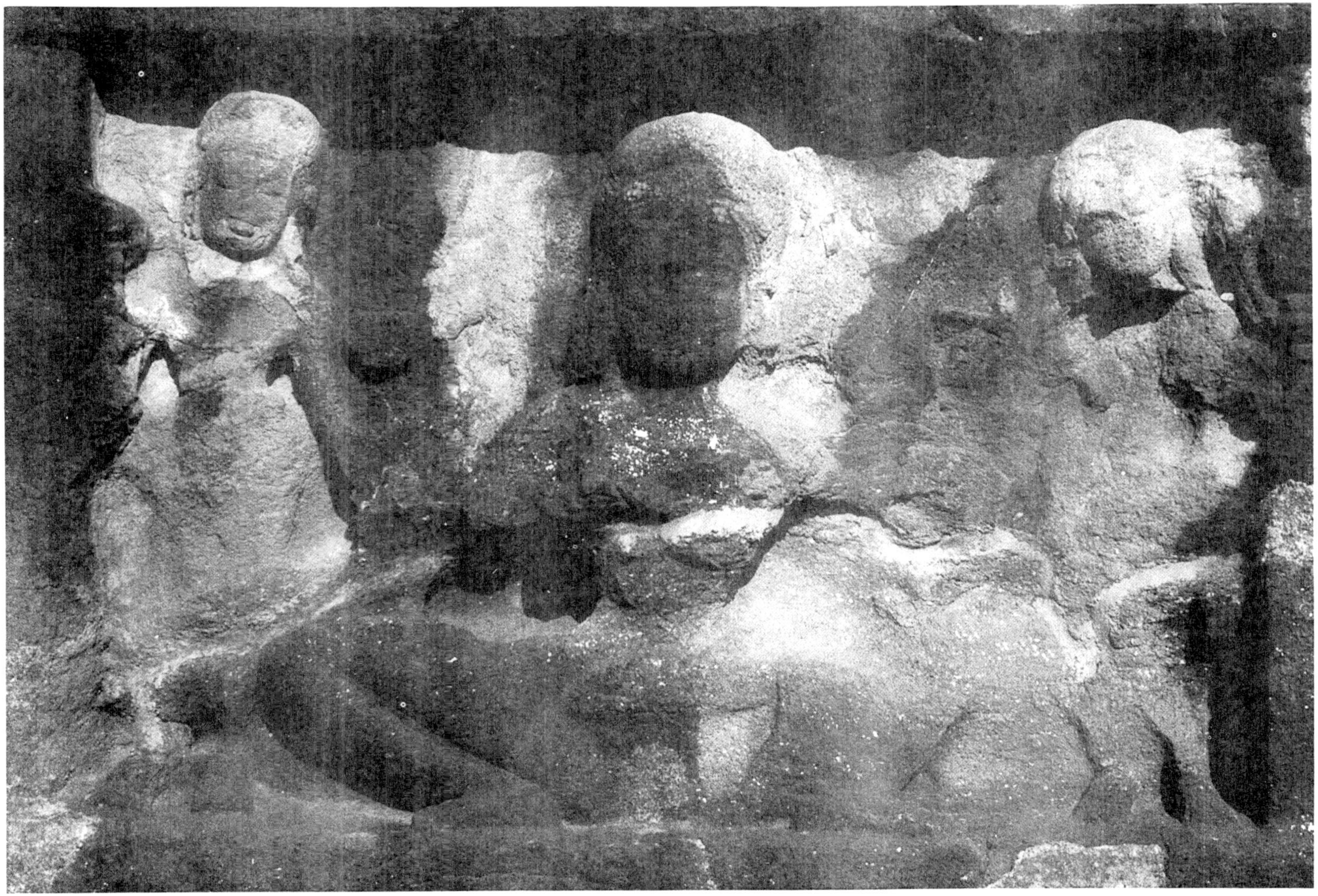

Fig. 75. Ellora, Rāmeśvara temple (21), Aurangabad District, Maharashtra, 50 × 77 inches, stone, sixth century

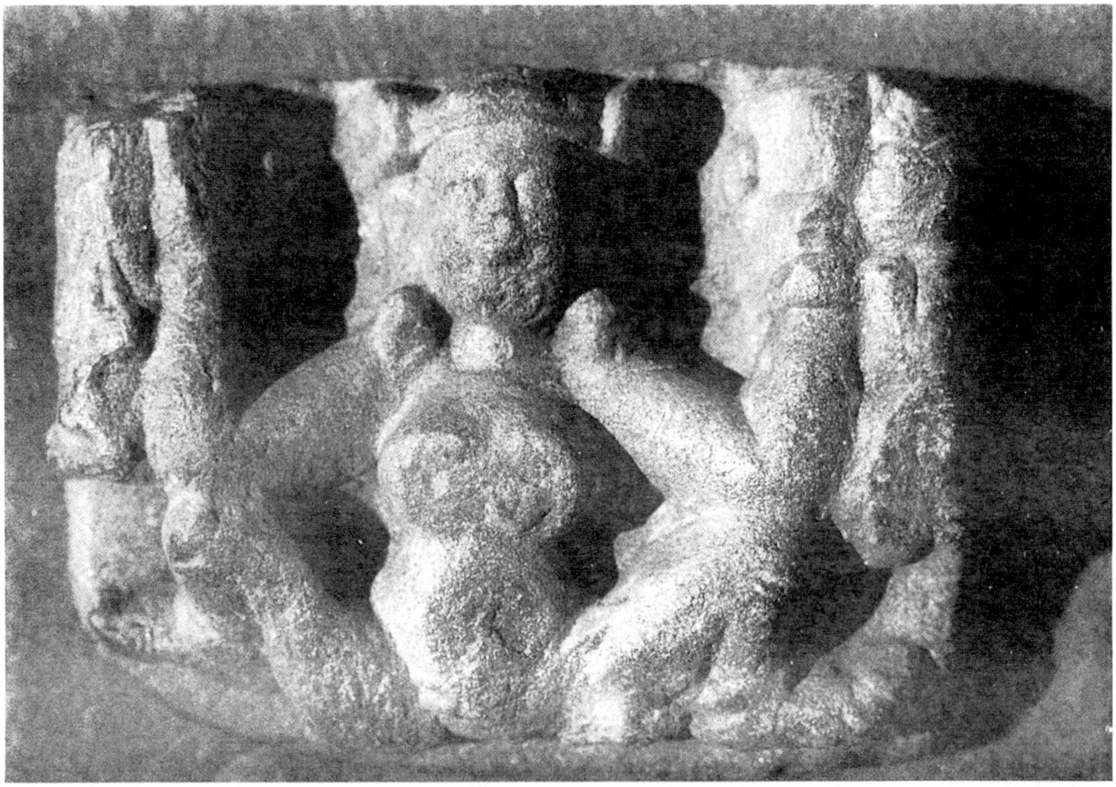

Fig. 76. Elephanta, Bombay District, Maharashtra, Prince of Wales Museum 81.7/1, 3 × 2 inches, stone, sixth century

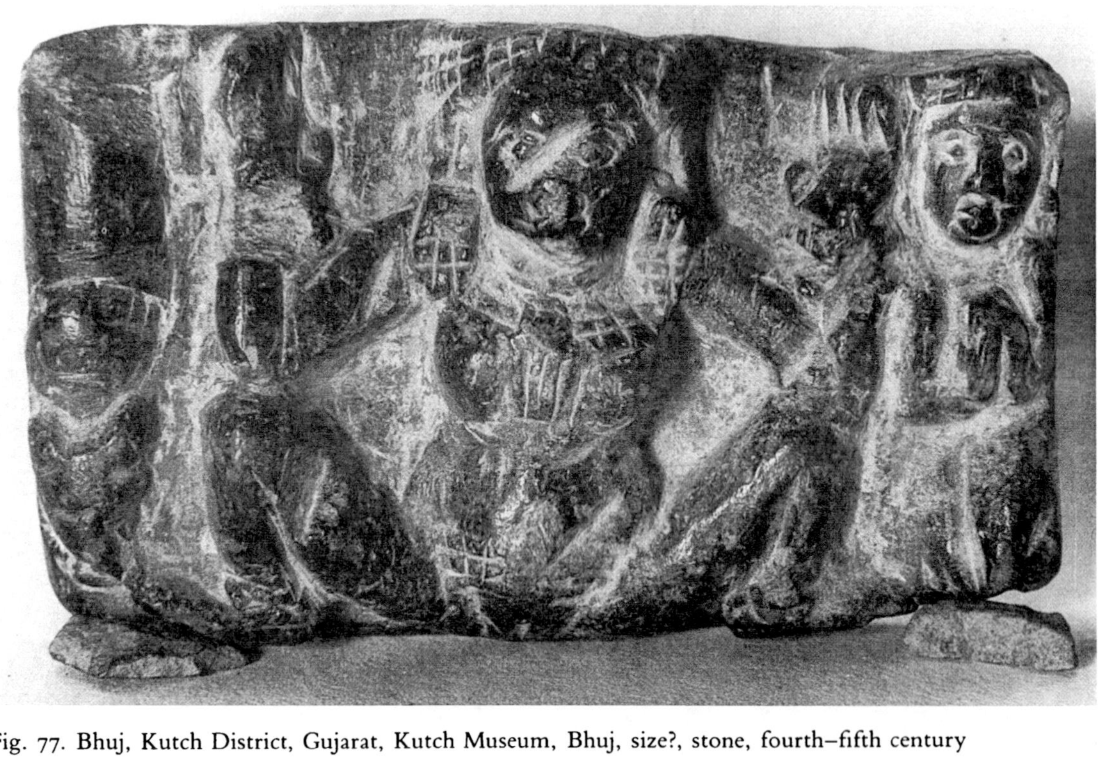

Fig. 77. Bhuj, Kutch District, Gujarat, Kutch Museum, Bhuj, size?, stone, fourth–fifth century

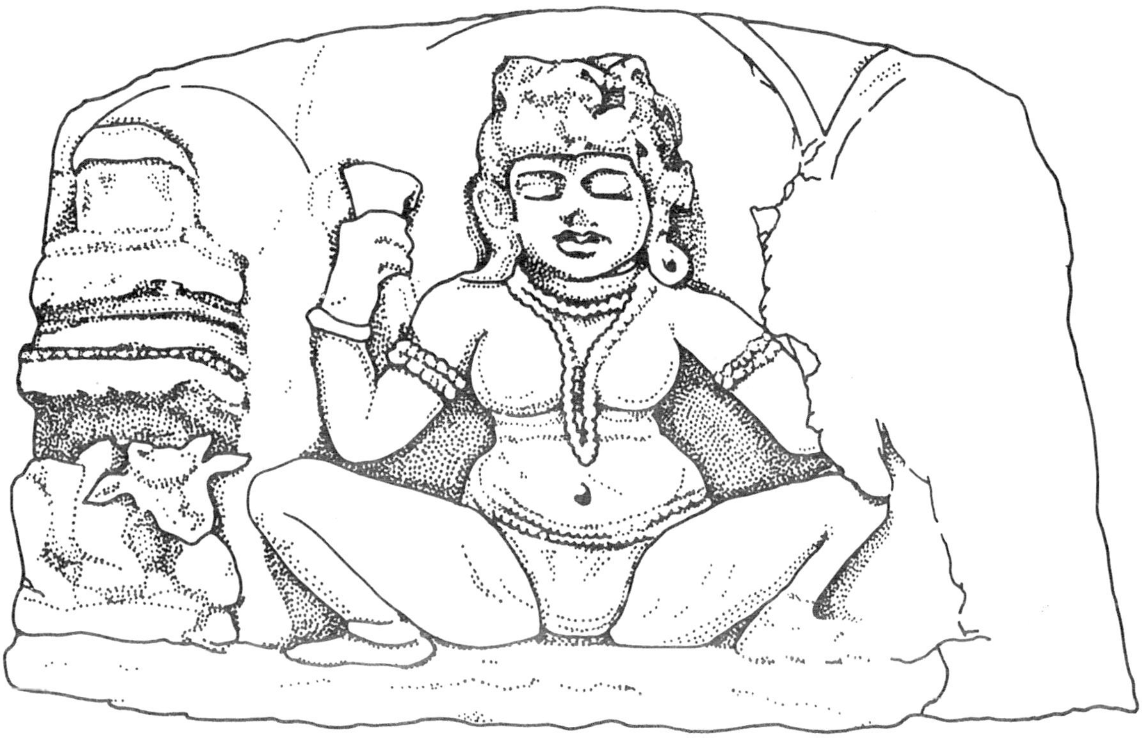

Fig. 78. Bhinmal, Jalor District, Rajasthan, size?, stone, seventh century

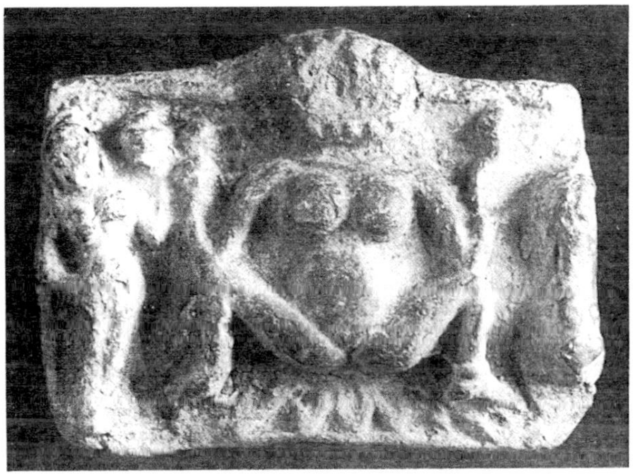

Fig. 79. Kanad, Surat District, Gujarat, Western Circle Office, Archaeological Survey of India, Baroda, 2 × 3 inches, terra-cotta, sixth century

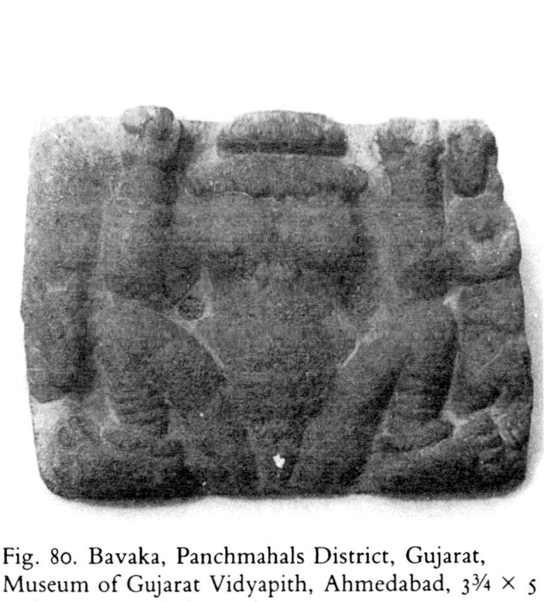

Fig. 80. Bavaka, Panchmahals District, Gujarat, Museum of Gujarat Vidyapith, Ahmedabad, 3¾ × 5 inches, stone, ninth–tenth century

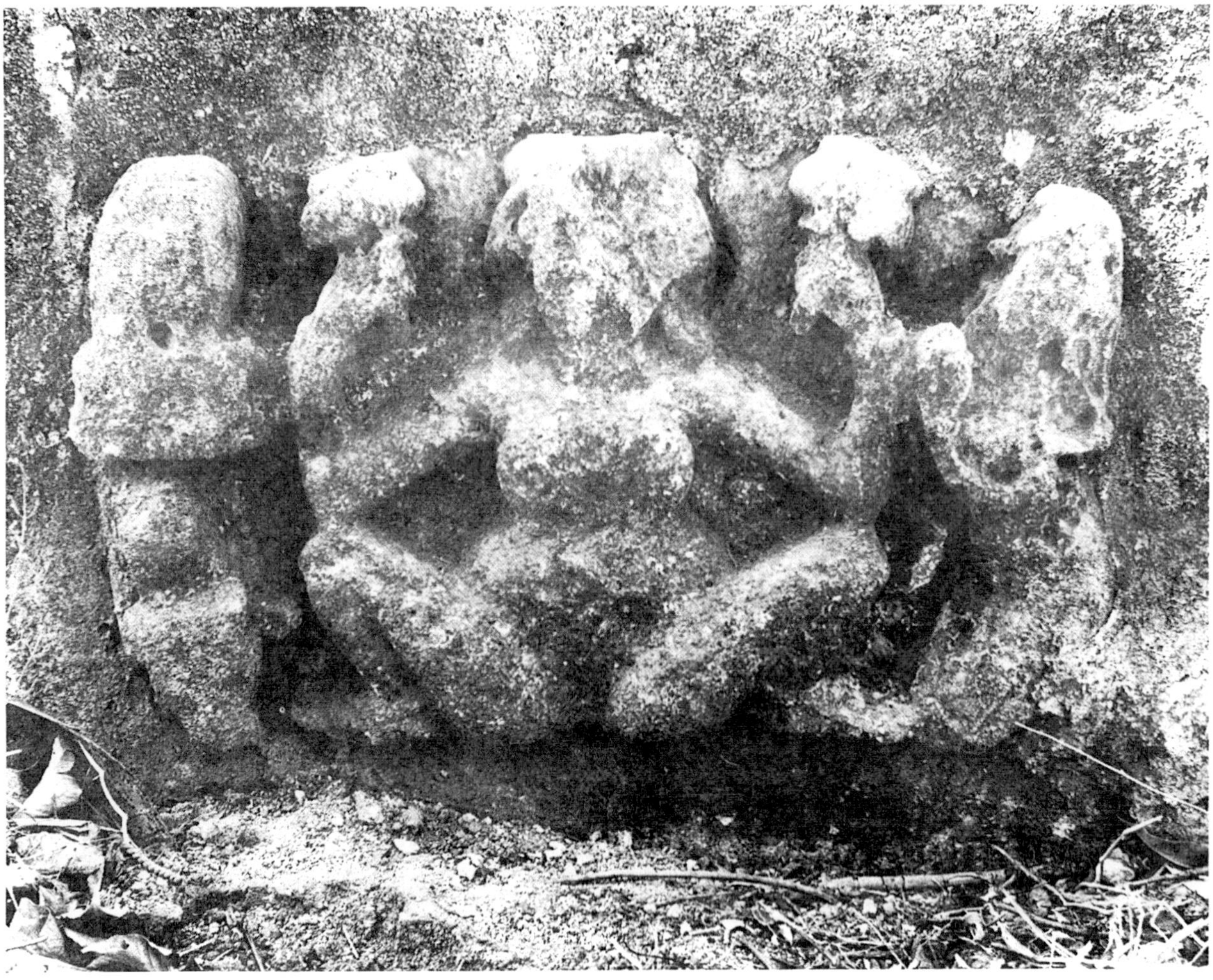

Fig. 81. Dhank (a), Rajkot District, Gujarat, size?, stone, seventh century

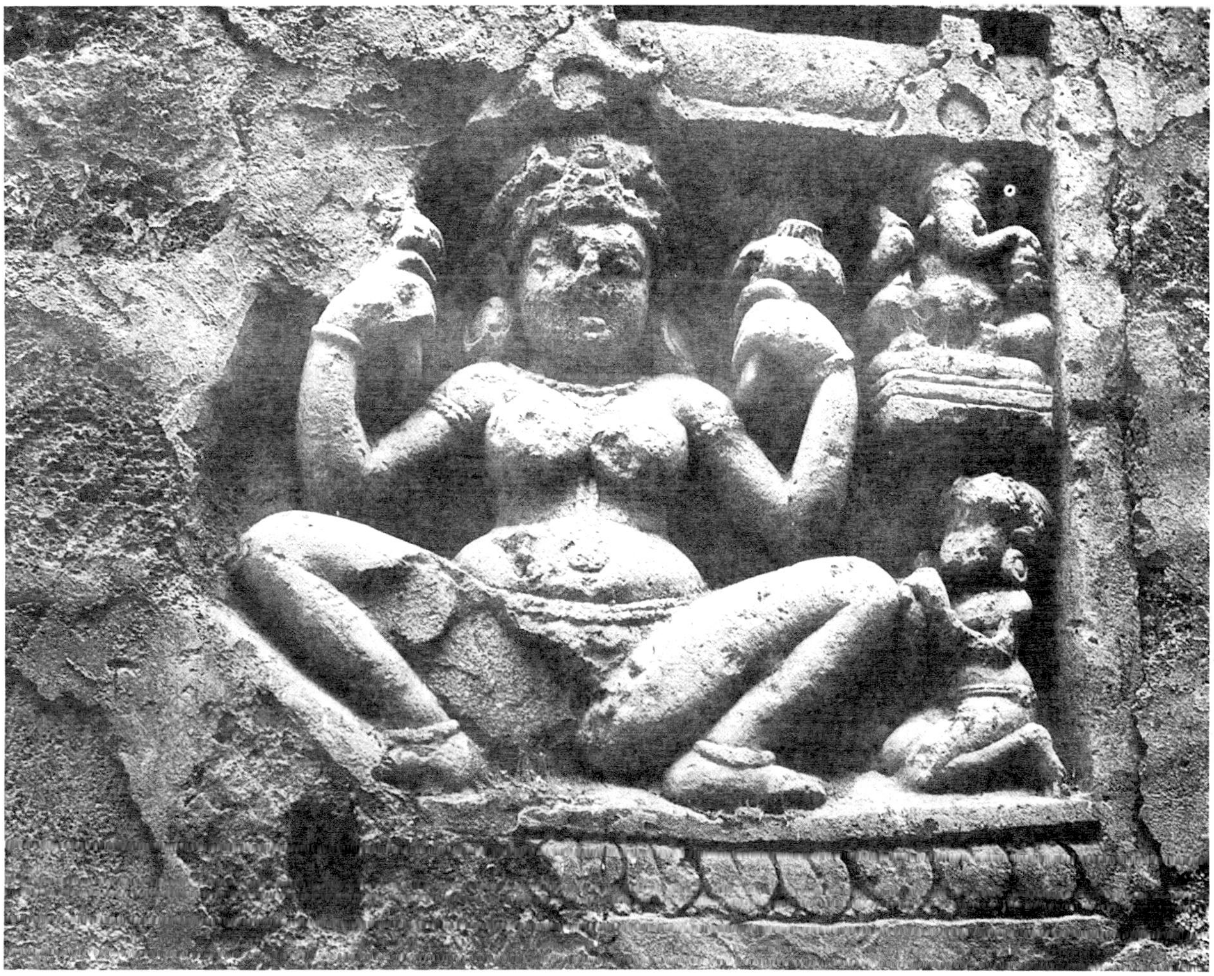

Fig. 82. Dhank (b), Manjusri *vapi*, Rajkot District, Gujarat, size?, stone, seventh century

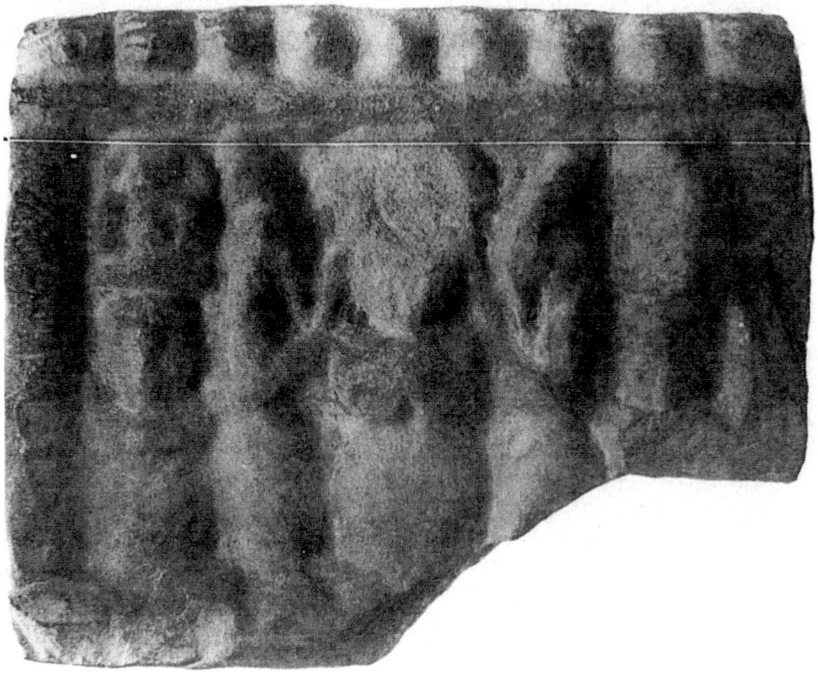

Fig. 83. Variavi, Surat District, Gujarat, Collection of U.P. Shah, 2 × 4 inches, stone, sixth century

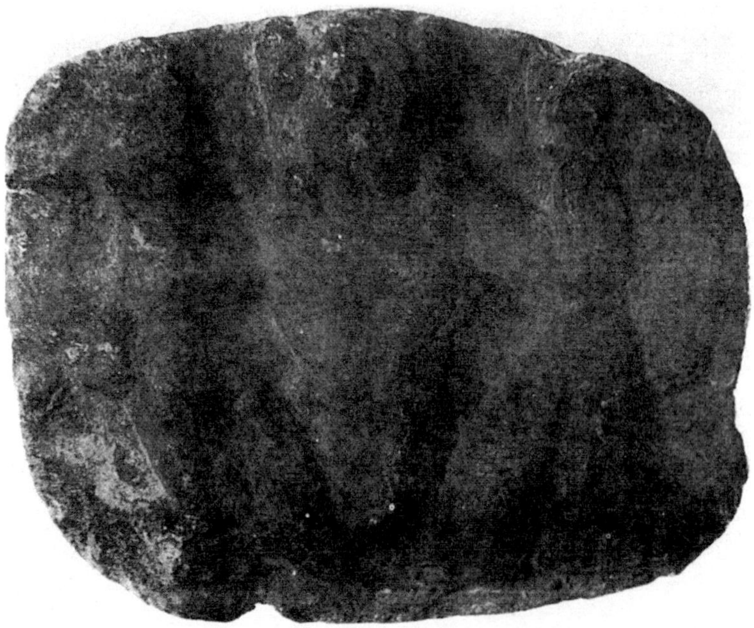

Fig. 84. Kavi, Broach District, Gujarat, Collection of U.P. Shah, 1¾ × 2 inches, stone, sixth century

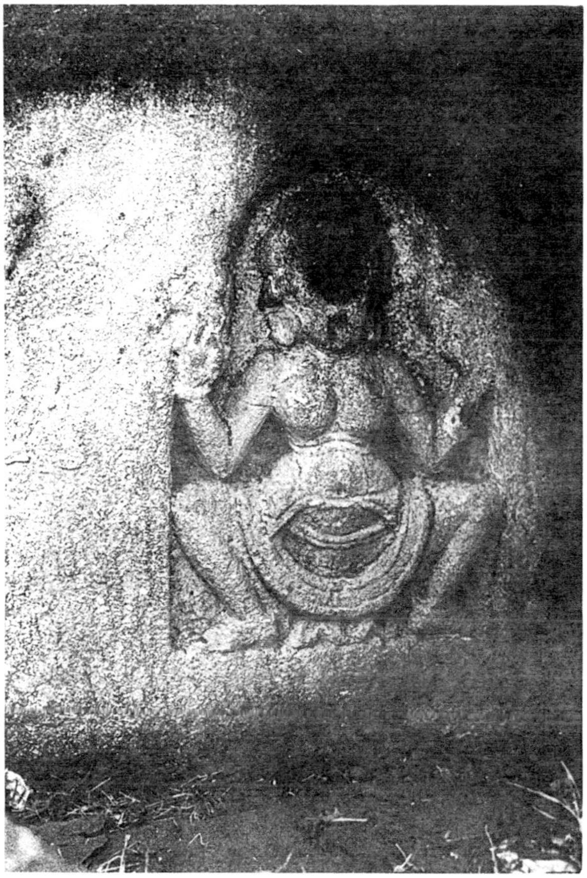

Fig. 85. Arna, Jodhpur District, Rajasthan, height 16 inches, stone, seventh century

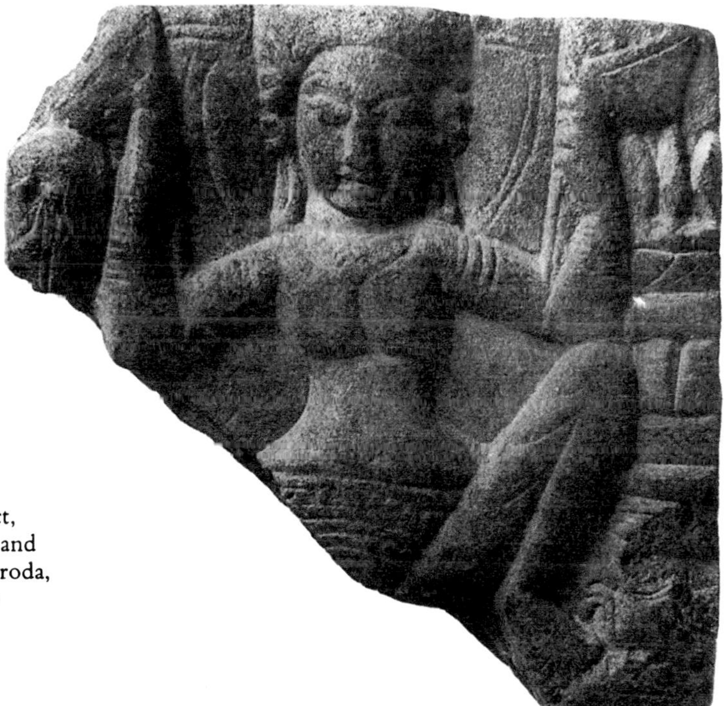

Fig. 86. Tarsang, Panchmahals District, Gujarat, Department of Archaeology and Ancient History, M.S. University, Baroda, 3½ × 3½ inches, stone, sixth century

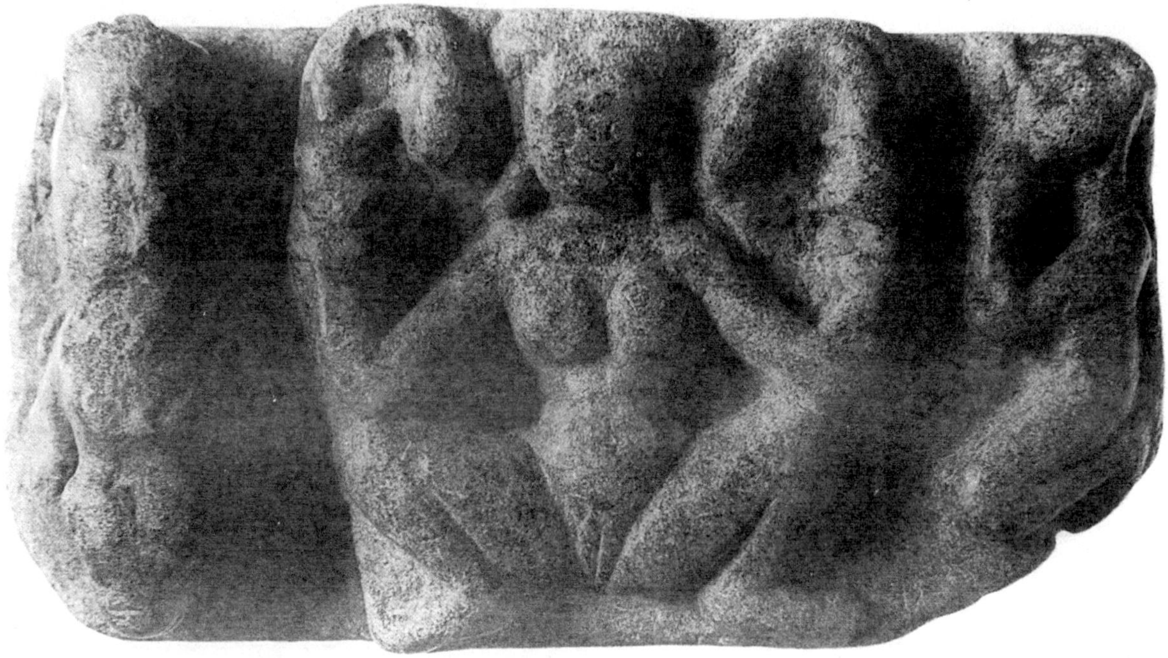

Fig. 87. Valabhipur, Bhavanagar District, Gujarat, Department of Archaeology and Ancient History, M.S. University, Baroda, 2½ × 4½ inches, stone, seventh century

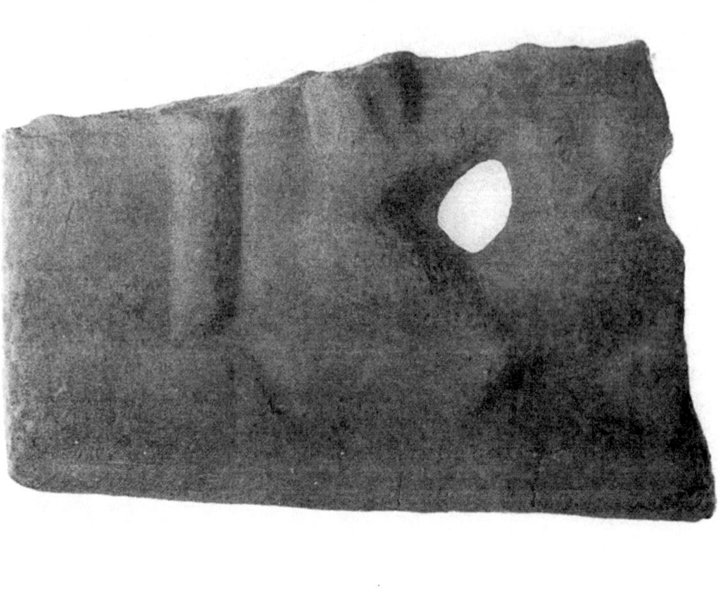

Fig. 88. Randelia, Bhavanagar District, Gujarat, Department of Archaeology and Ancient History, M.S. University, Baroda, height 2 inches (fragment), stone, date?

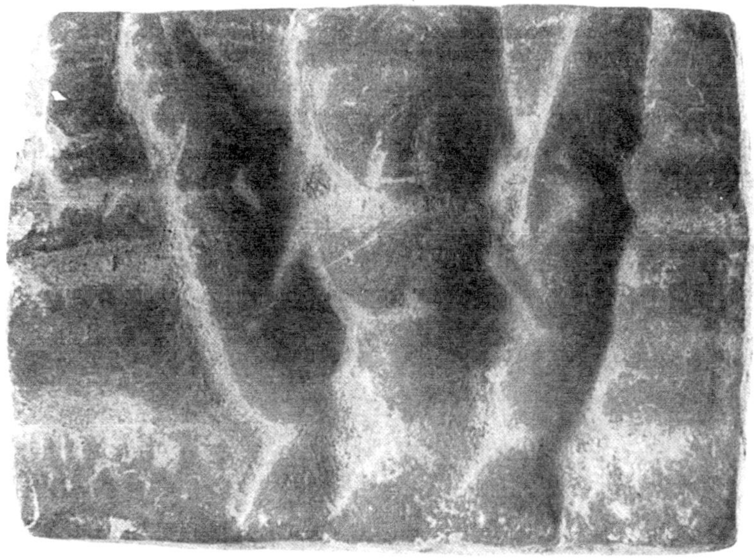

Fig. 89. Gadhali, Bhavanagar District, Gujarat, Department of Archaeology and Ancient History, M.S. University, Baroda, 2 × 2½ inches, stone, seventh century

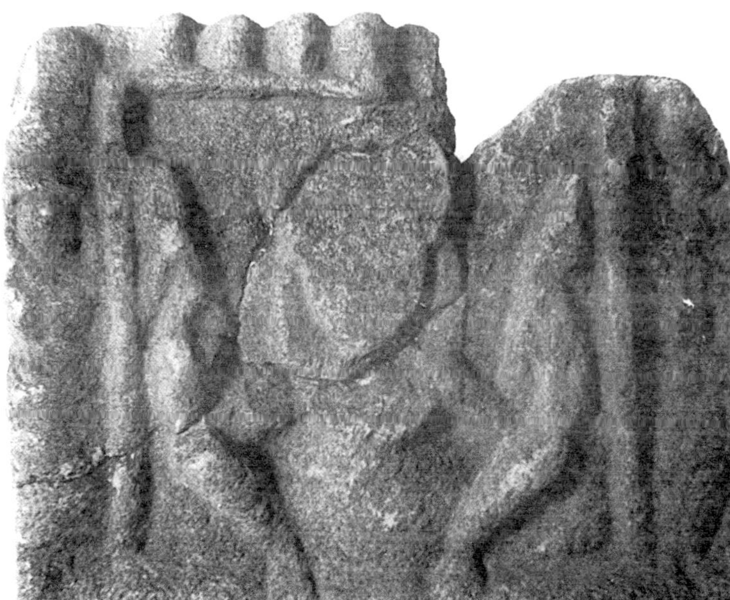

Fig. 90. Sathal, Ahmedabad District, Gujarat, Department of Archaeology and Ancient History, M.S. University, Baroda, 3 × 4½ inches, stone, fourth–fifth century

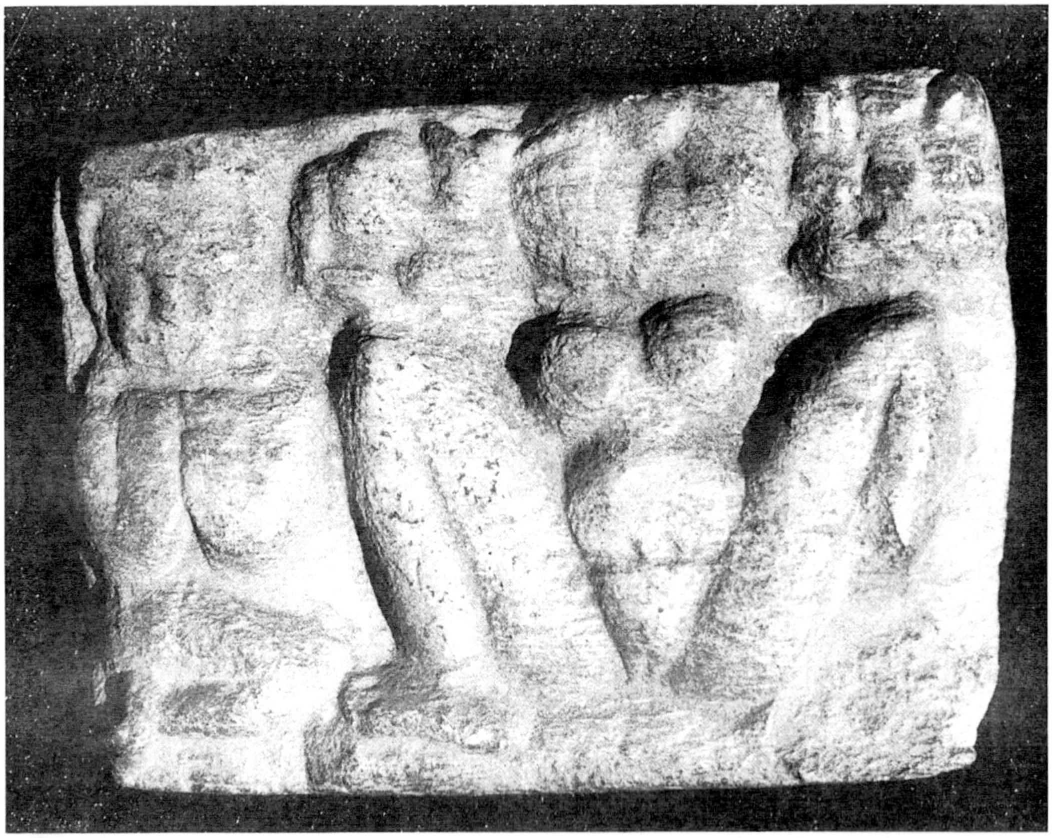

Fig. 91. Mandhal, Nagpur District, Maharashtra, Central Museum, Nagpur, 3¼ × 4 inches, stone, fourth–fifth century

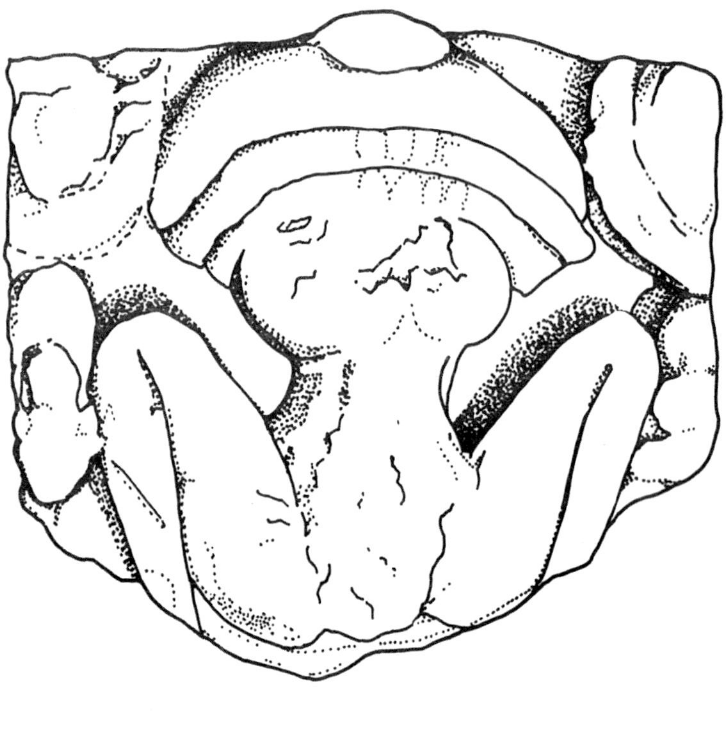

Fig. 92. Mahurjhari (b), Nagpur District, Maharashtra, Sarasvatī Bhavan Mahāvidyalaya (College), Aurangabad, size?, stone, seventh century

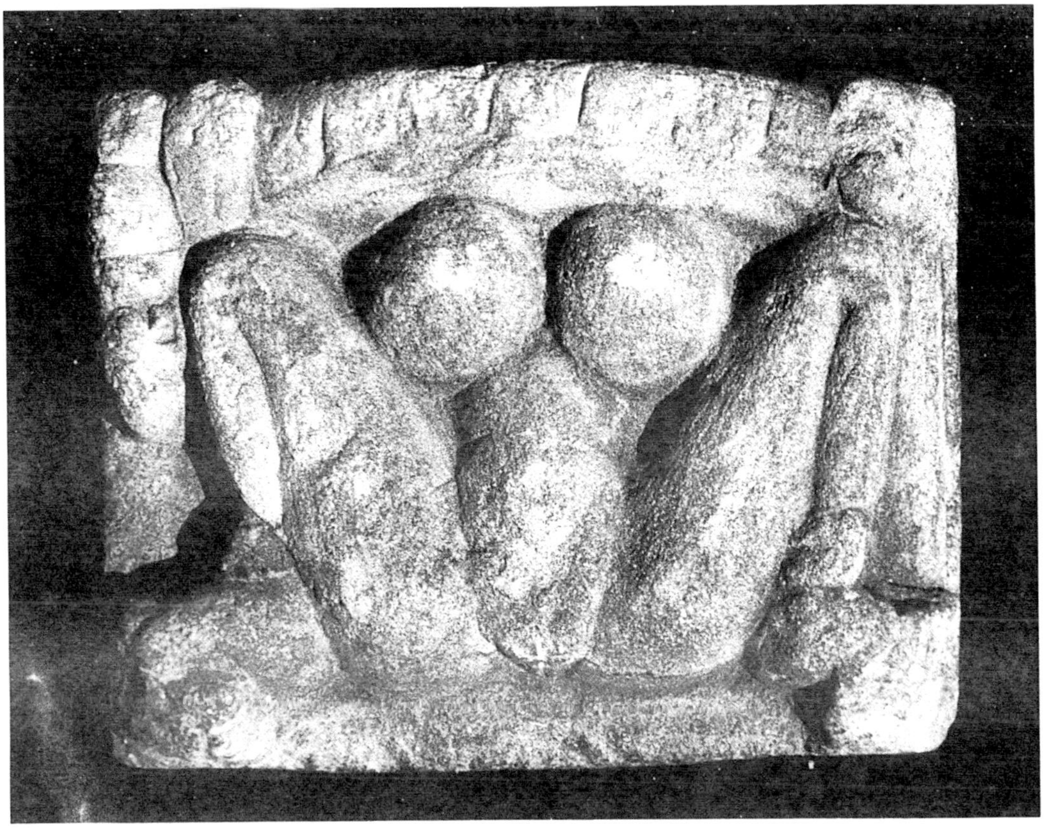

Fig. 93. Mansar, Nagpur District, Maharashtra, Central Museum, Nagpur, 4 × 3¼ inches, stone, fourth–sixth century

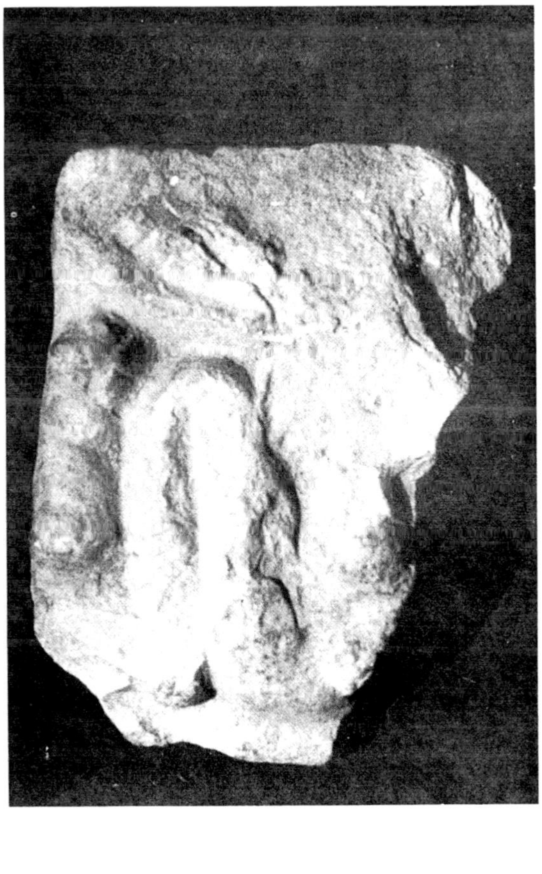

Fig. 94. Paunar (a), Wardha District, Maharashtra, private collection, 3¼ × 2¾ inches (fragment), stone, fourth–sixth century

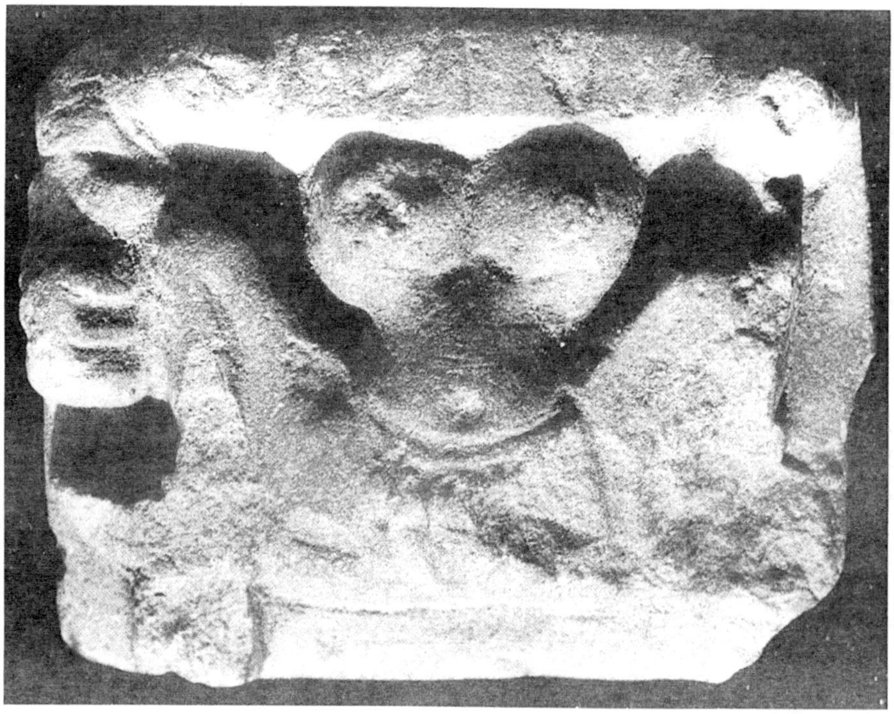

Fig. 95. Paunar (b), Wardha District, Maharashtra, private collection, 7 × 5¼ inches, stone, fourth–sixth century

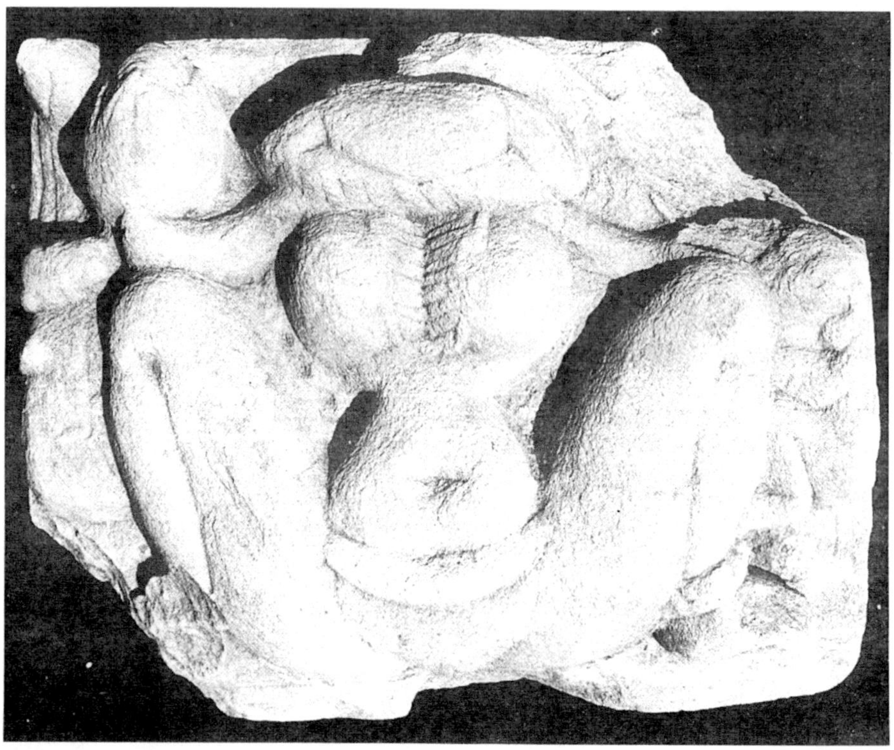

Fig. 96. Paunar (c), Wardha District, Maharashtra, private collection, 5¼ × 7 inches, stone, fourth–fifth century

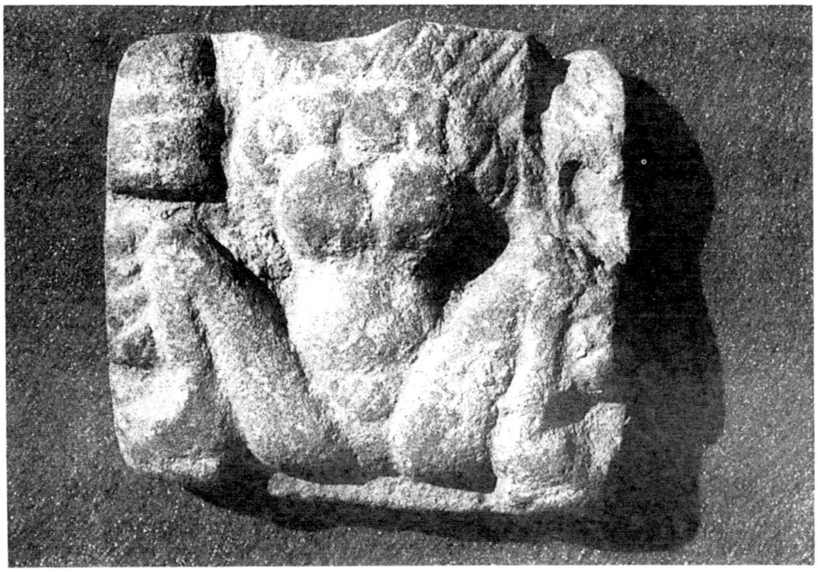

Fig. 97. Ter, Osmanabad District, Maharashtra, Ter Museum 9.168, 2 × 2¼ inches, stone, fourth–sixth century

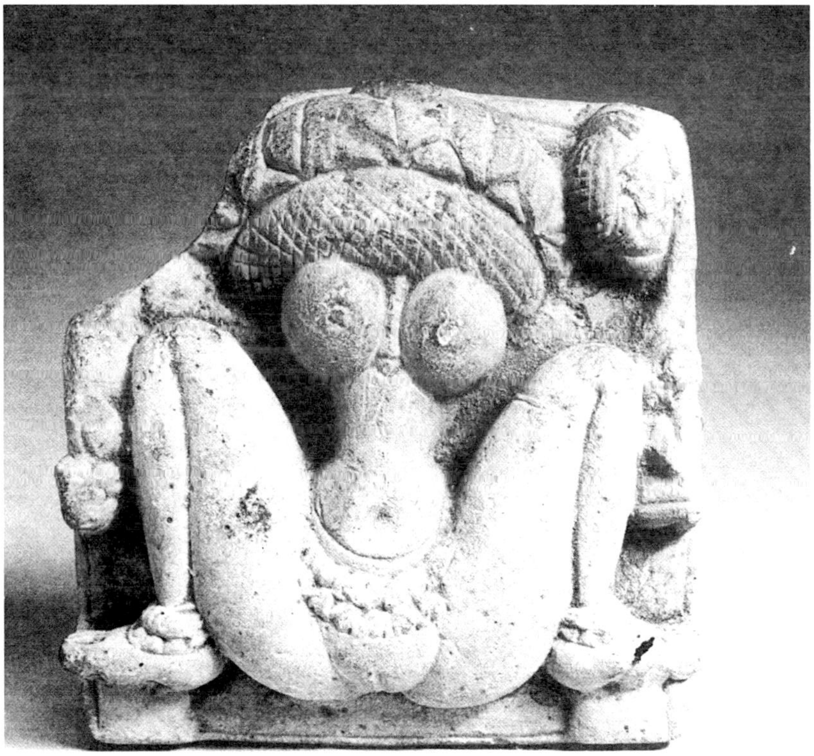

Fig. 98. Site unknown, Seoni District, Madhya Pradesh, Eilenberg Collection, London, 4 × 4 inches, stone, sixth–seventh century

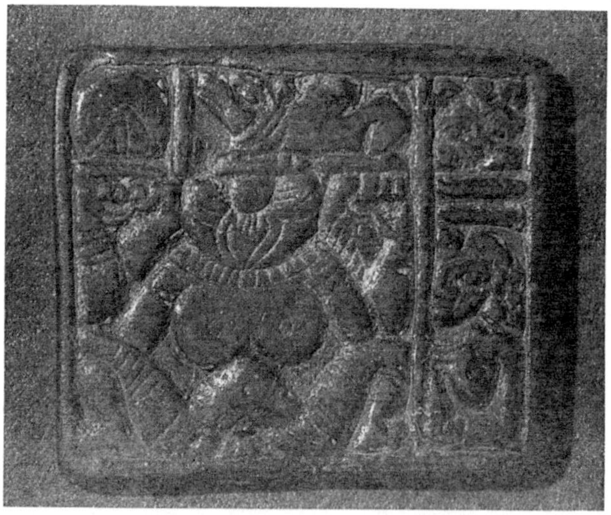

Fig. 99. Ter, Osmanabad District, Maharashtra, Ter Museum RC 8192, 2½ × 2¾ inches, stone, fourth–sixth century

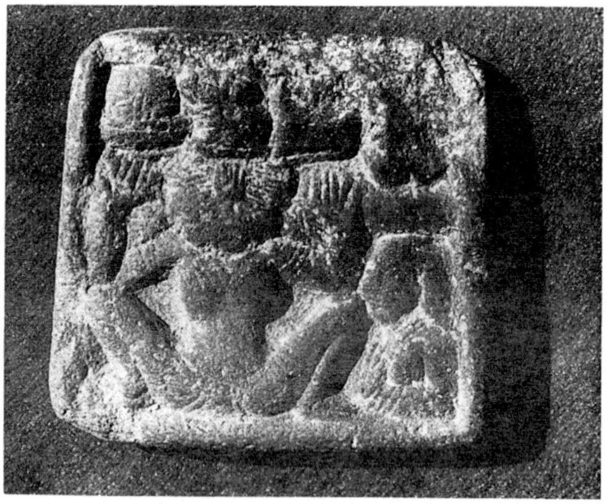

Fig. 100. Ter, Osmanabad District, Maharashtra, Ter Museum 9.166, 2½ × 2¾ inches, stone, fourth–sixth century

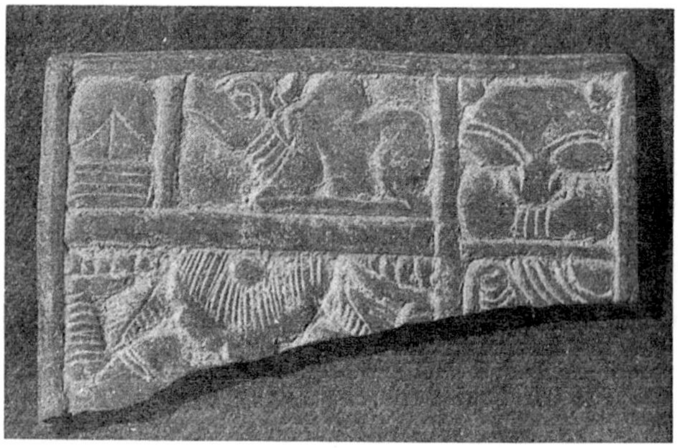

Fig. 101. Ter, Osmanabad District, Maharashtra, Ter Museum 9.154, width 3½ inches (fragment), stone, fourth–sixth century

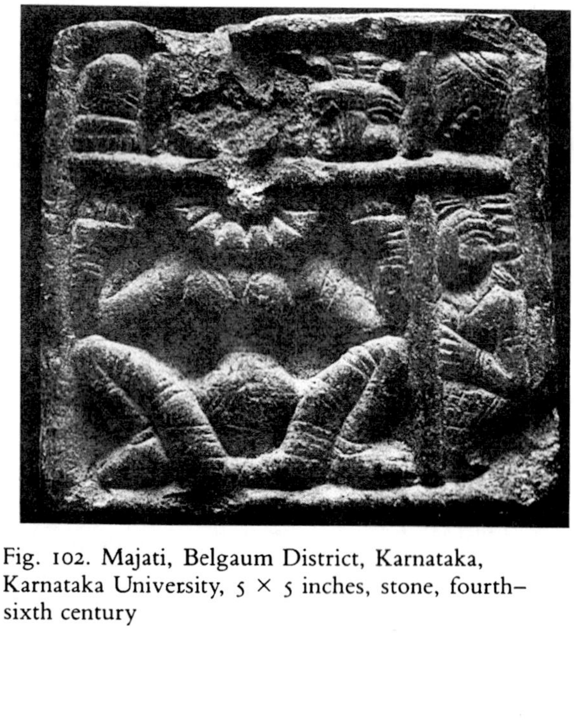

Fig. 102. Majati, Belgaum District, Karnataka, Karnataka University, 5 × 5 inches, stone, fourth–sixth century

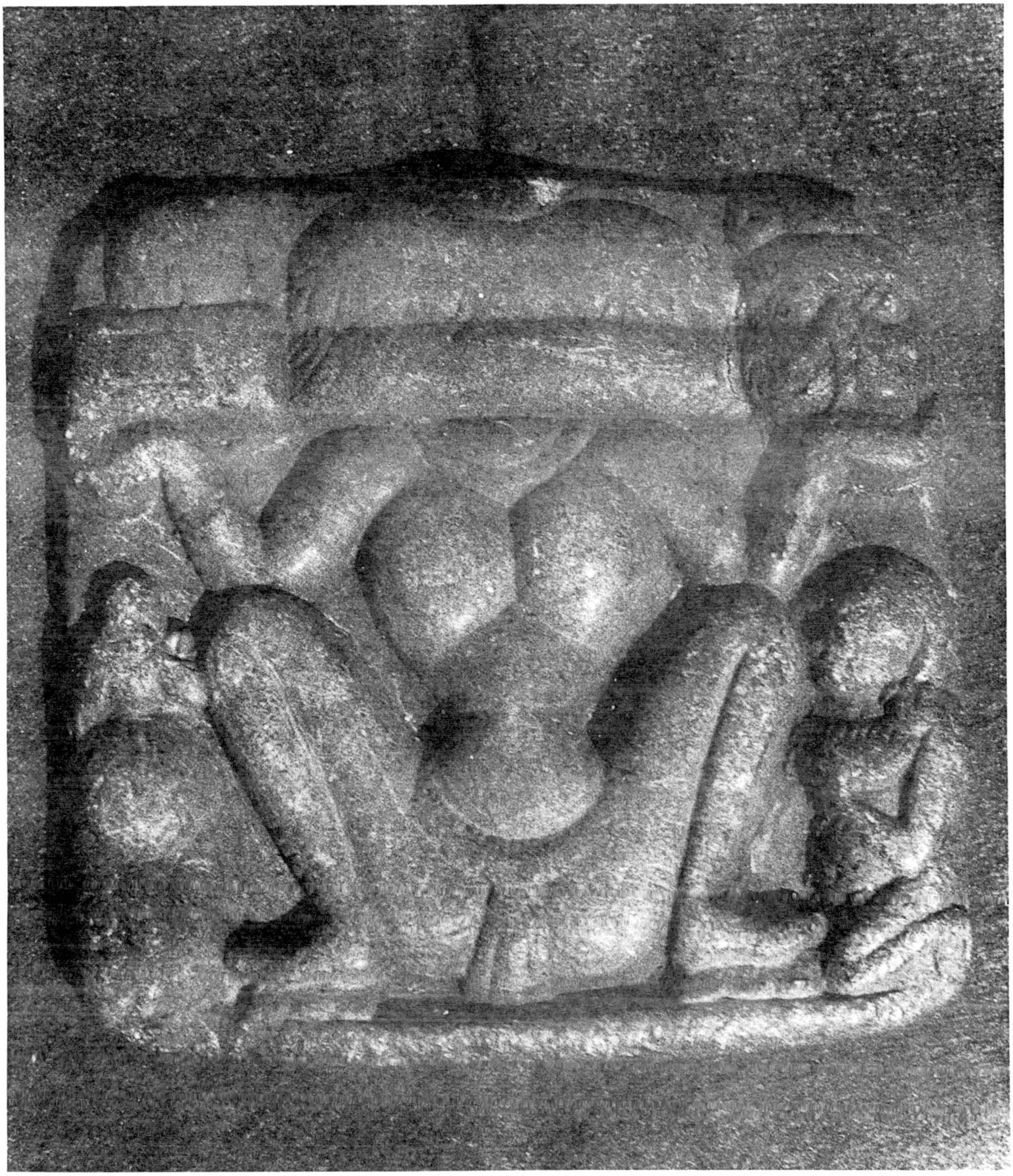

Fig. 103. Keesaragutta, Hyderabad District, Andhra Pradesh, Andhra Directorate of Archaeology and Museums, 4¾ × 4¾ inches, stone, fourth century

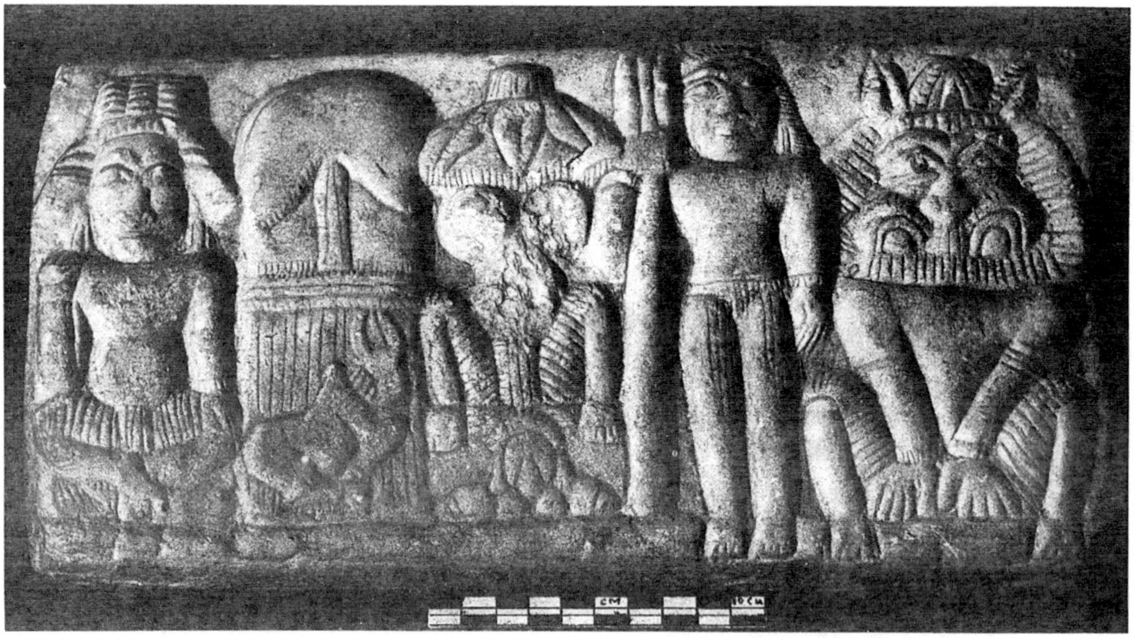

Fig. 104. Darsi (a), Prakasam District, Andhra Pradesh, Andrha Directorate of Archaeology and Museums, 5 × 10½ inches, stone, third–fourth century

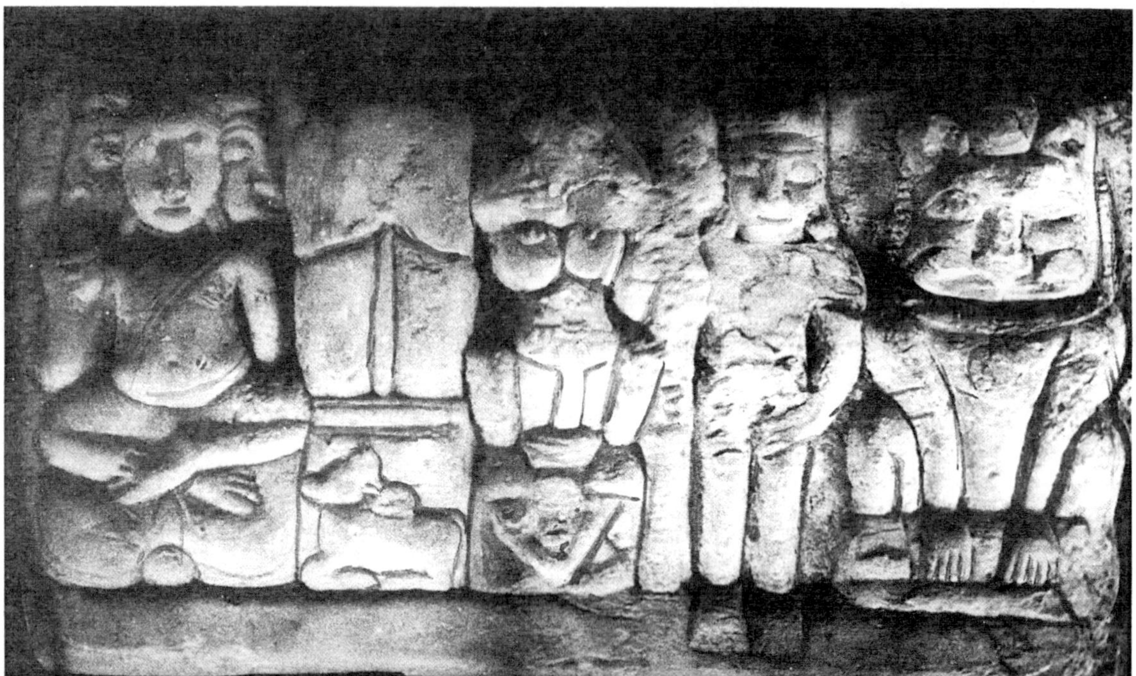

Fig. 105. Darsi (b), Prakasam District, Andhra Pradesh, Nellore Museum, 5 × 12½ inches, stone, third–fourth century

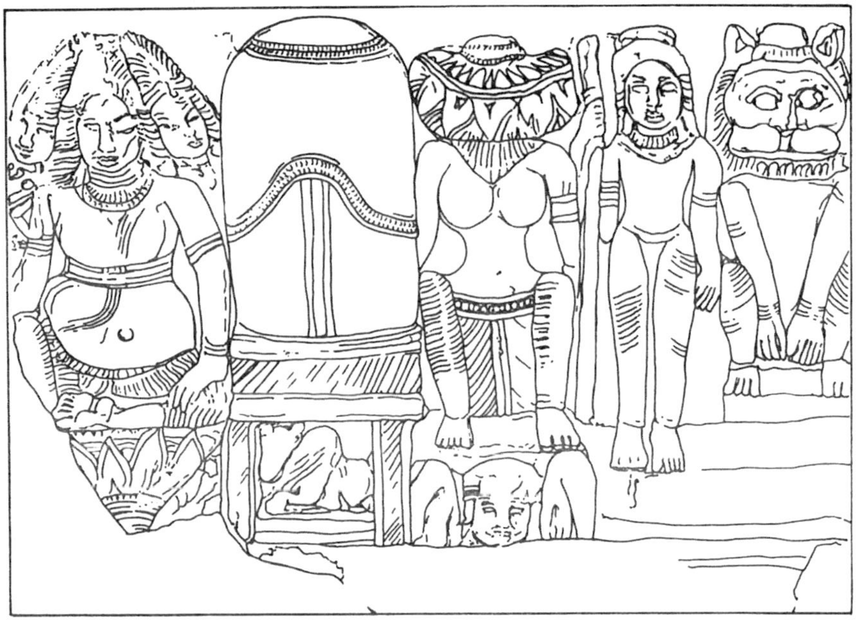

Fig. 106. Kunidane, Guntur District, Andhra Pradesh, current location unknown, 10½ × 7½ inches, stone, fourth–fifth century

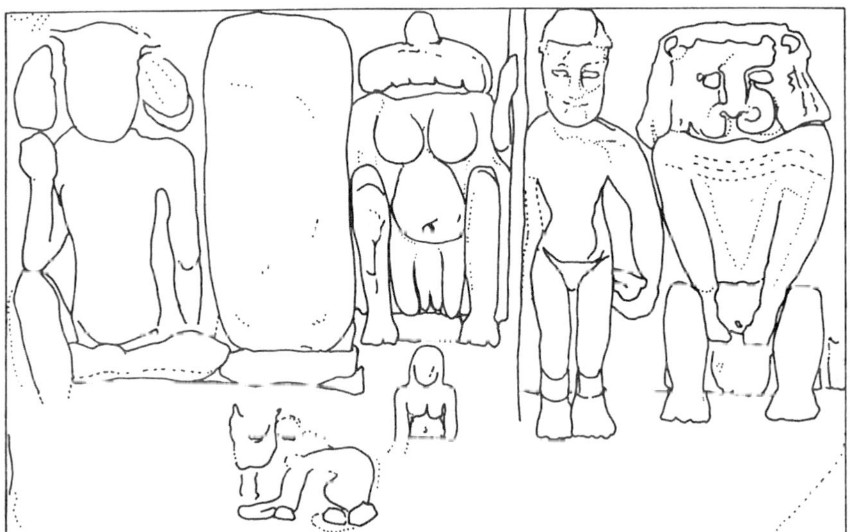

Fig. 107. Uppalapadu, Guntur District, Andhra Pradesh, current location unknown, size?, stone, third–fourth century

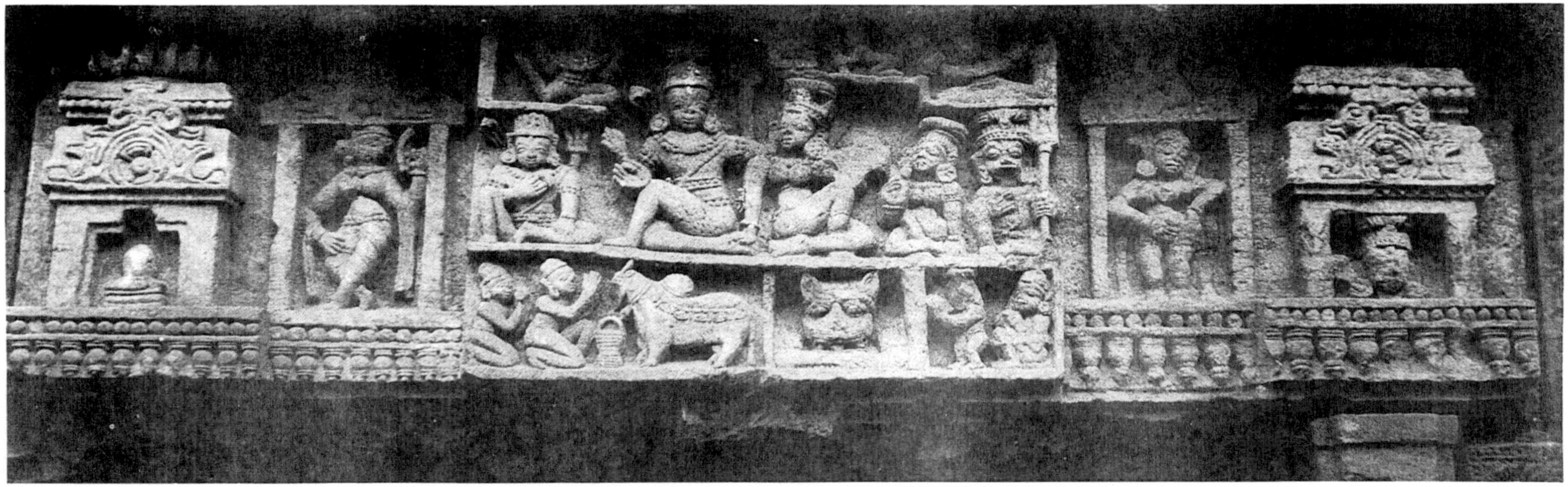

Fig. 108. Bhuvaneśvara, Puri District, Orissa, Satrugneśvara temple, lintel, stone, sixth–seventh century

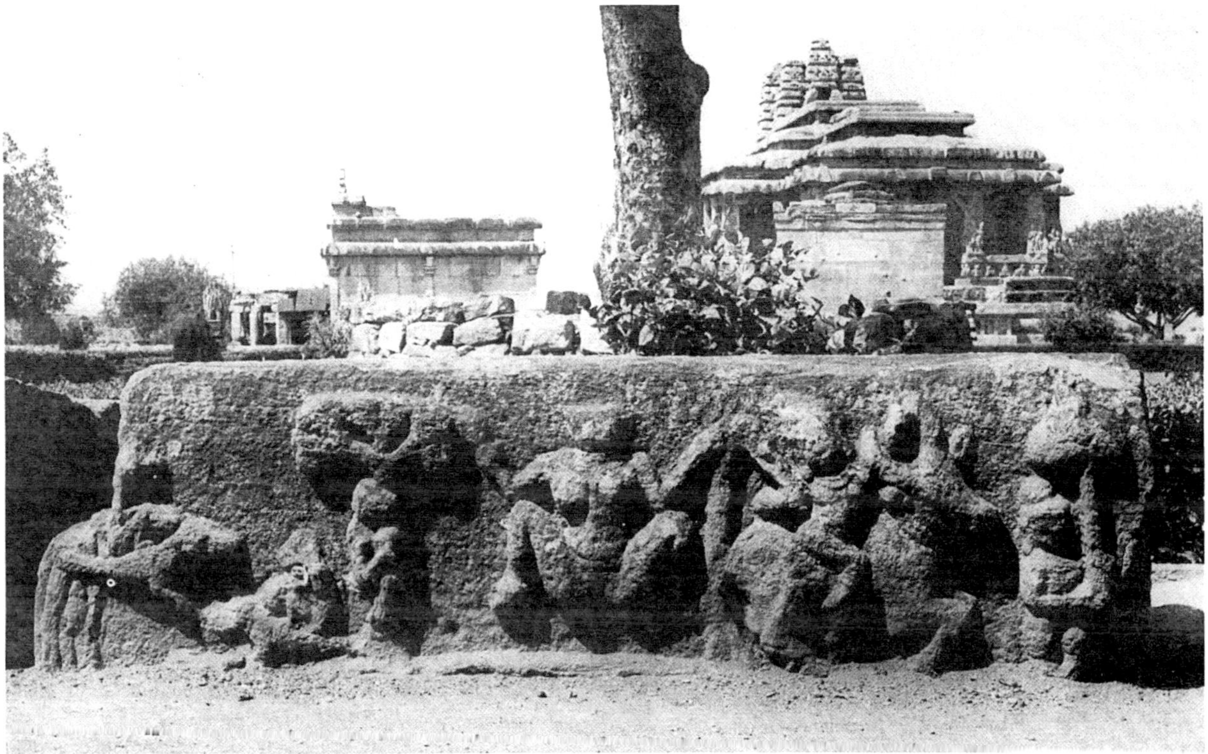

Fig. 109. Aihole, Bijapur District, Karnataka, Huchchapayya temple tank rim, Aihole Museum, 16 × 51 inches, stone, eighth–ninth century

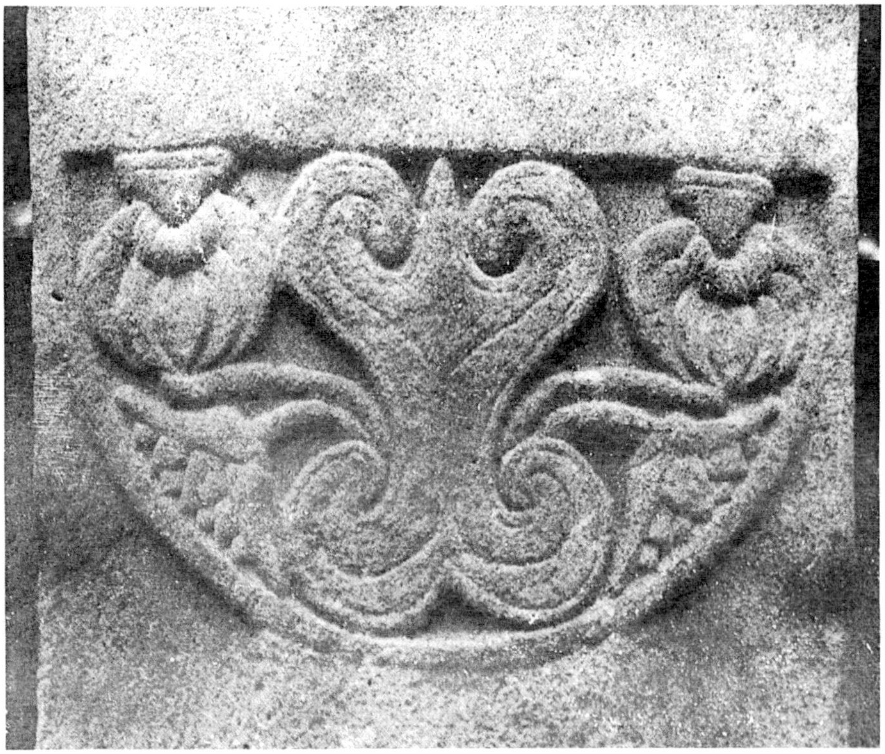

Fig. 110. Sanchi, Raisen District, Madhya Pradesh, *stūpa* II, railing medallion, first century B.C.

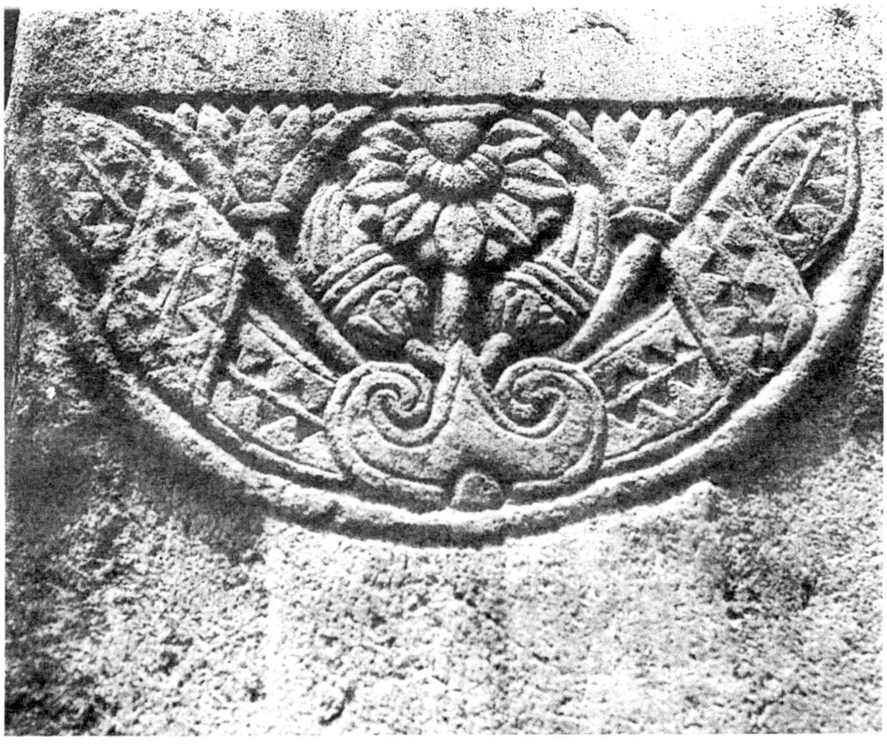

Fig. 111. Sanchi, Raisen District, Madhya Pradesh, *stūpa* II, railing medallion, first century B.C.

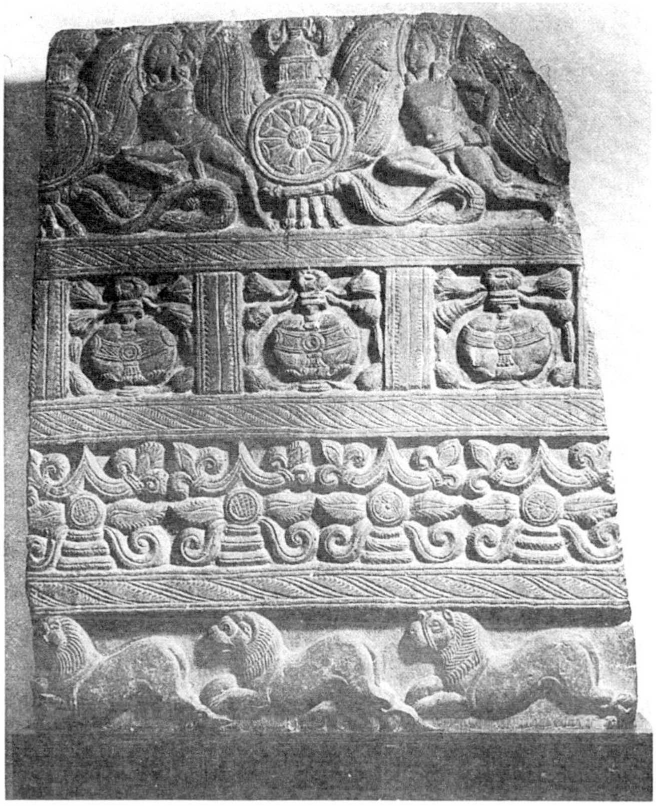

Fig. 112. Nagarjunakonda, Guntur District, Andhra Pradesh, *stūpa* casing slab, National Museum, New Delhi 50.19, stone, third century

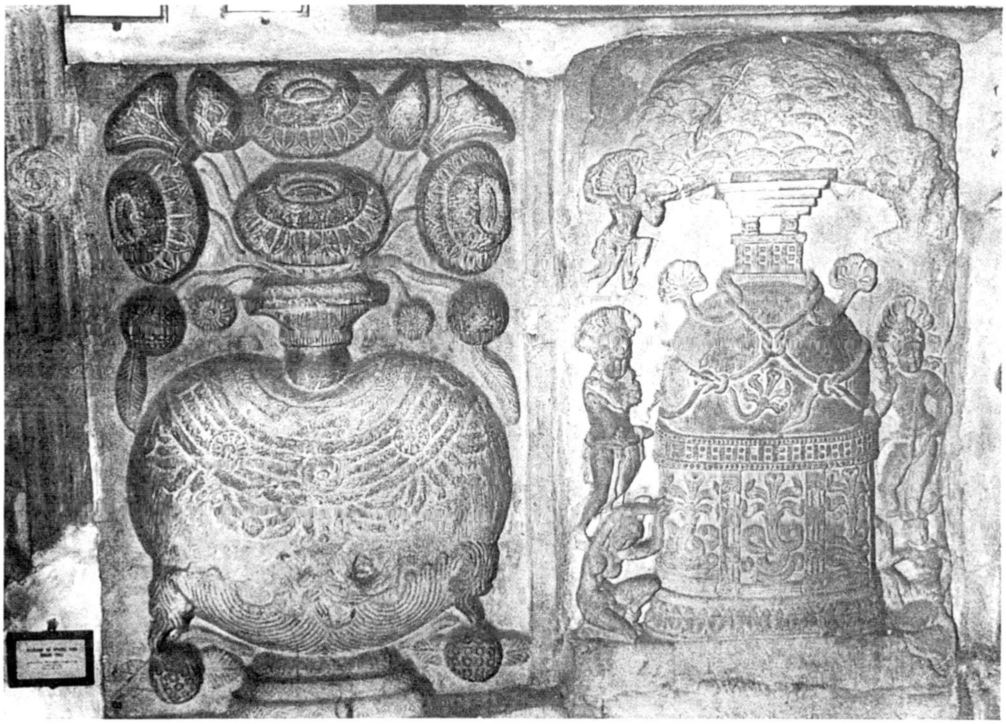

Fig. 113. Amaravati, Guntur District, Andhra Pradesh, *stūpa* casing slab, Madras Government Museum, stone, third century

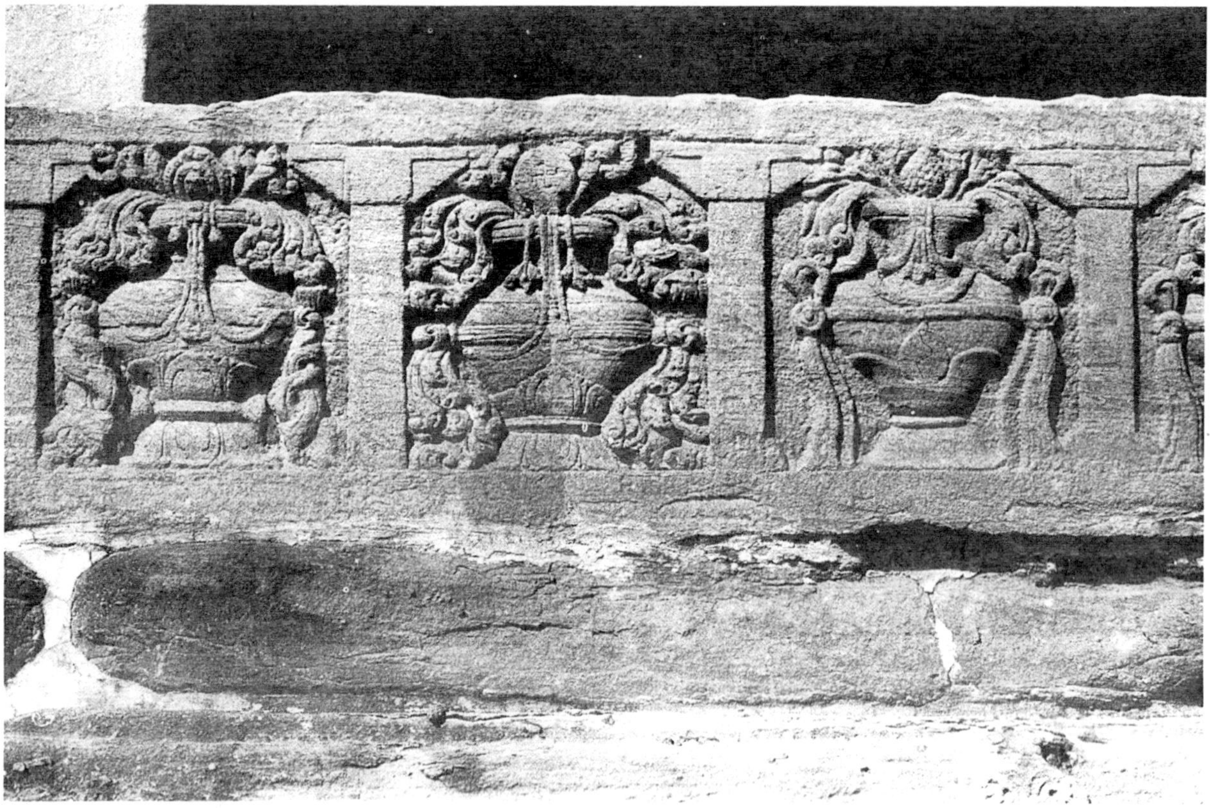

Fig. 114. Aihole, Bijapur District, Karnataka, Huchchimalli temple, balustrade, eighth century

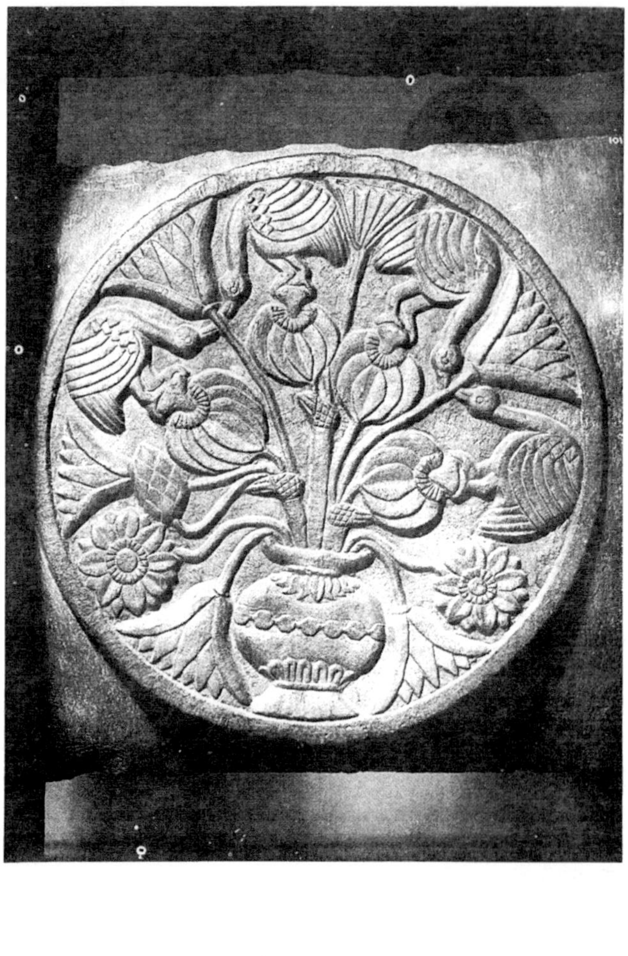

Fig. 115. Bharhut, Satna District, Madhya Pradesh, *stūpa* railing medallion, Indian Museum, Calcutta 90, stone, first century B.C.

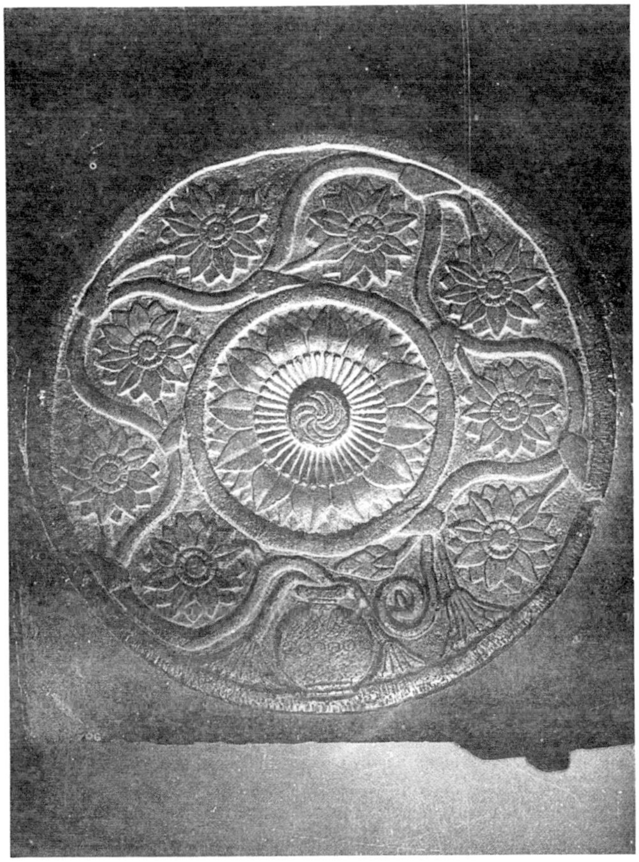

Fig. 116. Bharhut, Satna District, Madhya Pradesh, *stūpa* railing medallion, Indian Museum, Calcutta 101, stone, first century B.C.

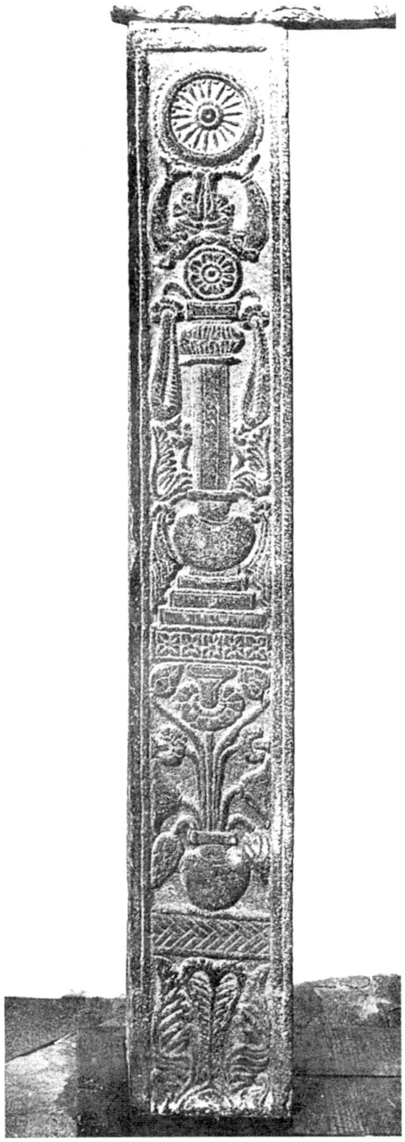

Fig. 117. Sarnath, Varanasi District, Uttar Pradesh, *stūpa* railing post, Archaeological Museum, Sarnath 120, stone, first century B.C.

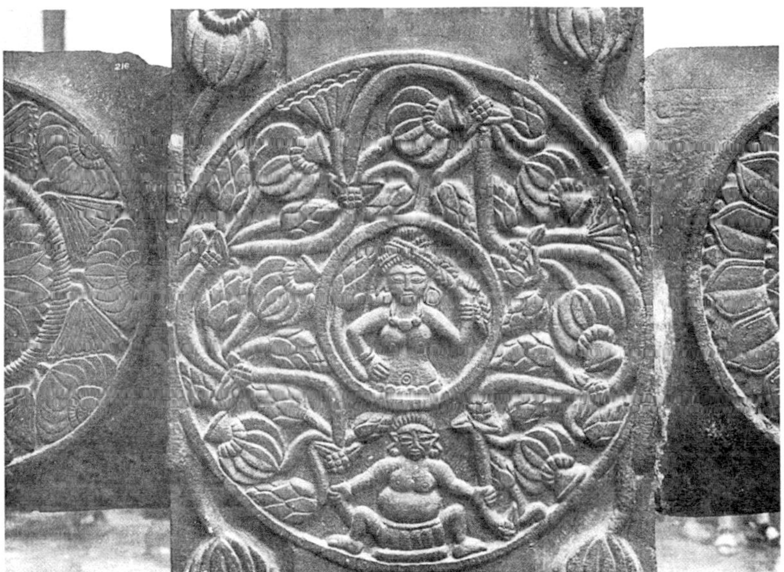

Fig. 118. Bharhut, Satna District, Madhya Pradesh, *stūpa* railing medallion, Indian Museum, Calcutta 219, stone, first century B.C.

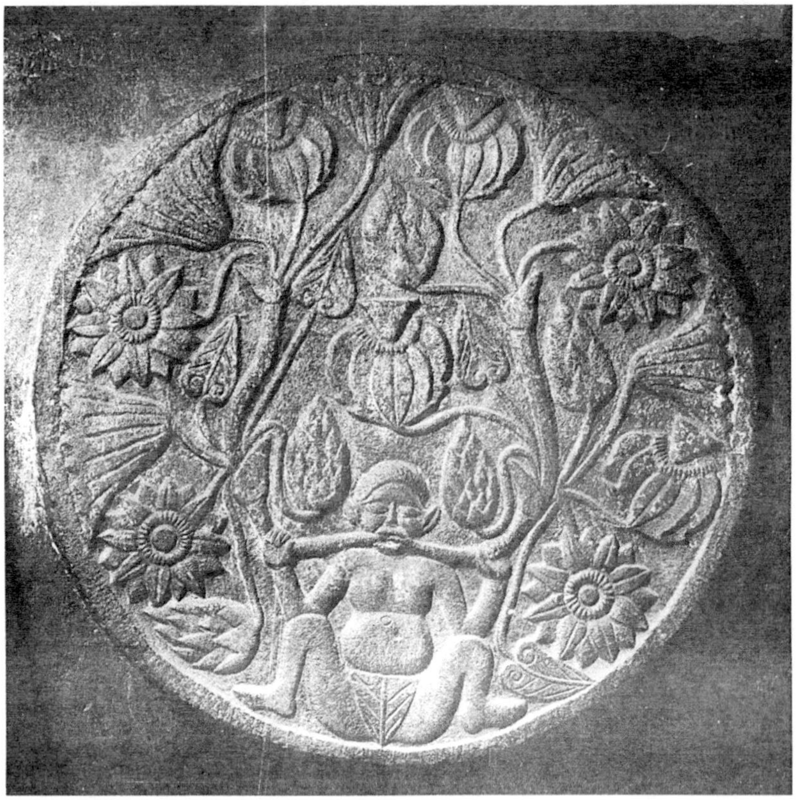

Fig. 119. Bharhut, Satna District, Madhya Pradesh, *stūpa* railing medallion, Indian Museum, Calcutta 279, stone, first century B.C.

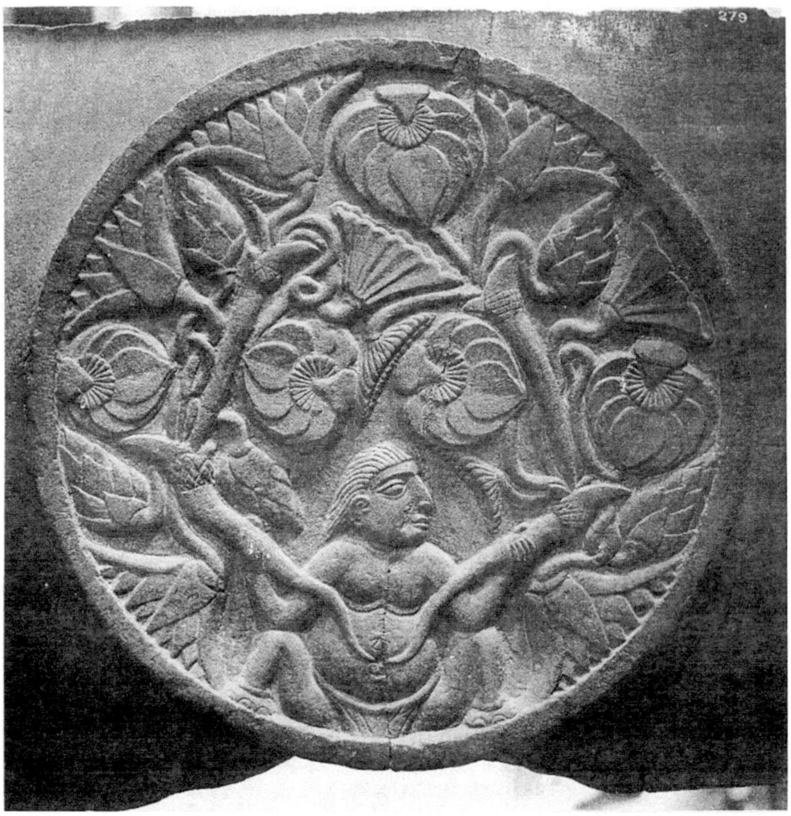

Fig. 120. Bharhut, Satna District, Madhya Pradesh, *stūpa* railing medallion, Indian Museum, Calcutta 83, stone, first century B.C.

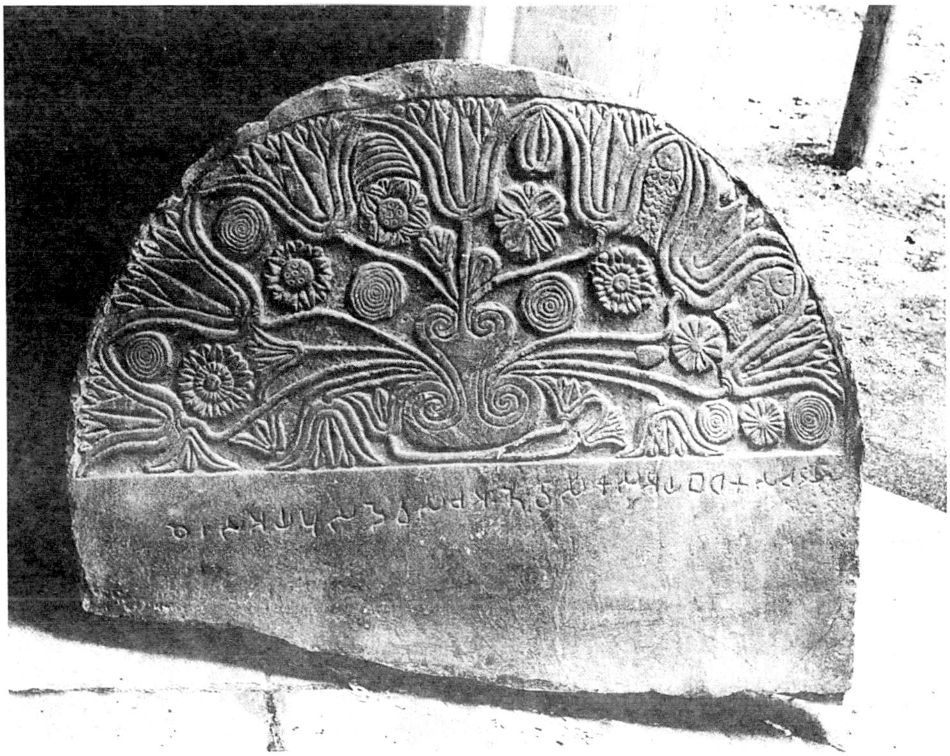

Fig. 121. Kesanapalli, Guntur District, Andhra Pradesh, shrine entry step stone, Andhra Directorate of Archaeology and Museums, 2 × 2½ feet, stone, third century

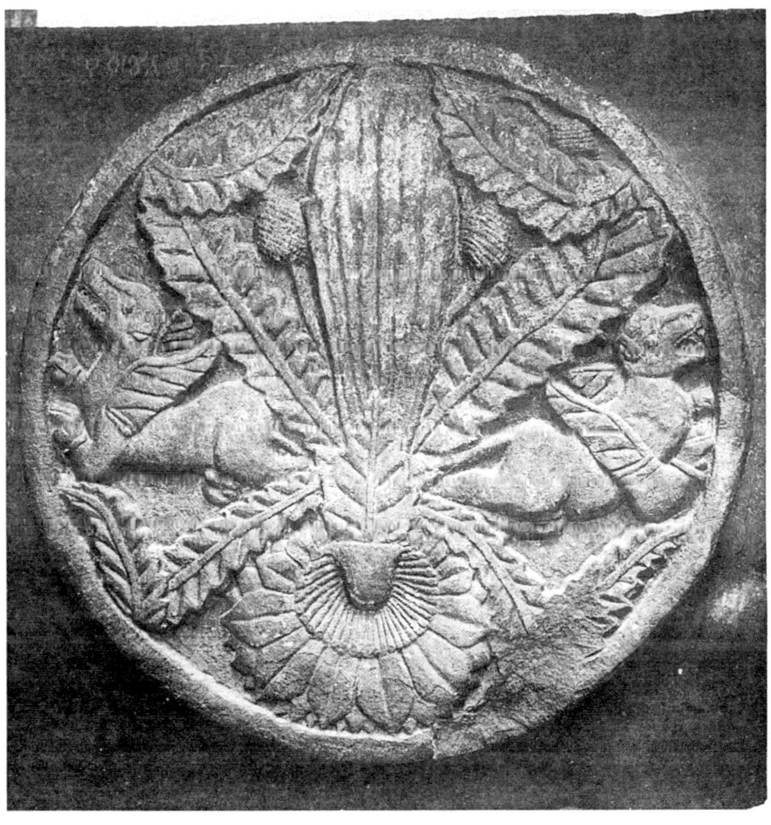

Fig. 122. Bharhut, Satna District, Madhya Pradesh, *stūpa* railing medallion, Indian Museum, Calcutta 131, stone, first century B.C.

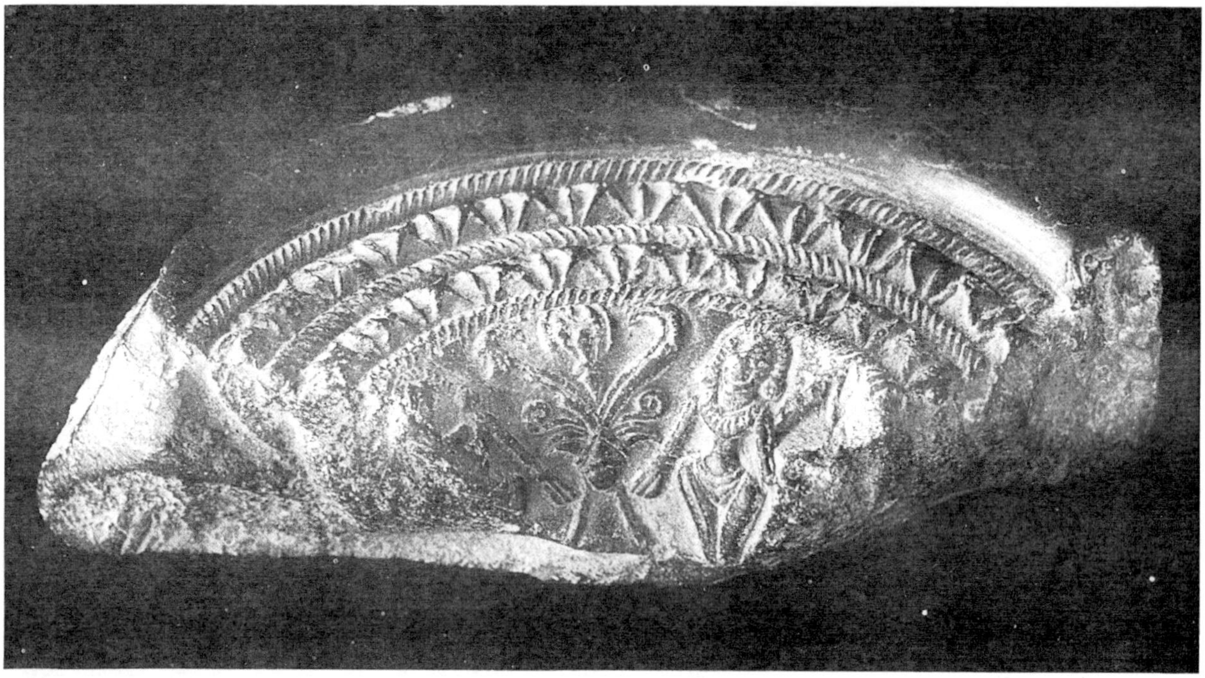

Fig. 123. Varanasi, Varanasi District, Uttar Pradesh, Bharat Kala Bhavan 2/5202, ring stone, 3 × 7/8 inches, stone, third century B.C.

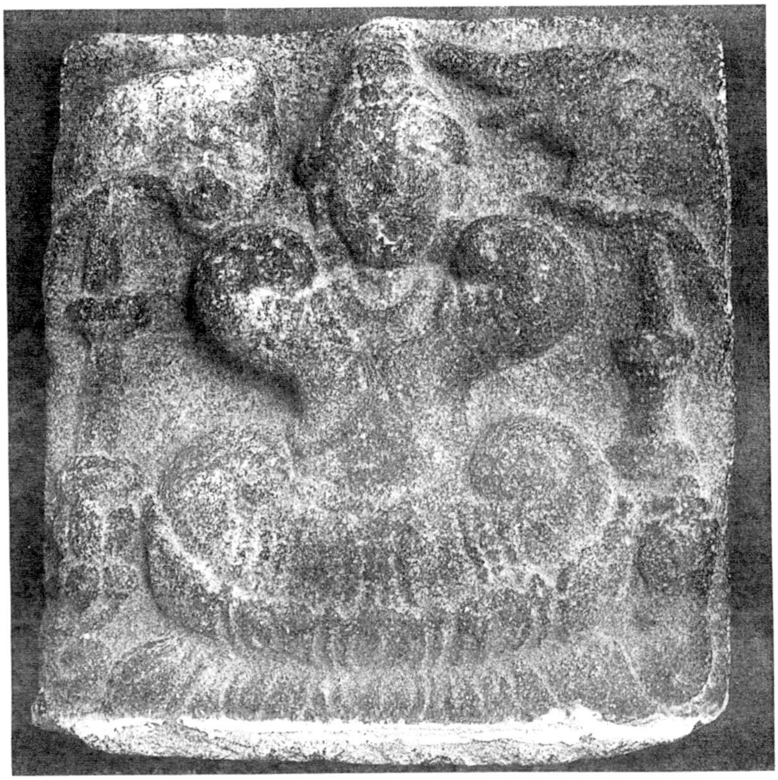

Fig. 124. Kaveripakkam, North Arcot District, Tamil Nadu, Government Museum, Madras 112/38-39, 13 × 11½ inches, stone, ninth century

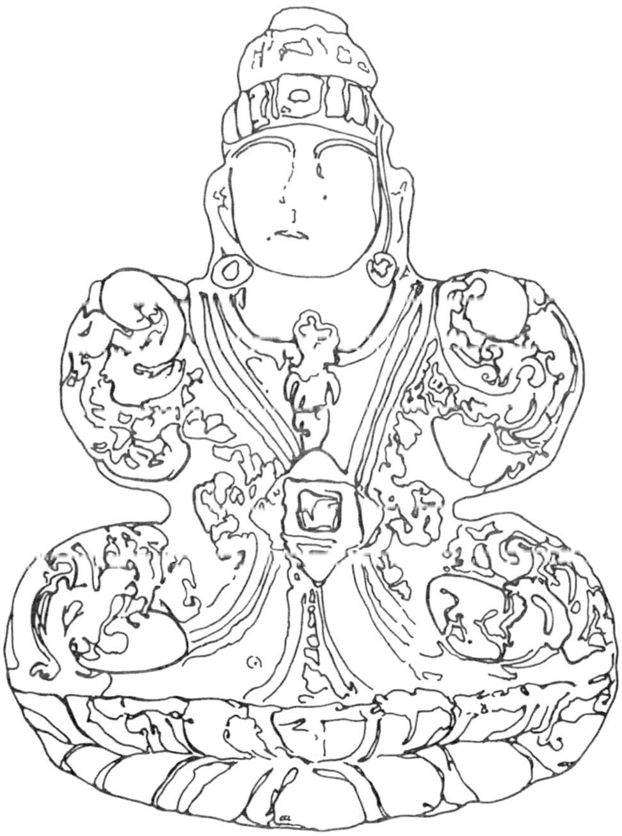

Fig. 125. Enadi, Tanjore District, Tamil Nadu, Government Museum, Madras 39/35, bronze, 2 × 1½ inches, ninth century

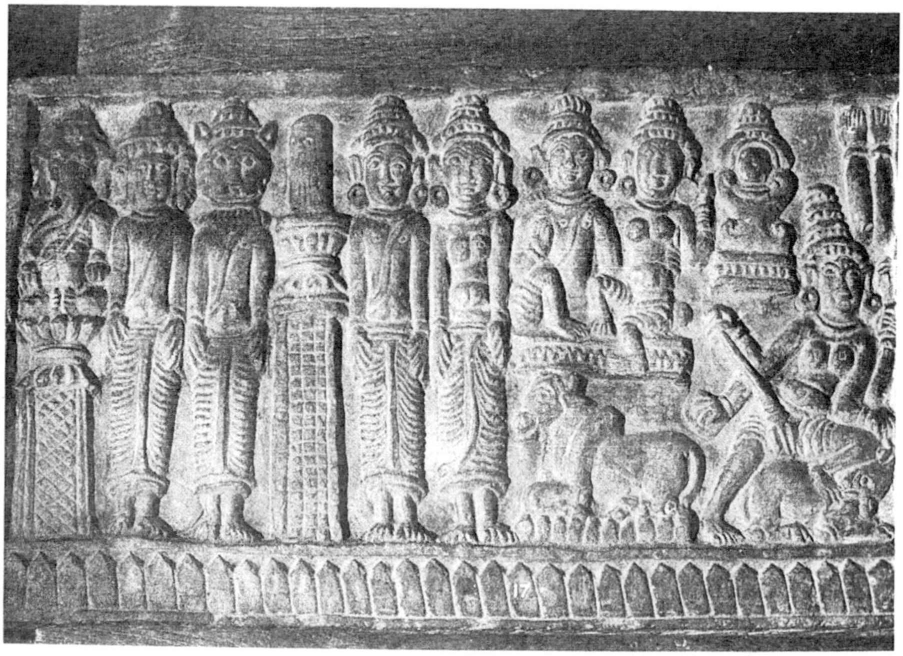

Fig. 126. Peddamudiyam, Cuddapah District, Andhra Pradesh, Government Museum, Madras
17, 10 × 16½ inches, stone, fourth century

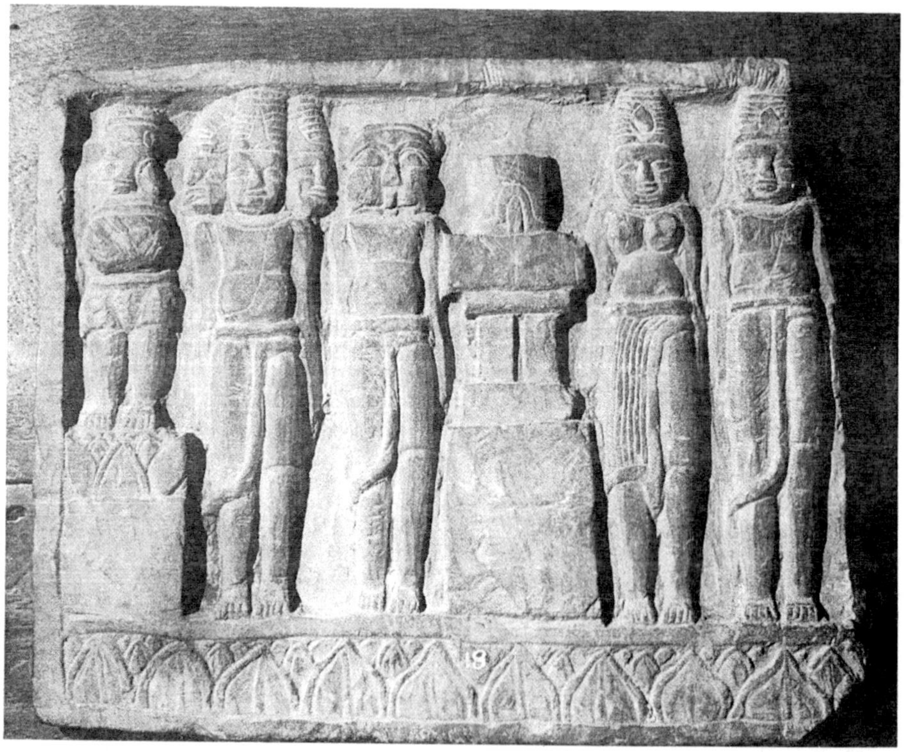

Fig. 127. Peddamudiyam, Cuddapah District, Andhra Pradesh, Government Museum, Madras
18, 9 × 10 inches, stone, eighth century

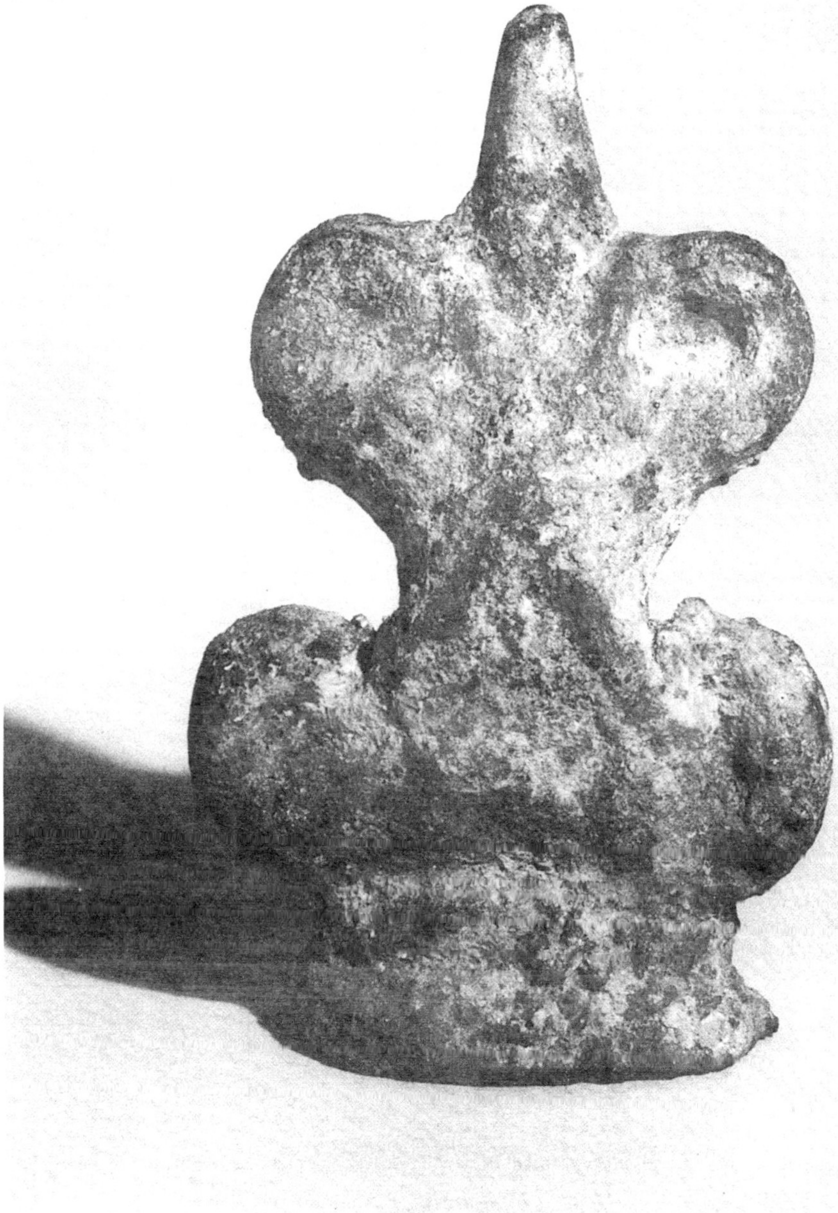

Fig. 128. Sri Lanka, *śrīvatsa,* British Museum 1898.7–2.102, bronze, height 5½ inches, 1000 B.C.

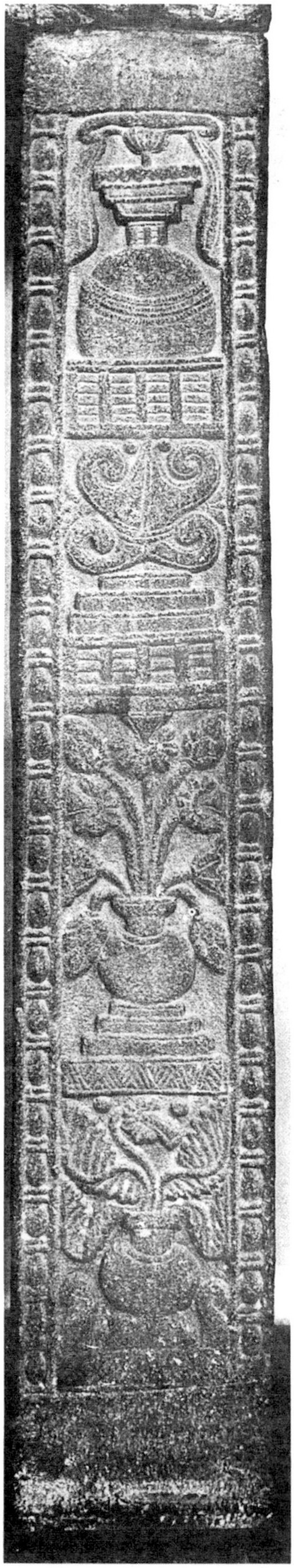

Fig. 129. Sarnath, Varanasi District, Uttar Pradesh, railing post, Archaeological Museum, Sarnath 422, height 4¾ feet, stone, first century B.C.

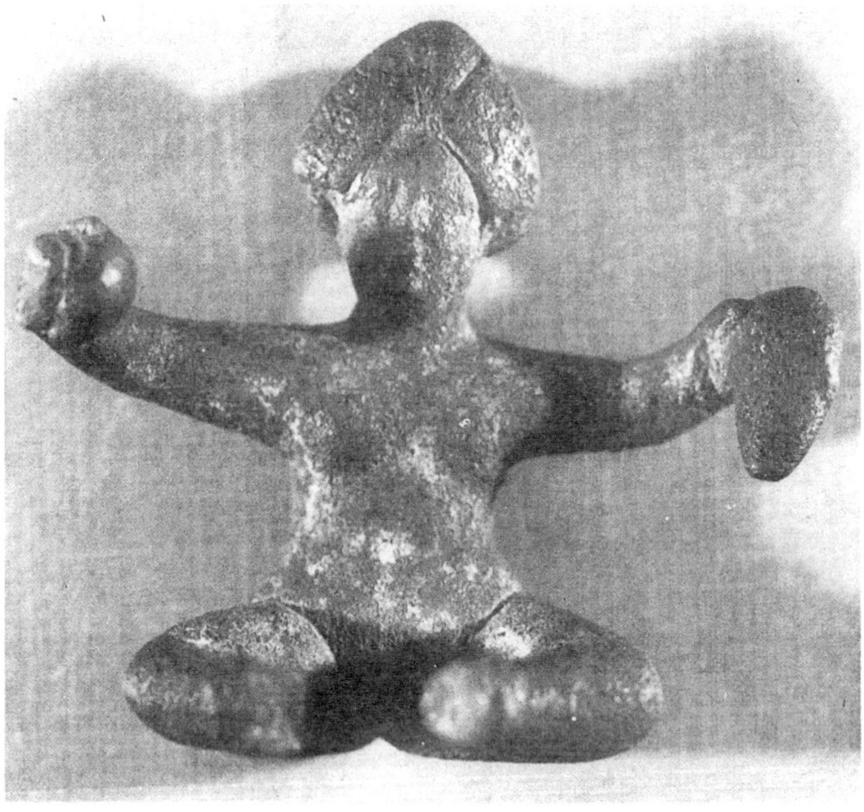

Fig. 130. Rome, Baubo, The David and Alfred Smart Museum, University of Chicago, Purchase 1984.3, height 3½ inches, bronze, second century